7
£45.00

Currents in Contemporary French Intellectual Life

Also by Christopher Flood

PENSÉE POLITIQUE ET IMAGINATION HISTORIQUE DANS L'OEUVRE DE PAUL CLAUDEL

POLITICAL MYTH: A Theoretical Introduction

POLITICAL IDEOLOGIES IN CONTEMPORARY FRANCE (*co-editor*)

Also by Nick Hewlett

MODERN FRENCH POLITICS: Analysing Conflict and Consensus since 1945

DEMOCRACY IN MODERN FRANCE

CONTEMPORARY FRANCE: Politics, Economics and Society (*with Jill Forbes and François Nectoux*)

UNITY AND DIVERSITY IN THE NEW EUROPE (*co-editor*)

Currents in Contemporary French Intellectual Life

Edited by

Christopher Flood
Professor of European Studies
University of Surrey

Nick Hewlett
Professor of French Studies and
Chair of the Centre for European Research
Oxford Brookes University

First published in Great Britain 2000 by
MACMILLAN PRESS LTD
Houndmills, Basingstoke, Hampshire RG21 6XS and London
Companies and representatives throughout the world

A catalogue record for this book is available from the British Library.

ISBN 0–333–71431–8

First published in the United States of America 2000 by
ST. MARTIN'S PRESS, INC.,
Scholarly and Reference Division,
175 Fifth Avenue, New York, N.Y. 10010

ISBN 0–312–23230–6

Library of Congress Cataloging-in-Publication Data
Currents in contemporary French intellectual life / edited by Christopher Flood
[and] Nick Hewlett
p. cm.
Includes bibliographical references and index.
ISBN 0–312–23230–6 (cloth)
1. France — intellectual life — 20th century. I. Flood, Christopher. II. Hewlett, Nick.

DC33.7 .C87   2000
306.4'2'0944 — dc21
                                                    99–086756

This book is printed on paper suitable for recycling and made from fully managed and sustained
forest sources.

10   9   8   7   6   5   4   3   2   1
09   08   07   06   05   04   03   02   01   00

Printed and bound in Great Britain by
Antony Rowe Ltd, Chippenham, Wiltshire

Contents

Notes on the Contributors

Laurence Bell is Lecturer in French Studies at the University of Surrey. He is co-editor of *Political Ideologies in Contemporary France* (1997) and author of a number of articles and chapters on French politics and society, in particular on political movements and social movements theory.

Máire Fedelma Cross is Senior Lecturer in French Studies at the University of Sheffield. She is co-author of *The Feminism of Flora Tristan* (with Tim Gray, 1992), and *Early French Feminisms 1830–1940* (with Felicia Gordon, 1996). She has edited *Voices of France: Political, Social and Cultural Identity* (1997), and *Population and Social Policy of France* (1997), and co-edited *La Société française* (with Sheila Perry, 1991). She is on the editorial board of *Modern and Contemporary France*.

Jacques Durand is Professor of English at the University of Toulouse-Le Mirail and formerly Professor of Linguistics at the University of Salford, where he was Chair of the Department of Modern Linguistics and first Director and Founder of the European Studies Research Institute. He is author of *Generative and Non-Linear Phonology* (1990) and has edited and contributed to a number of other books, including *Dependency and Non-Linear Phonology* (1986), *Explorations in Dependency Phonology* (1987), *Frontiers of Phonology* (1995) and *Current Issues in Phonology*, 2 vols. He has also worked on machine translation and published on a wide range of themes in general and French linguistics.

Christopher Flood is Professor of European Studies at the University of Surrey. He is author of *Pensée politique et imagination historique dans l'oeuvre de Paul Claudel* (1991) and of *Political Myth: A Theoretical Introduction* (1996). He has co-edited *Political Ideologies in Contemporary France* (1997) and two collections of essays on the politics of French intellectuals. He is co-editor of the European Horizons series for the University of Nebraska Press.

Jill Forbes is Professor of French at Queen Mary and Westfield, University of London. Her recent works include *Contemporary France: Politics, Economics and Society* (with Nick Hewlett and François Nectoux, 1994),

French Cultural Studies (with Michael Kelly, 1995), *Les Enfants du Paradis* (1997) and *European Cinema* (with Sarah Street, 2000). She is a member of the editorial board of *French Studies* and an associate editor of *French Cultural Studies*.

Hugo Frey is Lecturer in History at University College Chichester. He contributed to Berger, Donovan and Passmore (eds), *Writing National Histories* (1999) and has published articles in *Contemporary French Civilization*, *Modern and Contemporary France* and *Journal of European Studies*.

Seán Hand is Professor of French and Head of the School of Languages at Oxford Brookes University. He is editor of *The Levinas Reader* and author of articles on Levinas, Leiris, Jabès, Lacan, Memmi, Duras and postmodern ethics in journals which include *Paragraph*, *Romance Studies* and *Dalhousie French*. He has translated many contemporary French thinkers, including Levinas, Kristeva, Irigaray, Lyotard and Deleuze. He is author of forthcoming books on Michel Leiris and Emmanuel Levinas.

Nick Hewlett is Professor of French Studies and Chair of the Centre for European Research at Oxford Brookes University. He is author of *Modern French Politics. Analysing Conflict and Consensus since 1945* (1998) and *Democracy in Modern France* (2000), co-author of *Contemporary France: Politics, Economics and Society* (with Jill Forbes and François Nectoux, 1994) and co-editor of *Unity and Diversity in the New Europe* (2000). He has a number of articles and chapters in such journals as *Contemporary French Civilization, Modern and Contemporary France* and *Politics* and in edited collections.

Grahame Lock is Professor of Political Philosophy at the University of Nijmegen and Faculty Fellow in European Philosophy at the University of Oxford. He is author of *The State and I* (1981), *Wittgenstein: Philosophie, logique, thérapeutique* (1992) and a number of books in Dutch.

François Nectoux is Professor of Contemporary European Studies at Kingston University and co-author of *Contemporary France: Politics, Economics and Society* (with Jill Forbes and Nick Hewlett, 1994). He has published widely on French and European economic and environmental matters and his most recent articles have appeared in the *European Union Handbook* and the *Journal of European Social Policy*. He has also written articles and chapters on nationalism and culture. He is currently working on a study entitled *Unemployment and Social Exclusion in Contemporary France*.

Lieve Spaas is Professor of French Cultural Studies at Kingston University. Her books include *Lettres de Catherine de Saint-Pierre à son frère Bernardin* (1996) and *Robinson Crusoe: Myths and Metamorphoses* (co-edited with Brian Stimpson, 1997) and she is editor of *Paternity and Fatherhood: Myths and Realities* (1998). She is author of the forthcoming *Francophone Film: A Struggle for Identity* and is general editor of the Berghahn Books series, Polygons: Cultural Diversities, Mutations and Intersections.

Richard Wolin is Professor of History and Humanities at Rice University, Texas. He is the author of *Walter Benjamin: An Aesthetic of Redemption (1982), The Politics of Being: The Political Thought of Martin Heidegger* (1990) and two essay collections, *The Terms of Cultural Criticism* and *Labyrinths: Explorations in the Critical History of Ideas* (1995). He is currently working on a study of twentieth-century French political culture entitled *Left Fascism*.

1
Structure and Change in Contemporary French Intellectual Life

Christopher Flood and Nick Hewlett

Changing ideological and philosophical trends

The intellectual life of a society can be examined from many angles. For example, it can be approached historically in terms of the development of ideas over a span of time. It can be analysed in a more synchronic way to focus on the persistence of particular structural relationships within and/or between different currents of thought or fields of knowledge at a given period. It may take account of cross-fertilization with other societies. The approach may be sociological, considering the production, circulation and consumption of ideas across different socio-economic strata, different educational levels or different geographical regions, for instance. Alternatively, intellectuals themselves, considered either in terms of the words and actions of particular individuals, or viewed as an identifiable social group of culture-bearers and educators, may be the principal objects of investigation.

With regard to France, the aspect of intellectual life which has probably attracted more attention than any other is the involvement of intellectuals (men and women of letters, professional scholars) with political causes. Although there had been many earlier examples of this type of activity, the label of intellectual became current at the time of the Dreyfus Affair in the late nineteenth century to refer to the defenders of the Jewish officer who had been convicted of treason (Charle, 1990; Ory and Sirinelli, 1992). The term was applied to the left at that time, and since then has more often been used to refer to left-wing figures than to representatives of other political alignments. However, Maurice Barrès, the nationalist writer, journalist and politician who did much to popularize the term as a pejorative label for his ideological enemies, can himself be categorized as a politically committed intellectual of the

1

right. There have always been intellectuals of all shades of political opinion.

Throughout the twentieth century intellectuals have continued to play a leading role in the debates which have divided French society. Whether or not the wider public has taken them as seriously as they would have wished, intellectuals have justified their own interventions on the grounds that the trained intellect of the scholar, shaped by the benefits of a broad-ranging but rigorous education in the elite institutions of secondary and higher education, fulfilled a necessary function in speaking to and for the people. Whatever the particular field(s) of specialism followed by the intellectual in his or her professional activity, the mental and verbal skills have been assumed to enable lucid judgement of matters of principle, policy and practice in the political sphere.

Furthermore, while adopting partisan positions on public issues, intellectuals have been able to claim that they are not arguing from selfish motives but in the service of higher values because, unlike politicians, their careers have not normally depended directly on the outcome of the political controversies in which they have participated. Manifestos, quick-fire polemical books and articles in partisan periodicals, current affairs magazines or newspapers have been used as instruments of verbal warfare. Much of this activity has been concentrated in Paris, which has been the geographical centre of French intellectual production by virtue of the location of France's most prestigious cultural and academic institutions, headquarters of learned societies and intellectual clubs, alongside the main institutions of governmental, economic and media activity, with considerable interaction and transfers of personnel between them.

There have been many studies of the political aspect of French intellectual life (for example, Sirinelli, 1990; Winock, 1997). The period since the end of the Second World War has received particular attention in recent years as commentators have endeavoured to explain why there appears to have been a crisis of confidence and a process of self-questioning among many intellectuals since the mid-1970s or at least the 1980s (Jennings, 1993, 1997; Ross, 1991). Summarized schematically, the widely aired interpretation posits a chronological sequence of phases characterized by the dominance of particular ideologies among large sections of the intelligentsia. Thus, the temporary eclipse of the traditionalist and fascist extreme right in the climate of the post-Liberation purges of former collaborators and Vichyites coincided with the heyday of left-wing idealism of various shades – epitomized by the stance of prominent figures such as Jean-Paul Sartre, Simone de Beauvoir and

Maurice Merleau-Ponty – and particularly with the powerful pull of the Communist Party (PCF) as a pole of attraction in the light of its wartime resistance record, coupled with its call to emancipation of the oppressed.

Whereas the appeal of the Stalinist version of Marxism-Leninism and the positions of the PCF was already fading by the later 1950s in the wake of the invasion of Hungary, other versions of Marxism (in the manner of Sartre, Gramsci, Althusser, Lefebvre and others) continued to exert a powerful hold on many intellectuals, fed by social tensions arising from the processes of postwar modernization and by the conflicts over decolonization. This paved the way for the extraordinarily eclectic mixture of ideas circulating around the time of the events of May 1968, which in turn fed into emerging new ideologies centred on issues such as the environment, gender, sexuality, quality of life, participative democracy and third-worldism. With the benefit of hindsight, the preoccupation with individual self-expression and with the rights of special interest groups can be seen to prefigure further changes which were to fragment and eventually discredit traditional attachments to various conceptions of socialism or communism.

The increasing turn against Marxism, especially of the type associated with the Soviet Union, was famously spurred by publication of the French translation of Solzhenitsyn's *Gulag Archipelago* in 1974 and by the writings of ex-Marxist, anti-Marxist *nouveaux philosophes*, such as Bernard-Henry Lévi, André Glucksmann, Christian Jambet, Guy Lardreau and Jean-Paul Dollé in the later 1970s. This development foreshadowed an increasing disaggregation of the previously dominant left intelligentsia during the 1980s, amid withdrawal by some (the notorious 'silence of the intellectuals', as Max Gallo called it), disaffection with François Mitterrand's presidency and the governments of the left from 1981 to 1986 and 1988 to 1993, alongside a developing interest in liberalism and in questions of democracy and rights, whether conceived in the French tradition running from Constant and Tocqueville to Aron, or in the British and American traditions (Lilla, 1994; Mongin, 1994).

On the other hand, the rise of various forms of neo-liberalism has not gone unchallenged. While Marxism was subjected to relentless critique and the old ideological underpinnings of the left dissolved, there has been revulsion among left-wing intellectuals – shared by some social-liberals – against the version of neo-liberalism practised in the USA and Britain, overtly emulated by the Chirac government in 1986–88 and to varying degrees, but less overtly, by subsequent governments of the left as well as the right in keeping with the pressures of Europeanization and globalization. Rejection of the alleged economico-political inevitability of this model was captured in the dismissive label of *la pensée unique* ('one-track thinking') popularized by Jean-François Kahn in the left-of-centre current affairs magazine, *L'Evénement du jeudi*, in the early 1990s, then in a book of the same title (Kahn, 1995) before becoming one of the buzzwords of political discourse for a time. Similarly, voices have been raised in opposition to the type of claim made, for example, by François Furet and others in their book *La République du centre* (1988) to the effect that French politics had now, at last, entered a phase of normalization and relative consensus as regards fundamental values after two hundred years of division since the time of the Revolution. For example, Françoise Gaillard (1997) points out that democracy does not presuppose the exclusion of conflict from the sphere of legitimate political behaviour: rather, it implies pluralistic acceptance that an interplay of conflicting viewpoints is the very basis of politics (for variations on the rejection of 'consensus', see other French contributions to Goux and Wood, 1997). During the 1990s, amid much soul-searching over national identity and over the politics of 'collective memory' regarding the Occupation period (Conan and Rousso, 1994), and notwithstanding a tendency to focus more on single issues in the absence of a totalizing vision of the future, there were diffuse efforts to revitalize the left around reconceptualizations of a socio-economically and ethnically inclusive republicanism grounded on new definitions of citizenship and rights (Mathy, 1997). The task was spurred by the rallying call to antiracist struggle in face of the ideological and electoral drive of the Front National, itself powered by an influx of post-fascist intellectuals of the New Right during the later 1980s (Flood, 1997a, 1997b; Fysh and Wolfreys, 1998; Perrineau, 1997).

Of course, this schematization of the rise and decline of particular ideological currents among the French intelligentsia has only limited validity in relation to the real complexities of the intellectual-ideological sphere at any given time. In reality, innumerable shades of thought have always continued to coexist across the left–right spectrum and the environment has remained highly pluralistic – for example, even in the years immediately following the Liberation, the ignominy suffered by the extreme right did not mean that its intellectuals ceased to publish their views, nor did the intensification of rejections of Marxism during the 1990s after the collapse of the USSR mean that there were no longer Marxist intellectuals to carry the flag while awaiting better days.

Alongside and intertwining with the sphere of political commitment, a second aspect of French intellectual life which has been closely observed by French and foreign commentators has been the movement of philosophical and semi-philosophical ideas. In the course of the five and a half decades since the end of the Second World War various schools of thought have enjoyed periods of extraordinary attention among the intelligentsia because they have appeared for a time to offer particularly penetrating insights into the nature of social reality or even of the human condition in general (for useful overviews, see Goetschel and Loyer, 1994; Forbes and Kelly, 1995; and for topicality, the *Idées* section of the *Journal de l'année* published by Larousse each year). When stated crudely as a succession – again ignoring the real diversity of ideas at any given period – existentialism (of Sartre, Simone de Beauvoir, Albert Camus, Gabriel Marcel, among others), personalism (notably of Emmanuel Mounier and the group around *Esprit*) and phenomenology (of Maurice Merleau-Ponty, for example) occupied the centre of the stage during the later 1940s and the early 1950s. But by the end of the 1950s they were increasingly displaced by various forms of structuralism (with Claude Lévi-Strauss, Roland Barthes, Algirdas Greimas, Jacques Lacan, Michel Foucault and Louis Althusser among its leading exponents) and its near or distant relatives (including Fernand Braudel's approach to historical writing, for example, or Pierre Bourdieu's to sociological analysis). Structuralism had itself fragmented by the early 1970s to be overtaken by poststructuralisms (the later Barthes, the later Foucault, Jacques Derrida, Julia Kristeva, for instance) and theorizations of the postmodern (Jean-François Lyotard and Jean Baudrillard, among others).

There was a diffuse return in the 1980s and 1990s to more humanistic, ethical and subjective preoccupations, reflected by new interest in some older thinkers, such as Emmanuel Levinas or Paul Ricoeur, or by the emblematic reappearance of a former structuralist such as Tzvetan Todorov in the role of a humanistic moralist, and the prominence of younger philosophers, such as André Comte-Sponville, Alain Renaut and Luc Ferry, who have been highly critical of the antihumanistic spirit of thinkers such as Lacan, Foucault, Derrida and Bourdieu (Ferry and Renaut, 1985; and for interesting treatments of the links between these 'ideas' and the ideological climate in the 1980s, see Wood, 1991, 1998).

The relationship between philosophical fashions and the relative strength of particular ideological currents over a given period is extremely intricate. Suffice it to say here that the relationship is shaped in part by the fact that those intellectuals whose status is particularly high as producers of philosophical and semi-philosophical ideas at a particular time are often standard-bearers of political causes associated with ideological currents which are also pre-eminent among the intelligentsia at the same time. However, although association with ideas that are presented as radical and progressive in one sphere could easily be paralleled by association with radical ideas in the other, the coincidence has by no means been invariable. As regards their core concepts and morphology, there may be a greater or lesser affinity between a particular philosophical system and a particular ideology, but the philosophical systems (existentialism, structuralism, etc.) and ideologies (communism, socialism, liberalism, etc.) conventionally placed under generic labels are not solid blocks but assemblages which not only vary in detail from one exponent to another, but are also amenable to substantial adaptation and reinterpretation if an exponent wishes to do that.

Thus, existentialism and phenomenology could be adapted to fit with Marxism, as in the case of Sartre's *Critique de la raison dialectique* (1960) and Merleau-Ponty's *Humanisme et terreur* (1947), or in the writings of Edgar Morin, Kostas Axelos, Pierre Fougeyrollas and some other members of the group producing the review, *Arguments*, in the 1960s (Poster, 1975). On the other hand, some other existentialists and phenomenologists – Camus, Paul Ricoeur, Mikel Dufrenne and Emmanuel Levinas, for example – were non- or anti-Marxists. Indeed, echoes of existentialism can be found in the early writings of Alain de Benoist, a founding theorist of the New Right. Similarly, in the 1960s, exponents of the many diverse manifestations of structuralism, which did not even claim to be a philosophy but merely a method, included numerous Marxists, such as Louis Althusser, Etienne Balibar and Nicos Poulantzas in political theory, Maurice Godelier, Lucien Sebag and Emmanuel Terray in anthropology, the early Barthes and Julia Kristeva, in semiology, Michel Pêcheux and Françoise Gadet in discourse analysis, Lucien Goldmann, Pierre Macherey and Christian Metz in literary or film theory (Benton, 1984; Coward and Ellis, 1977; Dosse, 1992; Macdonell, 1986). Others, such as Foucault or Bourdieu in the 1960s, were close to Marxism while retaining a critical distance. Even when not explicitly linked to Marxism, structuralism lent itself readily to critique of liberal capitalist society, of bourgeois democracy and of bourgeois individualism and humanism. This was also true, for example, of Foucault's later, poststructuralist work on power/knowledge, or Gilles Deleuze's on Nietzsche and Lyotard's theorization of postmodernity, for example. On the other hand, even in the heyday of structural Marxism or Marxist structuralism, some structuralists, including the founding father, Lévi-Strauss, were never fully-fledged Marxists, and many others ceased to be so in due course.

Structures of intellectual life and scholarship·

In France intellectual debate is a topic of widespread fascination, not only for the producers and distributors of ideas, but also for a broader, highly educated public which has grown enormously since the 1950s thanks in large measure to the massive expansion of higher education and the increasing numbers of students and graduates produced by it. The development of the print and broadcasting media has likewise been an important factor: France is a country where substantial numbers of journalists and radio or television presenters make a specialism of following and helping to generate fashions in the sphere of ideas. It also sustains the tradition of reflective reviews specializing in ideas and current affairs (*Les Temps modernes*, *Esprit*, *Le Débat* and *Critique*, for example), the weekly current affairs magazines (such as *Le Nouvel Observateur*, which pioneered this form of journalism in the 1960s, *L'Express* and *L'Evénement du jeudi*) and the up-market press (*Le Monde*, *Le Figaro*, *Libération*). Moreover, there is nothing untoward about the radio station, France Inter, broadcasting a discussion between eminent philosophers for one and a half hours, complete with lengthy interventions by phone, e-mail or fax from listeners. For many years Bernard Pivot's television programme, *Apostrophes*, achieved an emblematic status as a showcase for exponents of philosophical and other ideas. Major booksellers, such as FNAC, have equally played their part in supporting this prestigious market by organizing promotional events such as the participation of celebrity thinkers in series of public debates on their premises. And, of course, there are the cafés which specialize in providing a venue for philosophical discussion.

As Louis Pinto (1994) has pointed out, journalists have exerted enormous influence on the field of ideas by bringing individuals to public notice, by labelling them as 'philosophers' and 'thinkers', by promoting particular subjects for attention, opening up debates, sponsoring discussions and seeking to stir confrontations between leading figures. Their endless demand for learned but accessible reflections on the state of the modern world and the situation of contemporary French society has helped to make careers for polymathic intellectuals, such as Bernard-Henri Lévy and André Glucksmann, specializing in media work alongside the writing of quickfire essays on burning issues of the moment.

Because many of the celebrities in the sphere of ideas have also been leading protagonists in political debates, by virtue of the expectations of the public role of the intellectual, some individuals have commanded an extraordinary amount of attention at particular times. Periodically it has been claimed that the era of towering figures has passed. The deaths of Sartre, Aron, Barthes, Lacan and Foucault – as well as the silence of Althusser after murdering his wife – in the early 1980s have sometimes been taken to mark a watershed in this respect. But this perception surely derives from a distortion of perspective arising from the confusion of value with status. If the disappearance of a very small number of unusually prominent figures was so important, even on the symbolic level, it would point to a desperate shallowness of French intellectual life. In reality, it says more about the cult of the all-purpose intellectual star, the *maître à penser*, and about the self-regarding nature of the Parisian intellectual scene in which individuals and factions (*chapelles, cénacles*) perpetually engage in fratricidal rivalries which are sometimes expressed as denunciations of (other) intellectuals in general. The alleged crisis of the intellectual in the 1980s, while corresponding, no doubt, to a crystallization of awareness of real social changes affecting the roles and status of intellectuals, can itself be considered a reflexive version of fashionable pessimism in the realm of ideas at the time: more recently there have been suggestions that the intellectuals are making a comeback. Changing times bring new figures to the fore, addressing new or old issues in new terms. In the 1990s the deaths of Emmanuel Levinas, Félix Guattari, Gilles Deleuze, François Furet and Jean-François Lyotard can be accorded similar significance, or insignificance, to the passing of the earlier series of major figures in the early 1980s. Popularly recognized intellectuals such as Bernard-Henri Lévy, Alain Finkielkraut and André Glucksmann, or rising stars such as André Comte-Sponville, Luc Ferry and Gilles Lipovetsky, who are prominent in the media today, are probably no more nor less despised, admired and envied by those who do not have that status than their predecessors were in earlier decades.

Whatever the case, the hothouse intellectual atmosphere of Paris continues to give intensity to debates. Over the course of time some individuals can still become the centres of entire micro-industries of intellectual production. For example, the sociologist Pierre Bourdieu has his institutional base as a professor at the Collège de France and as a director of studies at the Ecole des Hautes Etudes en Sciences Sociales. He and his academic disciples maintain the journal, *Actes de la recherche en sciences sociales*. He has connections with the publishing houses, Seuil, Editions de Minuit and Arléa. Closer to the politically committed end of his activity, he underpins the review, *Liber*, and the book series, Liber-Raisons d'Agir, which achieved impressively high sales for its low-price, small-format, polemical works. He is regularly interviewed or cited in *Le Monde, Le Monde diplomatique, Libération, Le Nouvel Observateur* and other media outlets. In short, he is a remarkable testimony to the rewards which can be gained by the cream of the elite in a set of academic and commercial institutions which he has subjected to relentless critique in his writings since the mid-1960s (for example, in Bourdieu, 1979, 1984, 1989, 1996; Bourdieu and Passeron, 1964, 1970). His political activism on the extreme left since the time of the students' and workers' strikes in the closing months of 1995 places him in contact with a number of the new social movements which have campaigned outside the sphere of mainstream politics in recent years, including Agir contre le Chômage, Droit au Logement, Observatoire de la Pauvreté and Réseau Société Syndicalisme, among others.

There is, then, an intriguing interplay between the realm of political commitments, fashionable ideas and a crucial third dimension of intellectual life, the education system which produces the intellectuals and provides many of them with employment as teachers and/or researchers in their various fields of scholarship. The education system has undergone many changes at all levels over the last fifty years, not least in terms of the numbers reaching the *baccalauréat* and hence of those entering higher education (Auduc and Bayard-Pierlot, 1995; Eicher, 1997; Renaut, 1998; Turner, 1997; Vasconsellos, 1998). In the former category, the rise from around 30 000 new *bacheliers* per year at the end of the 1940s to nearly half a million per year by the mid-1990s encouraged a huge increase in demand for higher qualifications. Consequently, student numbers in higher education – ranging from the prestigious, highly selective *grandes écoles*, with their corresponding preparatory classes, to the largely non-selective universities, the *instituts universitaires de technologie* and the *sections de techniciens supérieurs* – increased from around 150 000 in the mid-1950s to more than 500 000 by the late 1960s and onwards to more than two million by the mid-1990s.

The massive expansion of student numbers has placed enormous strain on teaching and other resources, especially in the overcrowded, underfunded universities, but the pursuit of research and the production of scholarly publications have by no means withered as a result. The Centre National de la Recherche Scientifique (CNRS), established in 1939 and relaunched after the war, has played an extremely important role in this regard, not only in the natural sciences, but across the full range of fields of knowledge. Financed by the state to an equivalent of roughly 1.7 per cent of GDP per year by the mid-1990s, supporting more than 1200 research groups (nearly 200 of its own and over 1000 in cooperation with the higher education institutions), the CNRS is a huge source of national funding, coordination and evaluation of research. At the time of the most recent report by its national committee (Comité National de la Recherche Scientifique, 1997), the CNRS directly employed some 11 700 full-time researchers, grouped within 40 sections, each of which included a set of related fields. Of the 38 000 professors and lecturers in pure and applied sciences, humanities and social sciences at that time, over 15 000 were carrying out research within CNRS-linked groupings, as were some 2000 post-doctoral researchers and 14 500 doctoral students. Researchers in the social sciences, humanities and the arts have always complained that they receive a very small proportion of the total funding. As a crude indication it is striking that whereas 8250 full-time researchers and 10 875 teacher-researchers in pure or applied sciences were associated with CNRS-linked groups in 1996, the corresponding figures for social sciences, humanities and arts taken together were only 2000 and 4000 respectively. On the other hand, there were large numbers (10 875, according to CNRS) of higher education teachers in non-scientific fields carrying out their research outside the orbit of the CNRS.

Production by scholars in higher education is not, of course, restricted to specialist monographs and journal articles aimed primarily at fellow-researchers in the same fields. It extends to more pedagogically oriented works for use by students, who provide a large readership for relatively cheap pocket editions of the type which began to be published in increasing numbers from the 1960s onwards, when Que sais-je? and Livre de Poche were joined by series such as Idées, Médiations and 10/18, prompting numerous imitators since that time and doing much to promote awareness of the development of the social sciences and humanities. Depending on the nature of the field and the potential demand, intellectual production could also feed into popularizing books and high quality magazines such as *L'Histoire, Sciences humaines* or *Le Magazine littéraire* aimed at a wider public.

The academic field which has traditionally had the most obvious relationship with the realm of fashionable ideas is philosophy, traditionally the jewel in the crown of French *culture générale*, as purveyed to the country's educated elites. Within the *lycées* there have been shifts in student demand in favour of the science and mathematics *baccalauréat* at the expense of the other combinations. Even so, with a requirement of eight contact hours per week in the classroom, philosophy still occupies the largest part of the curriculum in the final year of the *lycée* for students taking one of the *baccalauréats* in the L (literature) series, and carries an obligatory four hours per week for those taking the *baccalauréats* in the ES (economic and social) or the S (science) series (Auduc and Bayard-Pierlot,

1995). Students are thus compelled to develop a particular range of skills in verbal reasoning and rhetoric in response to abstract questions such as 'What is an injustice?', 'Can one deliberately forget?' or 'Is death thinkable?' (see Pinto, 1983). Philosophy remains a central element in the preparatory classes for the Ecole Normale Supérieure. Although it attracts small numbers of students in comparison with many social sciences or humanities, the subject still retains great prestige in higher education and those who go on to obtain the *agrégation* or the CAPES with a view to teaching the subject may well consider themselves practitioners of the queen of disciplines (Soulié, 1995).

The traditional prestige of philosophy as an academic subject, and the fact that very large numbers of highly educated people have at least a vestigial understanding of its characteristic concerns and modes of discourse, does much to explain the vigour of the market for ideas. It does not follow, however, that the philosophers who become well known in the media as representatives of innovative ideas are necessarily those who command most respect among professional philosophers in higher or secondary education. The programmes of the CAPES or the *agrégation* followed by those intending to become professional teachers of philosophy have not been immutable over the course of time, but they have remained heavily focused on the work of canonical thinkers such as Plato and Aristotle, Kant, Hegel and Nietzsche, Descartes, Rousseau and Bergson (Soulié, 1995). Even professional philosophers who seek to distinguish themselves from the mainstream have normally published previously on canonical authors. Thus, for example, Gilles Deleuze, later notorious with Félix Guattari as co-author of radical works including *Capitalisme et schizophrénie. L'Anti-Oedipe* (1972), among others, had previously written on Kant, Nietzsche, Bergson and Hume. Furthermore, as Pinto (1987) demonstrated on the basis of a comparison between several scholarly journals of philosophy (*Archives de philosophie, Etudes philosophiques, Revue philosophique, Revue de métaphysique et de morale*) and reviews specializing in ideas for a wider intellectual public (*Critique, Esprit, Débat*), there has been relatively little overlap of contributors between the two types of publication – only 7 per cent in his sample, and about 60 per cent of the contributors of more or less philosophical articles to the reviews of ideas were from outside the higher education system. Equally, there were significant differences in the types of subject discussed and in the tone of the writing. On the one hand, the topics of articles in the scholarly journals tended not to deal with current public concerns, but rather with questions relating to the history of philosophy or technical analyses in areas such as epistemology or logic, addressed in a dispassionate style. On the other hand, articles in the intellectual reviews tended to concentrate heavily on issues of contemporary public interest, such as matters relating to liberalism, postmodernism, the environment, bioethics or technology.

At the same time, while purists may have retreated into frosty indifference towards the non-specialist market, others have succeeded in moving deftly between the different spheres, using each to promote success in the other. As Niilo Kauppi (1996: 134–6) has shown, Michel Foucault was perhaps the classic example of this type of trajectory, dividing his work between academic scholarship and writing provocative articles for avant-garde intellectual reviews, then for major newspapers and weekly magazines until he had achieved the level of celebrity which earned him a chair at the Collège de France (compare Lamont, 1987 for an early study of Derrida on similar lines). More recently, Luc Ferry, a university professor of philosophy, has provided an interesting example of how a judicious mixture of philosophical scholarship and more popular theoretical writing on current issues – ranging from ecology to aesthetics, to philosophy of history, to the thought of Nietzegger and Heidegger, to the 'antihumanism' of the structuralists and poststructuralists, to the concept of reason, to the theory of rights – can make a very successful package, notwithstanding the fact that political philosophy has traditionally been a marginal field within both philosophy and political science in France.

Still, it is a little ironic that philosophical and semi-philosophical ideas have become such objects of interest in the course of a period when philosophy has been outstripped in its share of higher education students. It is easy to forget that structuralism represented itself as a challenge to the outdatedness of traditional philosophical and literary culture (Kauppi, 1996). It fed on, and to varying degrees into, the rising social sciences which had themselves drawn impetus from the prestige of science and technology in a period of rapid modernization. With the exception of economics, the social sciences had failed to establish firm institutional bases in higher education before the Second World War. The belated creation of teaching and research posts, accompanied by the development of more or less specialized academic qualifications in fields such as anthropology, sociology and political science from the 1950s to the 1970s was of enormous importance in this respect (Drouard, 1982; Guillaume, 1986). It also encouraged the transformation of older fields. For example, philology was overtaken by post-Saussurean structural linguistics, paving the way for generative grammar, pragmatics and neofunctionalist approaches. Literary-critical methodologies were revitalized by structuralist poetics and narratology, linking with and encouraging the development of semiological/semiotic approaches to other cultural forms including art, film and television. History writing, though charting its own remarkable course of renewal in the wake of Lucien Febvre and Marc Bloch who had founded the *Annales* during the 1930s, benefited hugely from the ability of its emerging stars around Fernand Braudel to represent their field as a crossroads or synthesis of the social sciences with its own distinctive notion of structuration in historical processes. The dynamics of this development, coupled with the sharing of a common culture, the cult of the polymath and the taste for generalization and systematization, encouraged prolific cross-fertilization between different fields of scholarship and stimulated interdisciplinary approaches to research based on new objects and methods of study.

Although the hegemony of the old philosophical-literary tradition in French culture was increasingly challenged from the later 1950s onwards within the field of ideas in the name of a supposedly more rigorous, scientific approach to the understanding of human beings and their societies, a great deal of common ground, or rather common culture, was shared by the challenged and the challengers. Given the fact that specialist academic training in most of the social sciences was not available to those who were students before the late 1960s, many of the leading challengers were themselves the products of a traditional philosophical (and literary) training at least as far as the *classes préparatoires* for the Ecole Normale Supérieure, and in some cases as far as the *agrégation*. Notwithstanding the aspiration to scientificity and the use of social-scientific models, statistical data and terminology, they too shared the culture of theoretical discourse, with a preference for abstract, deductive reasoning, systematization, use of copious references to canonical philosophers, a propensity to make universalistic claims concerning mankind in general and a certain contempt for Anglo-American empirical approaches (Kauppi, 1996).

For many intellectual fields the interaction between scholarly activity, popularization and contributions to media-dominated discussions of ideas has stimulated enormous dynamism. This was particularly true during the high period of institutional expansion from the 1950s to the early 1970s. Since that time the sense of momentum has diminished. Without the spur of the big systems of ideas which permeated the social sciences and humanities during that period there has been a widespread sense of dispersion and fragmentation. From a non-French perspective, the recent period might simply appear as one of normalization, as French academics adapt to the requirements of functional specialization and division of labour in an ever-expanding world of international scholarship where no individual can be sure of keeping up to date with the surfeit of scholarly publications even in the narrowest area of any subdiscipline. Nevertheless, there is no doubt that it has generated a sense of uncertainty, revealed in the number of references to a supposed crisis. In part, it is due to the fact that the humanities and social sciences which developed so vigorously have now been challenged from several directions in competition for students and to some extent in the market of ideas. The challenge has come from sciences, especially the newer biological and environmental sciences, from information technology and artificial intelligence, from vocational subjects such as management, administration and business studies, and from the emergent social-scientific field of mass communications. That was the rather uneasy climate in which the book, *Impostures intellectuelles* (1997), by the American physicist, Alan Sokal, and his Belgian collaborator, Jean Bricmont, caused such affront by drawing attention to the way in which a representative selection of France's leading philosophers/social theorists (Lacan, Derrida, Kristeva, Baudrillard, Deleuze, Latour, among others) had frequently misused the scientific concepts and terminology with which they had habitually larded their writings.

This malaise has fed into wider reflections on the possible end of French exceptionalism in a world increasingly dominated by Anglo-American culture and the English language. Of course, many French intellectuals have made visits to the United States or other anglophone countries to give conference papers or guest lectures. Some major figures hold visiting posts at prestigious American universities and many younger scholars work there for long periods or permanently, given the shortage of posts in France. Equally, some fields of the social sciences in France include more or less influential schools of thought which have much in common with Anglo-American approaches. This has been the case in political science, economics and sociology, for example (see Baslé, 1989; Chazel, 1988; Drouard, 1982; Guillaume, 1986; and relevant chapters in this collection). Recently, as Richard Wolin points out in his chapter for this collection, there has even been greater openness to the British and American tradition of analytical philosophy which had formerly been regarded as sterile and pedantic in comparison with French philosophers' taste for grandiose, universalistic systems of thought. Nevertheless, the sphere of intellectual production overlaps with other cultural spheres and is subject to similar preoccupations. Throughout the period since the Second World War, guardians of French culture have been concerned by what they have seen as excessive penetration of

France by the influence of the English-speaking cultures, and particularly of the United States (see, for example, chapters on cinema, television and linguistic policy in Perry, 1997). This anxiety had been voiced periodically even before the Second World War, but it has been more pressing since 1945, given the extent of American dominance of the West throughout the second half of the century. Since the end of the Cold War it has, if anything, grown more acute. In the cultural sphere it has been reflected in the protectionist thrust of government policy towards the arts, including the defence of French film production during the Uruguay round of the GATT negotiations. The same impulsion has been a factor in the direction of media regulation as the influx of American imports has been viewed as an important factor in dragging down standards. It has underpinned linguistic policy through attempts to prevent the swamping of French with anglicisms and through the promotion of the French language abroad, notably within the orbit of the Francophonie organization. In this respect, then, the ambivalence of many French intellectuals towards the United States is part of a much wider issue of what France is to become as a cultural entity in the future.

A short case study of the problems of a successful discipline

To illustrate some of the negative aspects of the changes which have affected the humanities and social sciences in recent years, let us take the case of history, since this shows the downside of a success story. We will borrow heavily from Gérard Noiriel's book *Sur la 'crise' de l'histoire* (1996) which nicely encapsulates the range of anxieties that have been widely aired by historians since the mid-1980s (themes recurring, for example, in several of the contributions to Boutier and Julia, 1995). Noiriel refers to a climate of uncertainty about the shape and future direction of the profession, despite the continuing popularity of history as a canonical subject which renovated itself very successfully during the postwar decades, earning a major international reputation in the process, and which recruits some 10 000 new students per year in higher education.

One aspect of the problem relates to conditions of service shared with other disciplines. The fragmentation of the professional community was caused partly by the end of the period of rapid expansion from the 1950s to early 1970s, followed by a long recession only partially reversed by renewal of recruitment in the 1990s. There had been a huge postwar expansion from about 100 established posts on the eve of the Second World War to 500 by 1968 and around 1200 by 1983, not counting a further 200 in the CNRS. Rapid expansion had destabilized the old networks of patronage and mutual support linking senior academics with junior ones – a process of incorporation in which the supervision/ writing of the *thèse d'Etat* had played an important part until its abolition in the early 1980s. Many more junior posts than senior ones had been created, heightening disparities of conditions as access to promotion became increasingly constricted. On the other hand, the crisis of recruitment in the 1970s and 1980s left many on the sidelines in non-established situations as few young scholars obtained established posts. Many would-be higher education teachers accepted post in schools instead. At the end of the 1980s and in the early 1990s the creation of new posts, though welcome, was inadequate to keep pace with the expansion of student numbers. In any case, it did not mark the start of a long-term process of renewal. Many teaching and research posts were based on short-term contracts, and teaching posts often carried very heavy contact hours. The general trend towards heavier teaching and administrative loads, coupled with quality assurance measures and staff appraisal, not to mention salary issues, gave university teachers a sense of being overwhelmed and increasingly distant from CNRS researchers and holders of posts in specialist or other elite institutions with good research opportunities.

All of these factors opened a gulf between those reaching the end of their careers having benefited from the heady years of expansion and those trying to make their way in a much harsher environment where distribution of posts was very bottom-heavy. Meanwhile, the internationalization of historical research had occurred on terms which were unfavourable to France. Internationally the field was dominated by the United States, including American historians of France. It was hard for French historians to integrate with international research because of the effort involved in acquiring sufficient mastery of English and of finding the funds to attend international conferences abroad. This created new divisions between those who did and those who did not enter the international arena, with some denouncing the provincialism of historical writing in France, while others denounced the damaging influence of American hegemony.

A second set of factors relate to the nature of historical study. The diversification of objects of historical study and methods of analysis had been seen as a sign of dynamism – exemplified by Pierre Nora's prestigious book series, La Bibliothèque des Histoires, published by Gallimard – during the heyday of the *Annales* in the 1950s and 1960s, as the discipline had rejuvenated itself by learning methodological lessons and absorbing new subjects of investigation from the rising social sciences. Already advocated by the founding fathers of the *Annales*, Marc Bloch and Lucien Febvre in the 1930s, it had become a hallmark of the paradigm, fostered particularly in the 6th Section of the Ecole Pratique des Hautes Etudes, then the Ecole des Hautes Etudes en Sciences Sociales, and encouraged by new university courses where history was taught alongside social sciences. However, euphoria was replaced in due course by an increasing perception of fragmentation and dispersion. Interdisciplinarity was a mixed blessing, since it left historians as an increasingly disparate body engaged in a bewildering variety of subdisciplines and interdisciplines. Furthermore, the traditional aspiration to objectivity had been challenged by exponents of the 'linguistic turn', such as Paul Veyne and Michel de Certeau, who focused on the history of representations and on the nature of historical discourse as a cultural phenomenon, thereby relativizing its claims to communicate knowledge of historical reality. By the 1980s the consequent sense of uncertainty as to the contours and borderlines of the field was underscored by history's loss of some of its primacy in relation to the newer social sciences which had by then become firmly established within the higher education system.

A further cause of fragmentation and questioning of professional roles relates to the issue of popularization. As the market for textbooks and accessible treatments of historical topics increased from the 1950s onwards and new formats were produced by publishers to cater to the rising demand, the further step was for the borders between professional historical activity and journalism to become blurred. Prominent academics contributed articles to magazines and newspapers, or participated in radio and television broadcasts, which benefited them by enhancing their public status. Popularization accentuated divisions between those who could gain prestige from this process and become directors of major series with big publishers and those who did more specialized work, or worked in unfashionable areas, as publishers offer fewer outlets for highly specialized monographs in order to chase the lucrative popular market. In any case, the 1990s saw a decline in the market for specialist historical works, which in turn rebounded on the quality of popularizations causing a decline in public taste for them as well, with consequent signs of saturation of the market.

Yet another facet of the process is the involvement of historians, not only as experts in public enquiries or in the show trials of Paul Touvier in 1994 and Maurice Papon in 1997–8, but also as commentators on sets of events which remain live political issues and have a high profile in the media. This aspect of the blurring of boundaries between historical scholarship and other forms of public activity applies particularly, though not exclusively (given the debates over the meaning of the

Revolution of 1789), to specialists in recent history whose fields cover the Second World War and the wars of decolonization, for example, which are controversial issues in relation to the notion of collective national memory of the past, and hence are viewed as central to national identity during a period of self-appraisal (for discussion, see the chapter on history writing in this collection). In these areas the distance in time which was traditionally taken to allow the historian critical distance from the events is shortened. In this arena works by professional histor-ians are offered to the public alongside works by historical journalists, each reviewing each other, sometimes collaborating, sometimes engag-ing in polemics, including those relating to the politics of managing collective memory. This further undermines the claim to professional authority based on the ideal of objectivity and critical distance from the subject of study.

From a different standpoint none of this need be seen as disastrous. It is the negative side of what can easily be represented as a story of great achievement. For example, Jacques Le Goff and Nicolas Roussellier (1995: 17) take a more balanced view of the matter when they argue that, notwithstanding the real challenges and changes facing the discip-line, the 'crisis' is more a question of mood and perception than of substance. Nevertheless, as regards the period since the end of the Sec-ond World War, history shows many of the characteristics of other fields: the institutional context which produces major differences of working conditions between the haves and the have-nots in the profession; the period of rapid expansion from the 1950s to the early 1970s, followed by constriction of resources and declining conditions of service for the less privileged majority; the diversification and fragmentation of the field, coupled with the benefits and dangers of interdisciplinarity; the rewards offered to some by the media and the blurring of borderlines between professional scholarship and journalism; the dilemmas as to the proper role of the scholar as educator, popularizer, expert commentator, produ-cer of 'ideas' and committed actor in public political debates; a growing awareness of the danger of insularity in an age when French language and culture are overshadowed by the English-speaking world and particularly the United States, making Gallocentric cultural universalism seem pretentious, parochial and archaic.

The collection

The present collection contains relatively little direct discussion of the politics of French intellectuals since there is already a very substantial literature on the subject in English as well as French. Instead the focus is primarily on scholarly work, some of which has contributed to or been influenced by the movements of ideas in the broader intellectual arena. The contributors to this book explore a range of key spheres of intellectual activity in the humanities and social sciences. They analyse influential bodies of thought, competing paradigms of knowledge, seminal debates and important moments of change. In the main, the work discussed in the book has been carried out by scholars who work in institutions of higher education. However, given that one of the most distinctive aspects of French intellectual life is the high level of production and consumption of scholarly work outside the confines of academic institutions, that is not invariably the case. The historical span of the book corresponds broadly to the period since the end of the Second World War, with particular emphasis on more recent developments, but it is not a compendium of historical overviews of the intellectual fields concerned. Contributors were invited to discuss their chosen areas from whatever standpoint they found most appropriate to capturing some of the most interesting and distinctive characteristics of French scholarship. In some cases, such as the chapters on philosophy and anthropology, authors have chosen to adopt a broadly chronological-thematic perspective by mapping out factors of change or continuity between schools of thought over the second half of the twentieth century. In other cases, such as the chapters on sociology and linguistics, the chronological dimension is less pronounced, as contributors have been more concerned to throw light on the essential features of particular systems of ideas or methods of analysis. Seán Hand's approach is the most radical. Instead of offering a conventional, analytical discussion of developments in literary theory, he produces a representation of the style and characteristic concerns of a certain type of French theoretical discourse. In articulating the assumptions involved in writing about his subject, he questions his own ostensible purpose, and that of the entire collection.

We have chosen to place the chapters in a sequence based on their historical situation within the institutions of the French education system, starting with the traditionally canonical fields (philosophy, literature, history), followed by the social sciences which began to be incorporated from the later nineteenth century onwards (linguistics, anthropology, sociology, economics, political science, psychoanalysis) then the two recently developed fields (feminism, film) which have crystallized as institutional areas of scholarship during the latter part of the twentieth century. There is no absolute, logical relationship between the different fields to dictate a more rigid ordering of chapters, since connections can be made in many directions as different affinities or areas of cross-fertilization are singled out, especially in view of the enormous amount of interdisciplinary work carried out in many of the fields under discussion.

References

Auduc, Jean-Louis and Jacqueline Bayard-Pierlot (1995) *Le Système éducatif français*, 4th edn. Créteil: CRDP.

Baslé, Maurice (1989) 'Economics and economists in France today', in Jolyon Howorth and George Ross (eds), *Contemporary France: A Review of Interdisciplinary Studies*, vol. 3. London: Pinter, pp. 205–18 (trans. George Ross).

Benton, Ted (1984) *The Rise and Fall of Structural Marxism: Althusser and His Influence*. London: Macmillan.

Bourdieu, Pierre (1979) *La Distinction. Critique sociale du jugement*. Paris: Minuit.

—— (1984) *Homo academicus*. Paris: Minuit.

—— (1989) *La Noblesse d'Etat. Grandes écoles et esprit de corps*. Paris: Minuit.

—— (1996) *Sur la télévision,* followed by *L'Emprise du journalisme*. Paris: Liber-Raisons d'Agir.

—— and Jean-Claude Passeron (1964) *Les Héritiers*. Paris: Minuit.

—— and Jean-Claude Passeron (1970) *La Reproduction*. Paris: Minuit.

Boutier, Jean and Dominique Julia (eds) (1995) *Passés recomposés. Champs et chantiers de l'histoire*. Paris: Autrement.

Charle, Christophe (1990) *Naissance des 'intellectuels', 1880–1900*. Paris: Minuit.

Chazel, François (1988) 'Sociology: from structuralist determinism to methodological individualism', in Jolyon Howorth and George Ross (eds) *Contemporary France: A Review of Interdisciplinary Studies*, vol. 2. London: Pinter, pp. 187–202 (trans. Jolyon Howorth).

Comité National de la Recherche Scientifique (1997) *Rapport de conjoncture 1996*. Internet version, http://www.cnrs.fr.

Conan, Eric and Henry Rousso (1994) *Vichy, un passé qui ne passe pas*. Paris: Fayard.

Coward, Rosalind and John Ellis (1977) *Language and Materialism: Developments in Semiology and the Theory of the Subject*. London: Routledge & Kegan Paul.

Dosse, François (1992) *Histoire du structuralisme*, 2 vols. Paris: La Découverte.

Drouard, Alain (1982) 'Réflexions sur une chronologie: le développement des sciences sociales en France de 1945 à la fin des années soixante', *Revue française de sociologie*, 23 (1): 55–85.

Eicher, Jean-Claude (1997) 'The recent evolution of higher education in France: growth and dilemmas', *European Journal of Education*, 32 (2): 185–98.

Flood, Christopher (1997a) 'National populism', in Christopher Flood and Laurence Bell (eds), *Political Ideologies in Contemporary France*. London: Cassell/Pinter, pp. 103–39.

—— (1997b) 'Pierre-André Taguieff and the dilemmas of antiracism', *L'Esprit créateur*, 37 (2): 68–78.

Forbes, Jill and Michael Kelly (eds) (1995) *French Cultural Studies: An Introduction*. Oxford: Oxford University Press.

Furet, François, Jacques Julliard and Pierre Rosanvallon (1988) *La République du centre. La fin de l'exception française*. Paris: Calmann-Lévy.

Fysh, Peter and Jim Wolfreys (1998) *The Politics of Racism in France*. London: Macmillan.

Gaillard, Françoise (1998) 'The terror of consensus', in Goux and Wood (1998), pp. 65–74 (trans. Jennifer Gage).

Goetschel, Pascale and Emanuelle Loyer (1994) *Histoire culturelle et intellectuelle de la France au XXe siècle*. Paris: Armand Colin.

Goux, Jean-Joseph and Philip R. Wood (eds) (1998) *Terror and Consensus: Vicissitudes of French Thought*. Stanford, CA: Stanford University Press.

Guillaume, Marc (ed.) (1986) *L'Etat des sciences sociales en France*. Paris: La Découverte.

Hazareesingh, Sudhir (1994) *Political Traditions in Modern France*. Oxford: Oxford University Press.

Jeanneney, Jean-Noël (1998) *Le Passé dans le prétoire. L'historien, le juge et le journaliste*. Paris: Seuil.

Jennings, Jeremy (ed.) (1993) *Intellectuals in Twentieth-Century France: Mandarins and Samurais*. London: Macmillan.

Jennings, Jeremy (1997) 'Of treason, blindness and silence: dilemmas of the intellectual in modern France', in Jeremy Jennings and Anthony Kemp-Welch (eds), *Intellectuals in Politics from the Dreyfus Affair to Salman Rushdie*. London: Routledge, pp. 65–85.

Kahn, Jean-François (1995) *La Pensée unique*. Paris: Fayard.

Kauppi, Niilo (1996) *French Intellectual Nobility: Institutional and Symbolic Transformations in the Post-Sartrian Era*. Albany: State University of New York Press.

Lamont, Michèle (1987) 'How to become a dominant French philosopher: the case of Jacques Derrida', *American Journal of Sociology*, 93 (3): 584–622.

Le Goff, Jacques and Nicolas Roussellier (1995) 'Préface', in François Bédarida (ed.), *L'Histoire et le métier d'historien en France 1945–1995*. Paris: Maison des Sciences de l'Homme, pp. 3–17.

Lilla, Mark (ed.) (1994) *New French Thought: Political Philosophy*. Princeton, NJ: Princeton University Press.

Macdonell, Diane (1986) *Theories of Discourse: An Introduction*. Oxford: Blackwell.

Mathy, Jean-Philippe (1997) 'Repli sur la république: la nouvelle donne des intellectuels français', *L'Esprit créateur*, 37 (2): 41–55.

Merleau-Ponty, Maurice (1947) *Humanisme et terreur, essai sur le problème communiste*. Paris: Gallimard

Mongin, Olivier (1994) *Face au scepticisme. Les mutations du paysage intellectuel et l'invention de l'intellectuel démocratique*. Paris: La Découverte.

Noiriel, Gérard (1996) *Sur la 'crise' de l'histoire*. Paris: Belin.

Ory, Pascal and Jean-François Sirinelli (1992) *Les Intellectuels en France, de l'Affaire Dreyfus à nos jours*, 2nd edn. Paris: Armand Colin.

Perrineau, Pascal (1997) *Le Symptôme Le Pen. Radiographie des électeurs du Front national*. Paris: Fayard.

Perry, Sheila (ed.) (1997) *Aspects of Contemporary France*. London: Routledge.

Pinto, Louis (1983) 'L'Ecole des philosophes', *Actes de la recherche en sciences sociales*, 47–8 (June): 25–38.

—— (1987) *Les Philosophes entre le lycée et l'avant-garde. Les métamorphoses de la philosophie dans la France d'aujourd'hui*. Paris: L'Harmattan.

—— (1994) 'Le Journalisme philosophique', *Actes de la recherche en sciences sociales*, 101–2 (March): 21–36.

Poster, Mark (1975) *Existential Marxism in Postwar France: From Sartre to Althusser.* Princeton, NJ: Princeton University Press.

Renaut, Alain (1998) 'Redéfinir les fonctions de l'Université', *Cahiers français*, 285 (March–April): 84–91.

Rousso, Henry (1998) *La Hantise du passé*, Interviews with Philippe Petit. Paris: Textuel.

Sartre, Jean-Paul (1960) *Critique de la raison dialectique I: Théorie des ensembles pratiques.* Paris: Gallimard.

Sirinelli, Jean-François (1990) *Intellectuels et passions françaises: Manifestes et pétitions au XXᵉ siècle.* Paris: Fayard.

Sokal, Alan and Jean Bricmont (1997) *Impostures intellectuelles.* Paris: Odile Jacob.

Soulié, Charles (1995) 'Anatomie du goût philosophique', *Actes de la recherche en sciences sociales*, 109 (October): 3–28.

Turner, Rob (1997) 'Higher Education', in Perry (1997), pp. 98–113.

Vasconsellos, Maria Drosile (1998) 'Les Lycées: évolutions et réformes', *Cahiers français*, 285 (March–April): 30–6.

Winock, Michel (1997) *Le Siècle des intellectuels.* Paris: Seuil.

Wood, Philip (1991) 'French thought under Mitterrand: the social, economic and political context for the return of the subject and ethics, for the Heidegger scandal, and for the demise of the critical intellectual', *Contemporary French Civilization*, 15(2): 244–67.

—— (1998) ' "Democracy" and "totalitarianism" in contemporary French thought: neoliberalism, the Heidegger scandal, and ethics in post-structuralism', in Goux and Wood (1998), pp. 75–103.

2
The Grandeur and Twilight of French Philosophical Radicalism

Richard Wolin

The irony of postwar French philosophy is that it found philosophy in its traditional Cartesian incarnation to be an embarrassment. Under the banner of the 'structuralist revolution' it strove to overthrow the reigning philosophical paradigms by any means available. To achieve this end, it borrowed concepts and methods from non-philosophical disciplines: anthropology, linguistics, psychoanalysis and the social sciences. These resources were mobilized in order to show that traditional claims concerning the autonomy of reason were untenable. In essence, philosophy knew not of what it spoke. Not only were its claims to intellectual sovereignty insupportable; they were pointedly ideological. They served to buttress a decrepit and unjust political system. As the jewel in the crown of the French educational system, philosophy was merely the window-dressing for a corrupt civilization. Thus, the itinerary of postwar French philosophy chronicles the triumph of non-philosophy over philosophy; it is a movement from 'idealism' to 'scientism'. The goal was to replace a philosophy of the subject with a cool and detached *structural anonymity*. At issue is the trajectory from Jean-Paul Sartre's celebration of 'consciousness' in *Being and Nothingness* to the impersonal 'discursive regimes' of Michel Foucault's 'archaeology'.

In 1945 Sartre proclaimed with great fanfare that 'existentialism is a humanism' (Sartre, 1995). He thereby sought to minimize the break with traditional Western values that had been implicit in his earlier work. In the politically charged atmosphere of the post-liberation period, he wished to show that the tenets of existentialism were compatible with the humanist values of the republican and socialist traditions. By proceeding in this way, Sartre emphasized his commitment, in good Cartesian fashion, to a philosophy of subjectivity. We can know the world and affirm human freedom, argued Sartre, in so far as we consciously fashion and shape it. Essentially, the world is a stage on which we realize human ends and purposes. Whatever the obstacles we may encounter, in the last analysis the ends of freedom are a matter of will and choice. 'Man is nothing else but what he makes of himself,' Sartre maintains. 'Such is the first principle of existentialism. It is also what is called subjectivity.' 'Man is nothing else than his plan,' Sartre continues; 'he exists only to the extent that he fulfills himself; he is therefore nothing else than the ensemble of his acts, nothing else than his life.' Could there be any more convincing testimony to the idealism of Sartre's philosophy than his famous declaration: 'Man is condemned to be free' (Sartre, 1995: 271, 278, 274)?

To a great extent, the intentions and aims of the structuralist revolution may be understood as an Oedipal rebellion against the philosophy of Sartre. At the same time, to employ a metaphor popularized by the structuralists themselves, the stakes of the revolt against Sartre were politically overdetermined. Much more was at issue than a family dispute among philosophers and intellectuals. In the eyes of his detractors and critics, Sartre's philosophy of consciousness became a figure for the inequities and injustices of Western humanism. From the failings of French republicanism – which prided itself on its universalist, civilizing mission – to the moral evils of communism – which, after all, claimed to be the rightful heir of the universalist legacy of the Enlightenment – the humanist tradition, on which Europe had placed such high hopes, an unrelenting and ruthless unmasking of humanism and the power claims subtending it presented itself as an urgent intellectual task; it was, moreover, perceived as an undertaking freighted with momentous political implications. And although Sartre himself was a staunch antagonist of France's Fourth Republic, his communist fellow travelling (especially in the aftermath of the 1956 Soviet invasion of Hungary) was unpalatable to many intellectuals of conscience.

The attack on the cognitive primacy of the epistemological subject came from a variety of quarters. One of the most influential critiques derived from the structural anthropology of Claude Lévi-Strauss. In the 1940s Lévi-Strauss had been introduced to the structural linguistics of Ferdinand de Saussure and Roman Jakobson. Saussure's famous *Course in General Linguistics* (1906–7) would become a towering influence on an entire generation of French postwar intellectuals. Saussure's *Course* had emphasized the primacy of *langue* – language as a preconstituted, self-referential system – over *parole* or utterance. In a similar vein, he also stressed the status of language as synchronic, non-temporal whole as opposed to its ephemeral, diachronic alterations over the course of time.

Saussure's characterizations of the structural nature of language – especially his claims about the priority of language as 'structure' *vis-à-vis* its ephemeral quality as 'event' – would become definitive for Lévi-Strauss's understanding of myth as well as for the structuralist movement in general.

For Lévi-Strauss structuralism offered a scientific explanation of myth, which was, he claimed, governed by the same types of fundamental binary oppositions Saussure had discovered operative in language. More generally, Lévi-Strauss was one of the first thinkers to recommend structuralism as a methodological basis for the human sciences in general. At the same time that the *Annales* school of historiography was downgrading the value of political history in favour of a series of more fundamental and gradual climatic and environmental shifts (the so-called *longue durée*), Lévi-Strauss sought to fulfil the time-honoured goals of anthropology as a 'science of man' by stressing the invariant nature of human mental structures. As he would observe in *Structural Anthropology*: 'All forms of social life are essentially of the same nature ... They consist of systems of behavior that represent the projection, on the level of conscious and socialized thought, of universal laws which regulate the unconscious activities of the mind' (Lévi-Strauss, 1963: 58–9). Just as Freud's doctrine of the unconscious presented an explanatory key to the workings of the conscious mind, Lévi-Strauss's search for unconscious 'universal laws' – or 'structures' – sought to lay bare the depth dimension of human social and cultural life.

Before the publication of his extremely influential autobiography in 1955, Lévi-Strauss's audience had consisted primarily of fellow social scientists. With the appearance of *Tristes Tropiques*, however (which sold a remarkable 60 000 copies), the situation changed drastically. Overnight, he became an intellectual celebrity. The timing could hardly have been more auspicious. France, which a year earlier had suffered a humiliating defeat in Indochina, was about to embark on a bitter struggle over decolonization in Algeria. The conflict would ultimately bring down the Fourth Republic and lead France to the brink of civil war. As an ardent champion of anti-colonialism, Lévi-Strauss proved the man of the hour. His rebukes of 'evolutionism' and 'progress' – doctrines that had served as ideological props for colonialism – as well as his impassioned rejection of Eurocentrism, found great resonance among philosophers who were similarly convinced that Western values were urgently in need of deconstruction. More generally, Lévi-Strauss's emphatic denunciations of European colonialism generated compassion for the marginalized

'Other', an orientation that, a decade later, would become one of the hallmarks of poststructuralism.

In *Tristes Tropiques*, Lévi-Strauss could hardly resist tossing an incendiary barb in the direction of Sartre and company. It was the superficiality and vacuity of French philosophical traditions – existentialism, phenomenology and other 'philosophies of consciousness' – he confessed, that had spurred his interests in the social sciences. Declining to mince words, Lévi-Strauss sought to parry Sartre's intellectual dominance:

> As for the intellectual movement which was to reach its peak in existentialism, it seemed to me to be anything but a legitimate form of reflection, because of its over-indulgent attitude towards the illusions of subjectivity. The raising of personal preoccupations to the dignity of philosophical problems is far too likely to lead to a sort of shop-girl metaphysics, which may be pardonable as a didactic method but is extremely dangerous if it allows people to play fast-and-loose with the mission incumbent on philosophy until science becomes strong enough to replace it: that is, to understand Being in relationship to itself and not in relationship to myself. Instead of doing away with metaphysics, phenomenology and existentialism introduced two methods of providing it with alibis.
>
> (Lévi-Strauss, 1992: 58)

Five years later, the publication of Sartre's massive defense of Marxism and dialectics, *The Critique of Dialectical Reason,* would incite Lévi-Strauss to new polemical heights. Sartre had argued for the evolutionary superiority of a 'dialectical' understanding of history. Lévi-Strauss rejoined that Sartre's approach, with its dogmatic insistence on the virtues of 'totalization' (a Hegelian urge to reconcile all social oppositions and antagonisms) was hardly an improvement over the compulsions of the 'savage mind' ('la pensée sauvage'). Sartre's ideological dogmatism was more or less the equivalent of the animistic worldview of a 'Melanesian savage' (Lévi-Strauss, 1966: 249).

In the early 1950s, France's leading psychoanalyst, Jacques Lacan, had also discovered the virtues of Saussure's structural linguistics. Since the 1930s Lacan's 'return to Freud' aimed to counter the influence of ego psychology and restore the primacy of the unconscious. Lacan's radical decentring of consciousness and its specious claims to autonomy would have a major impact on the course of subsequent French philosophy. For an entire generation of French philosophers, Lacanianism would become an obligatory rite of passage (*Lacan chez les philosophes*, 1991). Following Saussure, Lacan declared that 'the unconscious is structured like a language' (Lacan, 1977: 106). Its nature was forever unintelligible to the workings of the conscious mind. In direct opposition to the claims of the philosophy of the subject (the Descartes–Sartre lineage), Lacan maintained that the 'self' or ego represented a series of distortions and falsifications. The goal of analysis, therefore, was to overturn these distortions in order to return to a more primordial, presocialized stage of individual development (the 'real', which was impossible to reach as such). Thus, whereas the 'true self' was originally characterized by a series of fissures and clefts – which paradoxically entailed a corresponding measure of existential openness – the ego's ruthless will to unity attempted to cover up and repress the self's multidimensional origins.

But there were also growing intra-philosophical challenges to the legacy of existential phenomenology. In their zeal to abandon the paradigm of subjectivity, French philosophers had recourse to developments in German philosophy – above all, the sweeping critiques of reason articulated by Nietzsche and Heidegger. Already in the 1930s, Georges Bataille had attempted to preserve Nietzsche's unsparing critique of bourgeois society from appropriation by the Nazis (Bataille, 1985: 182–97). In Bataille's view, Nietzsche's standpoint of 'active nihilism' could be put to good use in delivering a death blow to the moribund value structure of Western civilization. In the early 1960s Gilles Deleuze would appropriate Bataille's understanding of Nietzsche as a philosopher of heterogeneity or radical, unassimilable 'otherness' in his landmark study, *Nietzsche and Philosophy*. For Deleuze, Nietzsche's infamous proclamation concerning the death of God represents an invaluable point of departure for philosophy. For by rejecting all transcendent, otherworldly sources of meaning, Nietzsche allowed philosophy to focus on the immanent values of life, materiality and difference. As Deleuze observes: 'For the speculative [Hegelian] element of negation, opposition or contradiction Nietzsche substitutes the practical element of *difference*, the object of affirmation and enjoyment. It is in this sense that there is a Nietzschean empiricism' (Deleuze, 1983: 9).

At least as influential as Nietzsche, however, was Heidegger's landmark remonstrance of humanism in his 1947 'Letter on Humanism', which was addressed to a French follower, Jean Beaufret. Heidegger's 'Letter' was perhaps the single most important philosophical text to appear in postwar France. For, at the precise moment that Sartre had staked his claim as the authoritative representative of French existentialism, Heidegger – the German father figure – intervened to say that Sartre had got it all wrong. Whereas Sartre had gone on record boldly proclaiming the 'humanism of existentialism', Heidegger contended, with equal boldness, that the end of metaphysics also signalled the end of humanism. While Sartre had treated the end of metaphysics as paving the way for a ringing affirmation of human existence, Heidegger countered that this affirmation remained caught in the metaphysical trap of the Cartesian 'I think'; that is, it remained a prisoner of the delusions of self-realizing subjectivity. In his radical assault on metaphysics, Heidegger proceeded, in a Nietzschean spirit, to condemn Plato's theory of ideas as sounding the death-knell of Western thought. For Plato had thereby introduced a fatal 'two-worlds' doctrine of reality, glorifying the disembodied forms or ideas and downgrading the realm of sensible appearance. Humanism, he claimed, predicated on the ideology of the 'subject', was an heir to this tradition of epistemological distortion. Sartre had claimed that, after Nietzsche's declaration concerning the death of God, we were left with a 'situation in which there were only human beings' (Sartre, 1995: 286). Heidegger, the 'poet of Being', disagreed profoundly, contending that, 'We are precisely in a situation where there is principally Being' (Heidegger, 1977: 214). And further: 'The history of Being is neither the history of man and of humanity, nor the history of humanity's relation to beings and to Being. The history of Being is Being itself, and only Being' (Heidegger, 1982: 221).

Heidegger's indictment of humanism, combined with his inspired polemics against modern technology, engendered an important French philosophical lineage that may be fruitfully designated as 'left Heideggerianism' – or, alternatively, 'left Nietzscheanism' (Ferry and Renaut, 1990a, 1997). In essence, a total critique of Western civilization that had been popularized by figures on the German right during the interwar years (Heidegger, Oswald Spengler, Ernst Jünger) was, in the postwar years, uncritically assimilated by the French philosophical left. In the aftermath of Stalinism, the Marxist critique of bourgeois society had forfeited its claims to radicalism. Marxism itself, in its predominant, orthodox guise, had turned into another ideology of domination or enslavement. Despite its unambiguously right-wing intellectual genealogy, the Nietzschean-Heideggerian lineage provided the French philosophical left with the conceptual leverage it needed to remain radical – anti-liberal, anti-technocratic, anti-parliamentarian – amid the blandishments of an affluent, postwar 'society of consumption' (Baudrillard, 1969). In the 1960s an entire group of philosophers who were originally attracted to a Marxist critique of capitalist society switched allegiances to a Heideggerian framework.

Representative of this trend is the philosophical path of Kostas Axelos. A founding editor of the leftist review *Arguments*, in the 1960s, Axelos, in books such as *Horizons of the World* and *Planetary Thought*, came to the conclusion that Heidegger's critique of reason was more all-encompassing – hence, more adequate to an age of bureaucratic domination – than was Marx's (Axelos, 1976). One might make a similar argument about the intellectual biographies of Jean-François Lyotard and Jean Baudrillard, both of whom switched from a type of 1960s leftism to a Heideggerian-inspired postmodernism (Lyotard, 1984; Baudrillard, 1994). Yet, at a later point, the philosophical left would pay a high price for its zealous rejection of democratic traditions. With the discourse of human rights paving the way for liberalism's return in the 1980s, the French Heideggerian left would find itself left out of the conversation.

Only with Michel Foucault would France finally discover a philosopher and engaged intellectual whose stature could rival that of Sartre (Miller, 1992). At times, Foucault's existential horror of classification ('Do not ask who I am and do not ask me to remain the same: leave it to our bureaucrats and our police to see that our papers are in order' – Foucault, 1972: 17) would cause him to passionately deny his indebtedness to structuralism (Foucault, 1970: xiv). Elsewhere, he would avow it quite readily: 'Structuralism', observes Foucault, 'is not a new method, it is the awakened and troubled consciousness of modern thought' (Dosse, 1997: i).

Modern thought made naive claims concerning its own intellectual self-sufficiency, claims that a structuralist approach was capable of demystifying and exploding. Under the methodological tutelage of the historians of science Georges Canguilhem and Gaston Bachelard, the early Foucault sought to explode the human sciences' claims to autonomy. According to Foucault, the sovereign claims of reason and rationality were in dire need of archaeological unmasking. Thus in *Madness and Civilization* (1961) he sought to show how social rationality, despite its pretenses to being 'value free', was inherently implicated in mechanisms of social control. Reason had a vested interest in either incarcerating or curing madness, which gave the lie to reason's exaggerated claims to benevolence. Displaying his intellectual indebtedness to Nietzsche, Foucault sought to show how Enlightenment reason, instead of setting us free, merely further immersed us in complex networks of domination.

In his breakthrough study, *The Order of Things* (1965), Foucault tried to demonstrate that the 'sciences of man' – and the logic of humanism that subtended them – comprised an intellectual grid, a series of inscriptions and classifications that aimed at subjugation and the constitution of human identity. In the twentieth century the project of the Enlightenment had grossly miscarried. Disaster radiated everywhere. Structuralism – or, to employ Foucault's preferred designation, 'archaeology' – tried to expose the geological fissures and exclusions that underlay the human sciences' grotesque miscarriage. For their apotheosis of 'man' threatened simultaneously to bring about his annihilation. Yet, Foucault discerned hope on the horizon in the form of a new, portentous epistemic-geological shift: a transformation that heralded the 'end of man' that would at the same time open up a space in which it was once more possible to think. By boring away relentlessly at the claims of the human sciences from within, Foucault believed he was facilitating the archaeological excavation of precisely such a space:

> Nietzsche rediscovered the point at which man and God belong to one another, at which the death of the second is synonymous with the disappearance of the first, and at which the promise of the superman signifies first and foremost the imminence of *the death of man*. In this, Nietzsche, offering this future to us as both promise and task, marks the threshold beyond which contemporary philosophy can begin thinking again; and he will no doubt continue for a long while to dominate its advance. If the discovery of the Return is indeed the end of philosophy, then the end of man, for its part, is the return of the beginning of philosophy. It is no longer possible to think in our day other than in the void left by man's disappearance. For this void does not create a deficiency; it does not constitute a lacuna that must be filled. It is nothing more, and nothing less, than the unfolding of a space in which *it is* once more possible to think.
>
> (Foucault, 1970: 342)

Sartre correctly perceived structuralism's dizzying success during the 1960s as an attack against his philosophy, but also as directed against Marxism's claims to political radicalism, and, more generally, the prospect of progressive historical change. Foucault, he charged, 'gives people what they want: an eclectic synthesis where Robbe-Grillet, structuralism, linguistics, Lacan, and *Tel Quel* are used in turn to demonstrate the impossibility of historical reflection' (Sartre, 1971: 110). Yet, despite these profound epistemological differences, in the 1970s the two representatives of intellectual *engagement* would often unite in the interest of shared political causes (Dosse, 1997: 337).

But in the 1970s Foucault himself began to perceive some of the limitations of the structuralist approach. True to its Saussurean inheritance, it was, he came to believe, excessively oriented toward the paradigm of language. In this sense, structuralism, by privileging language as a type of master code, was a form of idealism. Gradually the austere 'epistemes' of *The Order of Things* and *The Archaeology of Knowledge* were transformed into 'discursive practices', thereby indicating the change of focus to the non-linguistic dimension of lived experience (Foucault, 1972: 215–38). Correspondingly, Foucault's intellectual orientation began to shift from the problem of language to the problem of power. He baptized his new method, following Nietzsche, 'genealogy' (Foucault, 1984: 76–100).

At the same time, the fundamental epistemological assumptions that governed Foucault's earlier, archaeological period remained unchanged. 'Reason' was equated with 'instrumental reason': it was viewed as a tool of manipulation and control *simpliciter*. Foucault's understanding of reason bore pronounced affinities with Max Weber's conception of 'formal reason', that is reason as a mechanism of technical efficiency (Weber, 1969). Like Weber, with Foucault the idea of democratic legitimacy – that is of 'just' claims to political power – disappears from view. When reason is viewed from an exclusively functional standpoint as a form of social coercion, the question of what might constitute a legitimate or rational claim to authority appears unanswerable. Thus, there arose for Foucault the difficult question: with what justification or in whose name do we have the right to overturn the existing framework of social power? Since Foucault, motivated by a Nietzschean-driven cynicism concerning claims to 'right', had ruled out considerations of 'justice', there was only one response that remained open to him: one can resist power only in the name of a new, contrary claim to power. But this move has nothing to do with justice. As Foucault avows:

> The proletariat doesn't wage war against the ruling class because it considers such a war to be just. The proletariat makes war with the ruling class because, for the first time in history it wants to take power. And because it will overthrow the power of the ruling class it considers such a war to be just... One makes war to win, not because it is just... When the proletariat takes power, it may be quite possible that the proletariat will exert towards the classes over which it has just triumphed, a violent, dictatorial and even bloody power. I can't see what objection one could make to this.
>
> (Elder, 1974: 182–5)

With Foucault's later work on power, one is faced with a paradox. On the one hand, we are treated to magisterial and finely honed descriptions of the operations of 'biopower' – discipline, governmentality, the prescription of sexual identities and so forth – that, at times, border on the voyeuristic. At the same time, one runs up against the wall of an epistemologically driven political paralysis in so far as Foucault is at a loss to explain what might constitute genuine opposition or resistance to power. When the question is posed, one receives responses such as the following: 'Power is everywhere; not because it embraces everything, but because it comes from everywhere' (Foucault, 1980: 93); or, again, 'the point is not that everything is bad, but that *everything is dangerous*' (Foucault, 1984: 97). Yet, if what Foucault says is true and 'everything is dangerous', how do we go about discerning which forms of power are more dangerous and which forms of resistance are most serviceable for the ends of constructive social change? Or again: what are the essential differences between power and resistance if the latter can only resist in the name of power? In sum, one of the problems with the structuralist approach on which Foucault relies is that once the proverbial and much maligned 'subject' has been stricken from the interpretive framework, no social actors remain who might be capable of resisting 'power' as it has been theoretically described.

According to the conventional view, Derrida's work inaugurates the transition from structuralism to poststructuralism. Yet it is important to realize that, when all is said and done, there are as many continuities between the two schools as differences (Dosse, 1997: 17–41). On most issues of intellectual substance, structuralism and poststructuralism – in the guise of deconstruction – march arm in arm. Both are indebted to Saussure's methodological privileging of language as a systematic totality (*langue*) over utterances (*parole*). Consequently, both schools maintain that the status of modern philosophy must be relativized by the prior claims of the philosophy of language. Both structuralism and poststructuralism take strong issue with the epistemological model of transcendental subjectivity. Thus, whereas modern philosophy – Descartes, Kant, Husserl – treats the epistemological subject as a type of a priori given, both structuralism and poststructuralism consider it to be something secondary and derivative.

The major issue of dissensus between structuralism and poststructuralism concerns the ideal of scientificity or completion. Structuralism still adheres to the scientific ideal of epistemological wholeness or totality. It believes in the goals of scientific finality in which intellectual completion will have been attained and where all differences will be subsumed, classified and incorporated. Poststructuralism – once again, Derrida's deconstruction is the paradigmatic model – emphatically contests such claims to scientific finality. It insists that not only is such an ideal intellectually untenable, but that the very attempt to realize it constitutes an act of 'metaphysical violence' (Derrida, 1977: 79–153). The very act of attempting to systematize and classify differences, Derrida contends, is repressive. Instead, deconstruction insists on the ineffaceability of difference or *différance* (a term which suggests both temporal delay as well as spatial difference – Derrida, 1982: 1–28). Not only is the scientific ideal of totalization unrealizable. Viewed from a historical standpoint, the attempt to realize it has been an unmitigated nightmare.

In trying to reverse the traditional historical prejudices of reason and metaphysics, however, deconstruction succumbs to a series of prejudices of its own. One of its major methodological failings is that it opts for a totalizing rather than an immanent critique of reason. In essence, its condemnations of reason tend to be sweeping and unnuanced. In neo-Heideggerian fashion, 'reason' is abstractly held responsible for a wide variety of social ills – colonialism, patriarchy, totalitarianism and so forth. Yet such claims and accusations, while superficially plausible, are rarely grounded historically or supported empirically. They are merely asserted or assumed. To be sure, Derrida never makes the undialectical leap to philosophical irrationalism characteristic of many earlier critics of reason. At the same time, his refusal to make such a move seems intellectually inconsistent. Epistemologically speaking, one seems caught in a type of intellectual no man's land: the sins of reason are subjected to a series of withering criticisms; yet, Derrida also staunchly refuses to endorse the converse of reason: 'life', 'intuition', 'emotion'. On the one hand, one cannot help being impressed by deconstruction's ingenious philosophical, architectonic and conceptual pyrotechnics. On the other hand, when all is said and done, even sympathetic commentators and analysts find themselves at a loss to explain what it all means or whether following Derrida's labyrinthine exegeses is ultimately worth the effort.

Moreover, in recent years a series of chance external circumstances has severely compromised deconstruction's international standing. In the late 1980s it was revealed that one of deconstruction's most prominent North American backers, the Belgian-born Yale literary theorist Paul de Man, had actively collaborated with the Nazis during their occupation of the Low Countries during the Second World War. According to most accounts, Derrida's public defence of de Man was intemperate and manifestly apologetic (Derrida, 1989). Next came the so-called Heidegger controversy, provoked by new revelations concerning the German philosopher's allegiance to the Nazi regime during the 1930s. Here, too, Derrida, who had always acknowledged the deep affinities between deconstruction and Heideggerianism, was placed on the defensive. Lastly, in 1993, the *New York Review of Books* uncovered what came to be known as the 'Derrida affair', in which Derrida had threatened to sue a young author who had obtained the rights to reprint an interview with the French philosopher on the subject of Heidegger and Nazism (Wolin, 1993: ix–xx). Prior to these various high-profile public controversies and scandals, deconstruction's influence had already been on the wane, owing to its neglect of historical and political questions – e.g. the question of 'power', which was at the heart of Foucault's later work – and exclusive focus on questions of 'textuality' or the rhetorical construction of texts. Although Derrida possesses an extremely loyal and talented group of followers, it is far from clear that deconstruction can recover the momentum it lost as a result of these recent, high-profile, public setbacks.

During the 1970s a variety of historical circumstances unfolded to enshroud the structuralist/poststructuralist paradigm in a cloud of ethical suspicion. It seemed that the deconstruction of 'man' – of humanism, universalistic morality, and so forth – had gone too far. When it came to the pressing and urgent moral controversies of the day, which pertained to promoting the cause of human rights against a variety of authoritarian and despotic abuses, it was apparent that the structuralists and their heirs had very little to say. Their criticisms of Eurocentrism had been so vociferous that they ended up, *nolens volens*, endorsing a variety of oppressive regimes precisely in so far as they were non-Western. Foucault's rash support for Iran's revolution of the mullahs was perhaps the most egregious case in point (Miller, 1992: 306–14). During the late 1960s and early 1970s, the structuralist left became infatuated with Maoism – 'Le Vent de l'est', to employ the poetic title of one of Jean-Luc Godard's films from the period. Lacanians, the *Tel Quel* group (Philippe Sollers, Julia Kristeva), and Foucault all flirted with the charms of the Great Helmsman and the *gauchiste élan* of the Cultural Revolution (Foucault, 1980: 1–36). With the 1974 publication of Solzhenitsyn's *The Gulag Archipelago* – whose grim accounts of the Soviet camps reverberated like an earthquake across the left bank intellectual scene – all were caught with egg on their faces and compelled to make a prompt volte face. Later that same decade gruesome revelations concerning Pol Pot's killing fields, as well as the plight of the Vietnamese boat people, dashed any and every illusion about prospects for 'socialism with a human face'.

Human rights had become the battle cry of the hour. But, faced with such questions, the structuralist left had very little to contribute. Having laboured for two decades to deconstruct the ideological traps of Western humanism, it had become all but impossible to make up for lost time. A paradigm switch in French philosophy became evident in the mid-1970s. The 'new philosophers' – brash, telegenic, resolutely anti-*gauchiste* (despite the fact that all hailed from good Maoist backgrounds) – jumped on the anti-gulag bandwagon. In works like André Glucksmann's *The Master Thinkers* and Bernard-Henri Lévy's *Barbarism with a Human Face*, they vigorously denounced the complicity between philosophy and totalitarianism. The structuralist left itself was divided as to how to respond to this new challenge, and a major split developed between Foucault (favourable) and Deleuze (unfavourable) over the new philosophy's intellectual and political merits (Miller, 1992: 295–7). Seeking to remedy their earlier ethical shortfall, the poststructuralists hastily attempted to assemble a plausible moral programme that would not merely echo the fashionable pieties of human rights discourse. Thus the later volumes of Foucault's *History of Sexuality* focused on the relationship between ethics and aesthetics in ancient Greece and Rome (Foucault, 1984, 1986). Lyotard denounced the new 'slackening', or return of humanist paradigms, in his work of the 1980s, relying on Wittgenstein's theory of language games to denounce trans-contextual standards of justice (Lyotard, 1984, 1988). The ethical thought of Emannuel Levinas enjoyed a renaissance. His philosophy attempted to reverse the traditional Heideggerian preference for ontology over ethics (Levinas, 1969). His contention that the 'face of the other' confronts us with an undeniable and originary ethical demand gained significant currency.

Nevertheless, poststructuralist and neo-Heideggerian efforts to rehabilitate ethics seemed tainted by their earlier political and intellectual compromises. Moreover, their highly specialized and esoteric approach to philosophical topics seemed difficult to reconcile with the new mood of democratic openness. In France Western-style liberalism had always been weak. French philosophy of the 1980s set out to remedy this deficiency (Pavel, 1989; Lilla, 1994). Predictably, one of its initial moves would be to challenge the illiberal implications of the structuralist legacy (Ferry and Renaut, 1990b, 1997). The reaction against structuralism was so profound that one would be justified to speak of a veritable 'return of the subject' (Dosse, 1997: 324–36). Even committed structuralists such as Barthes and Foucault began flirting with the discourse of subjectivity (Barthes, 1994; Foucault, 1986). Evidence of a philosophical paradigm change was omnipresent. The hermeneutical approach of Paul Ricoeur made a comeback in the early 1990s. In 1991 the prestigious review, *Esprit*, devoted a special issue to his work. That same year a colloquium in his honour was held at Cerisy. As François Dosse has remarked, Ricoeur 'was able to preserve the dimensions of the Subject, of action, of the referent, and of ethics which were out of vogue. . . . He refused to accept that language was hermetic and always added the dimension of human action' (Dosse, 1997: 285). One tell-tale index of the dramatic shift in intellectual climate was the election of Jacques Bouveresse over Derrida to the prestigious Collège de France in the late 1980s. Bouveresse, influenced by Wittgenstein, was manifestly sympathetic to Anglo-American philosophical approaches (Bouveresse, 1996). Bouveresse

> contrasted the Anglo-Saxon practice of philosophy as an argumentative discipline with is literary status in France, which too often led to an indifference to content and argumentation. Bouveresse compared deconstruction or ultra-structuralism with the demand for clarity, which for Wittgenstein, defined philosophy's specificity, and differentiated philosophy from the spirit of science.
>
> (Dosse, 1997: 287)

In light of such considerations, deconstruction, seemed *passé*, representative of the old guard.

Generally speaking, French philosophy of the 1980s and 1990s assumed responsibility for rehabilitating concepts and traditions that had been declared obsolete by structuralism: the subject, ethics, humanism and history. In this connection it would be entirely appropriate to speak of a 'return of the repressed' (Dosse, 1997: 324–6). But the vanquishing of structuralism also came at a price. The intellectual 'export value' of French philosophy of the 1950s and 1960s – structuralism and poststructuralism – was predicated on its difference from Anglo-American philosophical traditions. French philosophy of the 1960s was radical, stylish, suffused with panache. A greater contrast could hardly be imagined with the staid seminar philosophy that dominated the English-speaking world from Oxbridge to Berkeley. French philosophical radicalism seemed tailor-made to suit the decade's political radicalism. But of course different times demand different philosophical outlooks. Now that the French have belatedly encountered Anglo-American modes of thought – pragmatism and analytical philosophy – French philosophy seems, predictably, to be of much less interest for practitioners across the Channel and across the Atlantic. Ironically, the theoretical claims of French philosophy of the 1990s have become more modest and more analytically sound; yet, by the same token, they have become proportionately less intriguing.

References

Axelos, Kostas (1976) *Alienation, Praxis, and Techne in the Thought of Karl Marx*. Austin: University of Texas Press.

Barthes, Roland (1994) *Roland Barthes*. Berkeley: University of California Press.

Bataille, Georges (1985) *Visions of Excess*. Minneapolis: University of Minnesota Press.

Baudrillard, Jean (1969) *La Société de la consommation*. Paris: Gallimard.

—— (1994) *Simulacrum and Simulacra*. Ann Arbor: University of Michigan Press.

Bouveresse, Jacques (1996) *Wittgenstein Reads Freud: The Myth of the Unconscious*. Princeton, NJ: Princeton University Press.

Deleuze, Gilles (1983) *Nietzsche and Philosophy*. New York: Columbia University Press.

Derrida, Jacques (1980) *Margins of Philosophy*. Chicago: University of Chicago Press.

—— (1988) 'Like the sound of a shell by the sea', *Critical Inquiry*, 14 no. 3 (Spring), pp. 590–652. Trans. Peggy Kamuf.

Dosse, François (1997) *History of Structuralism*, vol. 2. Minneapolis: University of Minnesota Press.

Elder, Fons (ed.) (1974) *Reflexive Water: The Basic Concerns of Mankind*. London: Souvenir Press.

Ferry, Luc and Alain Renaut (1990a) *Heidegger and Modernity*. Chicago: University of Chicago Press.

—— (1990b) *French Philosophy of the Sixties*. Amherst: University of Massachusetts Press.

—— *Why We Are Not Nietzscheans* (1997) Chicago: University of Chicago Press.

Foucault, Michel (1970) *The Order of Things*. London: Tavistock.

—— (1972) *The Archaeology of Knowledge*. New York: Pantheon.

—— (1977) *History of Sexuality*. New York: Pantheon.

—— (1980) *Power/Knowledge*. New York: Pantheon.

—— (1984) *The Foucault Reader*, ed. Paul Rabinow. Berkeley: University of California Press.

—— (1986) *Care of the Self*. New York: Pantheon.

Heidegger, Martin (1977) *Basic Writings*. New York: Harper & Row.

—— (1982) *Nietzsche*, vol. 4. New York: Harper & Row.

Lacan, Jacques (1977) *Ecrits*. New York: Norton.

Lacan chez les philosophes (1991) Paris: Michel Albin.

Levinas, Emmanuel (1969) *Totality and Infinity*. Pittsburgh: Duquesne University Press.

Lévi-Strauss, Claude (1963) *Structural Anthropology*. New York: Harper & Row.

—— (1964) *The Savage Mind*. Chicago: University of Chicago Press.

—— (1992) *Tristes Tropiques*. New York: Penguin.

Lilla, Mark (ed.) (1994) *New French Thought*. Princeton, NJ: Princeton University Press.

Lyotard, Jean-François (1984) *The Postmodern Condition*. Minneapolis: University of Minnesota Press.

—— (1988) *The Differend*. Minneapolis: University of Minnesota Press.

Miller, James (1992) *The Passion of Michel Foucault*. New York: Simon & Schuster.

Pavel, Thomas (1989) *The Feud of Language*. Oxford: Blackwell.

Sartre, Jean-Paul (1971) 'Replies to Structuralism', *Telos*, 9, 110–16.

—— (1995) 'Existentialism and humanism', in Charles B. Guignon and Derek Pereboom (eds), *Existentialism: Basic Writings*. Indianapolis: Hackett Publishers.

Weber, Max (1969) *Economy and Society*. Berkeley: University of California Press.

Wolin, Richard (1993) *The Heidegger Controversy: A Critical Reader*. Cambridge, MA: MIT Press.

3

It's Time for a Change: Mutations of Presence in Contemporary French Critical Theory

Seán Hand

> The future can only be anticipated in the form of an absolute danger. It is that which breaks absolutely with constituted normality and can only be proclaimed, *presented*, as a sort of monstrosity.
>
> (Derrida, 1974: 5)

My opening quotation above is designed to stand on an exemplary approach to the treacherous and paradoxical task of this essay, which is to delineate contemporary currents in French critical theory. As such, it states already what will be this essay's abstract failure, a failure it *should adhere to*, except that it will miss even that. That is, it offers the chance to take on board an absolute historiographical danger, and to work with that disastrous abeyance in order to come to a different kind of thinking and writing about the current. That is no doubt academically and pedagogically unacceptable, but – who knows? – it might just generate a prophetic if personal education

Two things have to happen at the same time in this essay's opening remarks. We have to state that the subject-mater is 'contemporary French critical theory', and that there are a number of ways, a few of which can be investigated here, in which these terms can be linked and conflated. And we have to state also, in a way that *is* indulgent *and* necessary, that to speak of 'contemporary French critical theory' is to speak of a supposed subject in a manner that reduces its own inhabitation *by* the current or the contemporary. An objectivist or simply chronological presentation of the title's subject-matter, then, can only betray what lies at the heart of that subject, the real alien danger within the establishment of reputation and status, and the ungraspable element preceding the subject-matter already in the title: namely, the *time* for a change, the unsatisfactory thematic preoccupations of post-humanist presence, and the privileging by theory *qua* theory as well as by contemporary theorists concerned with ethics of the temporality of presence. Such a temporality has been termed (in a no less paradoxical and agonised way) being-for-the-other.

My borrowed quotation tries to exist in that mode, to be an exemplary epigraph for contemporary French critical theory. Its attempt to recognize the deflection of the reality of the future through phantasmal anticipations relates to a key symptom of contemporary French critical theory, more generally of postmodern speculation, more particularly of my own failed opening, and logically of itself: that is, the attempt to denounce from within critical postulation the archival pretensions we are supporting and repeating. The quotation itself comes from Derrida's *Of Grammatology*, at a point where that text tries to raise the connections between temporality, presentation and monstrosity as part of an ethical explosion of the categories framing its task. Here I am obviously imparting such an attitude in order to make much of the conflation of terms and the directions their collective operation safely steers us in. Let me note, then, just in passing the paths quite clearly not taken before we present our safely dangerous 'constituted normality'.

Hypocrite lecteur. We all go along with the phrase '*critical* theory' as a convenient but disabling categorization, when the thought that there is an *uncritical* theory is, however paradoxically, a theory in itself that is more exciting and dangerously disorienting. Is it for reasons of responsibility or timidity that we step back from that violent orthodoxy? Or is it *just* a paradox? We all go along with the phrase 'critical *theory*', as though the critical were the authentic entry into the undifferentiated, acting as the temporal penetration of space, when the ethical experience of experience is that the future is not to be grasped as experience, that is, that one is acted upon by the apprehension of spatiality and its eruption within time. In this regard, the theory is absolute, irrevocable and unsatisfiable; and the critical is but a belated answer. Is it the radical passivity of this position, its religiously suffering demanifestation that frightens us? Or is it just the professional and psychic necessity of having a position, an anxiety occasionally sublated by the language of political engagement? Above all, we go along with the presentation of a *French* critical theory, as though the critical and the theoretical were somehow to be retained and enhanced phylogenetically, cloned from and transmitted within a singular, coherent culture. This is, of course, the *French* critical theory of Bakhtin, Saussure, Gadamer, Husserl, Heidegger, Freud and Marx; as borne out in the *French* critical theorists Derrida, Cixous and Levinas. This is also the *French* tradition resulting from a post-1870 pedagogical projection and a post-1794 linguistic cleansing. And this is also no doubt the ethnic singularity of thought reflected comparatively, in the now infamous statement by Heidegger made in the first section of *An Introduction to Metaphysics*, delivered originally in the summer of 1935, and acting precisely as a rehabilitation of metaphysical constitution in the service of political and historical singularity. Thus, speaking of Germany in the way in which one might think of any self-constituting, self-sustaining and self-answering national tradition, Heidegger insisted:

> [I]t is the most metaphysical of nations. We are certain of this vocation, but our people will only be able to wrest a destiny from it if *within itself* it creates a resonance, a possibility of resonance for this vocation, and takes a creative view of its tradition. All this implies that this nation, as a historical nation, must move itself and thereby the history of the West beyond the centre of their future 'happening' and into the primordial realm of the powers of being. If the great decision regarding Europe is not to bring annihilation, that decision must be made in terms of new spiritual energies unfolding historically from out of the centre.
>
> (Heidegger 1959: 38–9)

Notwithstanding the appeal to acephalic urges, these are in fact all cautious and defensive demarcations. I am, of course, hedging my bets even in speaking about them. Beyond their vocational assertiveness, however, we can glimpse the evasion of a more fundamental and transnational *fort/da* in which critical theory is in fact always fully engaged: the death-drive of thinking (as) the contemporary. This is *true* critical theory, which we can perhaps only reveal by dyeing it, staining it, with particular contextualizations. Those which I shall choose are normally thought of as 'French'; but I shall present them as part of a desire to get through certain theories of resolution and presence, towards an increasingly deracinated ethical disruption of the triumph of temporality over the spatial, and, with it, a transgression of national, discursive and conceptual limits. I am uncomfortably aware of how this still constitutes a 'constituted normality', how it is still a presentation, for all its affected distortion of chronological and thematic progress, of how I am managing merely to construct a very domestic *fort/da*. But this is going to be inevitable, and not just because it is what I am supposed to do. I try to suggest this play-off, and the double *fort/da* it works with, incidentally, in my title's chiasmic and specular form. By at least opposing the terms of change and mutation on the one hand, and time and presence on the other, I want these convergences to suggest what is really at stake in the archivization of the rest, which is the necessary pretension of conceptualizing the current. Once we make the mistake of letting ourselves go, and of allowing a bifocal discourse to emerge, we have to acknowledge the death-drive inherent in our present activity which acts as the opposite of the 'current' it purports to describe.

One way of turning this back into practical use is to note in passing the persistence of this attitude also in the course of French critical theory this century. To plot it crudely, this course has involved a move away from the humanist apprehensions and sensitivities acting as its dynamic and (class-based) legitimization, and subsequently through an increasingly scientific and anthropological specialization and self-constitution, and so reaching a present point where, as part of the experience of the end of modernism, we have begun to return to what has remained absolute and unabsorbed: the unconstitutable and unnormalizable at the origin of the responsibility that is lived out as the critical. The three forms of simultaneous rejection and recognition are linked on the surface by the history of contemporary French intellectual life, and in more subterranean ways by renunciation. There is certainly enough potential genealogy here for us to make progress. I shall now work against a historical and chronological backdrop that characterizes contemporary French critical theory as having two phases: a move from humanist existentialism to quasi-scientific objectivization; and a return of the repressed. We can make this approach more energetic by following through the specifically virile nature of anxieties (given that 'French' feeling and thinking are often amusingly associated in a way that 'German' or 'British' counterparts are not, with physical and even sexual dynamics).

I shall begin, therefore, by isolating the moment of *crisis* that is the concern with devirilization running from the 1930s through to the 1950s and beyond. Crisis is here taken to mean an unavoidable problem of collective projection. Such a moment is intended to act obviously as a genealogy in the Foucauldian sense.

Foucault's approach is here crucial to a mutational presentation of the contemporary, in terms both of his importance as a critical theory and of his exemplification of the resistance to the archivization on which he so depended. In other words, in his archival work the discursive formation remains part of (or even really) the object of analysis and as such presents a chiasmal and effective practice of conscious change and self-depostulation. Thus Foucault's genealogical approach can be thought of as ethical, in the sense that its insistence on discussion at the origin of enquiry obliges historiography to break with the determined temporal order and the silent institutional enforcement of continuities, and effectively provokes the turmoils of cognition normally erased in the course of detaching a philosophical result from the history of its formation. (Where Foucault nonetheless speaks of a modernist vision of progress is in his scientific prophetism: the revolutionary fervour with which he presents this approach as liberating and curative (no more so in fact than in the anti-normative championing of exceptionality: here the structure of blasphemy becomes all too imprisoning).

My analysis begins with the formative reaction of the Collège de Sociologie to the Munich crisis. I shall then try to pursue the transformation of this theme by immediate postwar existentialism; and then attempt to link it to a further transformation within structuralist optics. What I have specifically in view here is the theme's continuity through mutation and its strategic relation to the refounding of the contemporary. In the case of writers such as Bataille, Sartre and Robbe-Grillet, therefore, we individually and compulsively, that is to say repeatedly, witness both the reinventions of the contemporary in terms of an authentic confrontation with raw reality, and the parallel projection of a new, critical (yet not simply counter-cultural) notion of 'Frenchness'.

Founded in 1937 by Georges Bataille, Michel Leiris and Roger Caillois, the short-lived Collège de Sociologie sought to pursue a study of modern social structures in a transformational rather than academic manner. Resembling a revolutionary cell, in that it took itself to have a radical mission on a political as well as aesthetic level, the Society's founding declaration (Hollier 1988: 3–5) nonetheless went beyond the political in three main points which it emphasized: firstly the study of social structures was henceforth to focus on the *contemporary*, and to affect as a consequence the prevalent modalities of research itself; secondly, this *activist* form of knowledge should effect a refounding of intellectual life as a *moral* community; lastly, this activity is properly speaking a *sacred* sociology, where 'sacred' signifies the link between the obsessive patterns of individual psychology and the currents of social structure. Our reaction to this is equally threefold: the programme of collective desubjectification advocated here is obviously anti-functionalist and to that degree constitutes an *artistic* radicalism; the tenor is nonetheless a committed one, and as such prefigures the later existentialist legitimation of radical refounding; as with the existentialist project, the pretension of conceptualizing the current is here ultimately an academic one in its depoliticizing analysis of expenditure: in other words, it projects a utopia.

These tensions are brought to a high point in the Collège's declaration on the International Crisis of 1938, which was published simultaneously in the November issue of three different journals: the *The Nouvelle Revue Française, Esprit* and *Volontés* (Hollier 1988: 43–6). What is particularly obvious in the Collège's reaction is its desire to comment at once on the current, that is the September events (it is dated 7 October 1938) 'while there is still time', and before 'restorative oblivion' is permitted to seal the political (lack of) will to reimpose constituted normality, to present the danger and monstrosity of the future as a non-event. Equally obvious is the desire to do so *in order to legitimate itself* precisely through crisis, and by demanding the (political) current as a lie. For our purposes, this also involves placing in abeyance the geographical and social demarcation of French interests:

> The College of Sociology is not a political organism. Its members hold whatever opinion they please. It does not think it is obliged to consider the particular interests of France in the venture. Its role is solely to draw the lesson it is bound to draw from the events, and do this while there is still time, that is to say before everyone is completely persuaded that in the heat of the event he effectively demonstrated calm, dignity, and resolve.
>
> (Hollier, 1988: 45)

It is at this point, once the contemporary, French interests, and political or intellectual quiescence are raised and scorned, that the Declaration introduces unambiguously its refounding of the event as a collectively visceral and specifically virile challenge:

> The College of Sociology regards the general absence of intense reaction in the face of war as a sign of man's *devirilization*. It does not hesitate to see the cause of this in the relaxation of society's current ties, which are practically nonexistent as a result of the development of bourgeois individualism.
>
> (ibid.)

The solution logically proposed is that of a vitalistic disclosure of the 'absolute lie' of the current, together with its geographical/social definitions, and a celebration (that ambiguously partakes of the masculine being-unto-death it implicitly decries in the fascist threat) of a virile initiative before the event-into-nonevent that is the highpoint of mortality:

The College of Sociology... urges those, for whom the only solution anguish disclosed is the creation of a vital bond between men, to join with it, with no other determining factor than the awareness of the *absolute lie* of current political forms and the necessity for reconstructing on this assumption a collective mode of existence that takes no geographical or social limitations into account and that allows one to behave oneself [*d'avoir un peu de tenue*] when death threatens.

(Hollier 1988: 45–6)

Here the anguish of the moment produces an intellectual affirmation of a non-intellectual vitalism, an anti-collective collectivism based on the acephalic absorptions of the current into a modernist vision of prehistory marked by the sacred and the ecstatic, where these are assumed to be expressly virile. This monstrosity, designed to contribute a supranormality, and partaking of the mythopoetics of fascism even in its opposition to it, has the at least historiographical merit of throwing into abeyance the politically resolved categories of contemporaneity, Frenchness and realpolitik (or by extension intellectual life). That it does so not only by raising these questions, but also by echoing the macho homophilia of the right-wing intellectuals who have been bewailing French degeneration and the mutation in maleness effected by a changing economy (by 1906, 38 per cent of the French workforce was female), suggests that its radical refounding in itself partook of a tradition of such erasures and proclamations, a tradition that links some of the main 'French' theories of social, political and aesethic presence in the twentieth century: specifically, surrealism, ethnography, existentialism and structuralism.

Turning now to Sartre's contribution to this *tabula rasa* programme, it is logical that he should legitimate his version of the current with a degeneration of both the surrealist and Bataillean overcoming of events. In *What is Literature?* (Sartre, 1948) Sartre dismissed surrealism's destruction of subjectivity as a purely formal surpassing that never effects a passage from potentiality to action, while in the article 'A new mystic' (Sartre, 1947), he similarly castigates Bataille for a specious intuitive ecstasy that effectively opposes what we *are*: namely a *project*. Bataille's response (Bataille 1973), consistently enough, involves a contestation of the deterministic implementation of Sartre's Hegelian teleology, and a reinstated preference for the agony of process over the certainty of project. 'Perpetual overcoming' and 'project' are of course key elements in Sartre's existentialist vision of the refounding of authentic presence as the grasping of one's own essence, as articulated in *Being and Nothingness*.

That text is of course all the more a masculine vision of authenticity and a programme of virile redressing for the fact that it does not see itself as such. But both in its general aggression and in its particular cameos (such as the asserted bad faith of the woman in the café who kids herself that she is not engaged in seduction with a man) there occurs within the totalizing ontology a 'constituted normality' that is specifically sexual, and virile, in its aggressive regulations. This comes interestingly to the fore (in our present context of the refounding of the current and of presence in relation to the political [French] realities leading up to and including the Second World War) in the polemically and self-validating essays produced at the end of France's war, where the symptomatology of sexual exceptionality, or monstrosity, coexists with the proclamation of existentialism as constituted normality of authentic contemporary history and critical reactions. The founding 'Presentation' of the first issue of *Les Temps modernes* in 1945 significantly focuses on Proust, and in erasing one canon obviously seeks to present itself as the virile successor in terms that are as merciless (and intimidatingly collectivist) as they purport to be metaphysical: 'we refuse to believe that the love of an invert presents the same characteristics as that of a heterosexual ... For us, what men have in common, is not a nature, but a metaphysical condition' (Sartre 1945: 12–13). In *Situations III*, Sartre extends this existentialist refounding, which might be compared with a Gaullist historical re-imagining, to an overdetermination of the *épuration* that relies on and derives from virile definitions. As a result, in 'What is a collaborator?', we are firstly presented with a fantastical vision of Fascism as a dynamic that encouraged 'relations between France and Germany as a form of sexual union in which France plays the role of the woman' (Sartre 1949: 58). Into this *mise-en-scène* he then introduces collaboration as 'a climate of femininity' and more particularly as a beguiling, seductive, masochistic homosexual who 'pretends to play on the attraction that French culture exerts, according to him, on the Germans'. Sartre concludes, unambiguously: 'Parisian homosexual circles, moreover, provided many dazzling recruits' (ibid.). This French collaboration becomes fetishized, depoliticized and dismissed as a singular sexual aberration, against which there stands the inclusive, masculine integrity of a resistance and refounding that confuses ideological and sexual presence. Sartre may conclude that the finally triumphant resistance showed that 'the role of man is to know how to say no' (1949: 61): it is obvious here how one identificatory crisis has been transformed into a collective projection designed to define and control the contemporary.

Viewed in this manner, we can see how the Sartrean crisis is connected not only to expenditure as analysed and endorsed by the Collège de Sociologie, but also in a symptomatic way to later quasi-structuralist purgations. This may seem paradoxical, given the structural attenuation of selfhood and the frequent subversion of political commitment by textual obsessionality in, say, a Robbe-Grillet. But the links are also compelling, including of course on the level of virile violence, while the denigration of Roquentin in *Pour un nouveau roman* is not only necessary to the logic of self-founding which we are here following through, but acknowledges in the process Sartre's recognition of 'the cleaning power of the gaze' (Robbe-Grillet 1967: 66). As a typical product of postwar refounding, this text is remarkable for the vigour with which it pursues a post-existential project of redemptive hygiene. Everything is washed, stripped, cored. The reinvention of Frenchness in the 1950s and 1960s, which depended of course as much on the *tabula rasa* of metaphysical speculation as on advertisements for Gallic lifestyles, preserves and secretes (as its own return of the repressed) the *épuration* of the war's end as an intellectual cleaning-up operation wherein the unknowable or non-recuperable to theory is trapped as filth. I do not have the space here, unfortunately, to begin to relate this domestic anxiety and its accompanying violence to the increasingly obvious obsession in Robbe-Grillet with sadomasochistic reversal and fetishization, nor to develop this, as I should wish to do, into a counter-critical reading of Lacanian schematization. But I do want to contend here that this *fort/da* of the (sexually) monstrous, together with the oppressive geometrism of structuralist orthodoxy that came to be associated with it, bring to a logical endpoint for French critical theory the apprehension of devirilization that can be traced back to the crisis years of colonialism at the end of the nineteenth century but is particularly active and determining in the rapid reformulation of contemporary French intellectual life dominating the pre-and postwar periods, to be internalized thereafter by succeeding refinements/abandonments.

If the war provided a simple feature for national-cultural resistance in this period of critical theory (including its almost militaristic antipathy to critical theory not its own), the end of the war both physical and ideological mutates in a subsequent historical period into a more complex (in part since now more temporarily agonised) unfolding of the mutation of critical theory. In this period I also want to focus on an interactive nucleus of writers that in distinct but related ways work through the (non-) resolution of the death-drive of thinking (as) the contemporary. My primary texts in this section are thus: *Roland Barthes par Roland Barthes* (1975), which we might say inverts the Sartrean project and with it the Sartrean contemporary and authentic existence; Jean Baudrillard's *L'autre par lui-même* (1987), which tries to outdo Barthes's metacritique with such *nec plus ultra* essays as 'Why theory?'; and Jacques Derrida's *Aporias* (1993) which turns both the return to metaphysics in the Baudrillard and the binarist exposition of metaphysics in the earlier Derrida towards the presupposition underwritten by the collection of essays of which this one forms a part, that is the national/linguistic/cultural singularity imposed on critical theory. Using the syntagm 'my death', Derrida crosses three privileged borders as limits: the national, the discursive and the conceptual. This brings to a new level of realization our presumptions to conflate the terms 'contemporary', 'French' and 'critical', and specifically introduces into each the deep resonance of the *fort/da*, the carefully marked mortality of the legatee, at the heart of intellectual *life*.

Pleasure, fascination, ignorance, imaginary. Working through and beyond semiotic determinism, *Roland Barthes par Roland Barthes* returns critical theory to its repudiated incentives, the groundless grounds of *writing*. In the process, it provides an exemplary destabilization of the assumption governing the construction of this collection, given the text's attempt to release and yet preserve an autobiographical dismantling of the legacy of Western internalization. Barthes's pitch here is to present his thinking (both as object and as mode of analysis) as 'tenacious and floating' (Barthes 1977: 74): as with the Freudian membrane (and it is significant that he speaks in this section, 'The echo chamber', of transference as well as 'the Sartrean system'), the presence of theory, as coming from the other, and as representing the constituted normality, undergoes a mutational effect ('doctrinal vibration') that reintroduces the monstrous and resurgent decategorizations of the authentic and the ethical. In the process of realizing this, of truly *realizing* his 'contemporary French intellectual life', Barthes takes unto himself the pleasures of the imaginary and the temporal interlude that is normally reserved for this supposedly unrealized and pre-conceptualizing stage. He both promises and constructs the 'conceptual infatuations, successive enthusiasms, perishable manias (Barthes, 1977: 110) of the childhood revisited and the critical theory divested. His imaginary autobiographical relation now advances by 'amorous fits' (it should be obvious I have inadequately aped this decision in my own text). In terms of this essay's reviews what we are returned to most forcefully is the second degree reality of writing, the basic metacritical point that critical theory is itself a textual organism open, firstly, to its own analysis of enunciation, and released thereafter into the liberating danger of enacting itself. From the ideological point of view, this is unacceptable persuasion, designed to turn political rigour back into aesthetic aporia. What it reveals, of course, is the erotics *of* the political rigour: 'One can, then, either assume the subject of contradiction or else induce from this contradiction an astonishment, even a critical return: and what if there were, as a second perversion, *a pleasure of ideology?* (Barthes, 1977: 104). An important dimension of this critical return is also the anti-heroic and specifically *devirilized* nature of the monstrous body projected. Almost programmatically (but in suite rather than symphonic mode), Barthes makes again the collective resolutions common to the previous set of critical positions we reviewed, and again to the ethical end of *realizing* that 'in the field of the subject, there is no referent' (Barthes, 1977: 56). The mutation, then, works off those sensitivities so ostracized by Sartre, and proclaims delightfully subversive new indicators of critical insight: migraine, digestion, boredom, flab. In a telling phrase, Barthes insists that this 'deliberate loss of all heroism, *even in pleasure*' (Barthes 1977: 44) carries an 'ethical force'. And to be half in love with easeful death in this way also allows the text to come closer to the source of the echo than the resolute refusals of our previously reviewed critical positions. Oblivion everywhere tempts the voice of *Roland Barthes par Roland Barthes*, and is given anti-heroic grandeur via the language of love and the gesture of self-sacrifice. The mother's body is an important site of affect in this respect, and is canonized beyond the loquela of the last by the opening blurred image of a pre-verbal totality (the mother on the beach, balanced ambiguously against the text's closing reference to the monster of totality and the anatomical plate of the body minus skin, muscles, bones and nerves). Devirilization and anti-heroism are thus bodied forth in a *fort/da* of affective theory.

This form of mutational self-inhabitation was quite explicitly exploited by Jean Baudrillard in his 1987 *L'autre par lui-même*. Both the title and the review of earlier critical positions betray the debt to Barthes's text; in addition, the subtitle of Baudrillard's work, 'Habitation', while referring technically to the presentation and defence of the totality of one's work for a doctoral degree, plays conveniently on the autobiographical habitation constructed by Barthes. Logically, it both repeats many of the lessons of Barthes's complex revisioning and in simulating the Barthesian approach seeks to outdo and nullify it. Another temporal stage of *fort/da* is enacted. The ground for this, including the mutated observation of our earlier reviewed critics, had already been laid in Baudrillard's earlier works *L'échange symbolique et la mort* (1976) and *De la séduction* (1979). The former extends the logic of Barthes's *Fashion System* to postulate the feminization of society, the fetishization of the phallus and the mutation of the law of the father into the desire of the mother. Beyond this monstrosity what is in turn suggested as even more fundamental is the *fort/da* of death as incurable deviance whose exclusions operate a will-to-power within Enlightenment totalizing discourse. Direct links back to Bataille, Durkheim and the Collège de Sociologie, and implicit criticisms of the Sartrean project, interact with the Barthesian mode of genealogy to produce a dangerous return of the critically repressed; here, as elsewhere, Baudrillard provokes a glimpse of the *unheimlich* of socialization. The work on seduction operates in a similar manner, reviewing and encouraging a seduction of history (and/or seduction of seduction) that can critique both Marxian notions of falsity and feminist imprisonment within productivist models while recalling to mind the metaphysical imaginary of Bataillean eroticism. *L'autre par lui-même* is both an extension of this anti-project of the end of a philosophy of subjectivity, and a specific metacritical mutation that deals with hasty denunciations of his undialectical hypercriticism. Reviewing the course of his own analysis (and influence), from reification to simulation and then to the radical exteriority of the object, from exchange-value to the ironic fatality of the object that has become indecipherable (Baudrillard 1987: 77), Baudrillard effectively conflates Marxist apprenticeship with metaphysical 'objective passion' in order to get to the point of asking: 'why theory?' The reply to the question is a provocative summation of the passage traced, and recalls many of Barthes's more radical *aperçus* in his autobiographical implosion. Language and theory no longer act as a mode of production, but as a mode of disappearance; their end is no longer analysis but the preservation of enigma (1987:83). Critical nihilation is profoundly non-moral in its non-adherence to the effect it describes dialectically; a Bataillean auto-destruction must return to theory to make of it an event in the world it envisages. This resembles Barthes's desubjectivation of the referent and make an important reassertion of temporal and eschatological resistance to the summation and conceptualization interiorized even by this volume of essays. What Baudrillard proposes, then, is *active* mutation: an anticipation of theory's future failure of nihilation in the monstrosity and deviation of writing: 'if the world is fatal, let us be more fatal than it. If it is indifferent, let us be more indifferent than it. We must conquer the world and reduce it through an indifference that is at least the equal of its own' (1987:86).

The critical responses to this return to metaphysics can be quickly noted. Sign-fetishism and stoic aestheticization do not account for continuing atrocities. Post-Marxist provocation does not discredit critical social theory. More tellingly, the metaphysical imaginary retains all the dialectical apparatus it derides having in cases merely replaced production with signification and subjectivity with the passion of the Object. But we can also note in passing the simple failure in such reactions of an entrenched leftist critique. The historical critique of post-historical speculation merely begs the question; political agency cannot be simplistically opposed to aestheticism; dialectical materialism has its own powerful fatality. The temporal determinisms and resolute will-to-power of these critical reactions, evident in critics even such as Kellner (1989), serve here in fact to emphasize how all of our critics have been working towards but within the aporia of death as the non-thematizable (but destabilizing) future that helps to actualize theory. It is precisely this possibility that forms the basis of Derrida's *Aporias*.

Aporias enacts a critical return of the overflowing of borders in the primary and preconceptual realm of the limits of *Dasein*. This return is structured broadly by a two-part presentation that begins with 'Finis' before moving on to 'S'attendre à l'arrivée', a move and a phrase encapsulating Derrida's speculations on the famous §50 of *Being and Time* where, '[W]ith death, Dasein stands before itself [steht sich . . . bevor; s'at-tend lui-même] in its own most potentiality-for-Being' (Heidegger 1962: 294). The metacritical, and autobiographical or rather autothanatological, elements of this return are signalled clearly from the start: in the context of a conference on the crossing of borders (*le passage des frontières*). Derrida recalls Diderot's remark that he could not read the third chapter of Seneca's *De brevitate vitae* without blushing, since it was the story of his own life, before adding that the text itself contains among other things a rhetoric of borders. He then, of course, proceeds to enact in this, his own text, what he has set up as anticipatory *mise-en-scène*, working for and against the anticipated end that moreover can only be death as *anticipated* end. Thus, both commenting on and repeating one's distortion and dissimulation of one's being-unto-death, and preparing us with comments about one's lack of preparedness for the imminence of death, Derrida traces the borders of his meditation on death by opening up/with the negative/active cited phrase: 'death has no border' (Derrida 1993: 6). The indiscriminate and overwhelming nature of the phenomenon, in its pre-social and supra-political abnormality, its existential absolute and monstrous indifference have all underpinned, as we saw, the distinguishing critical positions of the theory of presence reviewed. Derrida chooses at this early point to delimit this fatality with a significantly temporal and linguistic, rather than territorial, sentence: 'Il y va d'un certain pas [It involves a certain step/not; he goes along at a certain pace]' (Derrida 1993:6). Pointing out, in a very Levinasian moment, that the one belonging to which the phrase unambiguously belongs is that of the French *language*, and extending this idea into that of a shibboleth, that is the essential foreignness and supra-discursivity of the phrase, Derrida links identity and difference, familiarity and hospitality, host and guest (or later ghost) via the constant crossing of borders, through which we (can only) anticipate the threshold of death. Defining this already as a possibility of the impossible (this essential Heideggerian definition being pored over later at greater leisure), and designating this by the term *aporias*, Derrida now logically enacts this anticipation in a manner that relates him closely to the dynamics at least of Barthes and Baudrillard (the absence of reference to these theorists being here *absolutely* irrelevant even if one thinks naturally of his 1981 essay, 'The Deaths of Roland Barthes'). Anticipation as confirmation and repudiation of limit here leads Derrida to trace/limit the presence of aporia in his work to date, in the course of which he reviews no fewer than 14 of his own works, spanning the previous 25 years, and all abutting an unresolvable structure of temporality and 'a *différence* in being-with-itself of the present' (1993: 17) that interrupt 'the relation to any *presentable* determination' while 'maintaining a presentable relation to the interruption' (ibid.). recognizing in this recall the memory of what was carrying the future, or in my terms the promise in the contemporary of the intention of presence, Derrida now comes to the existential question: 'Is my death possible?' (1993: 21). It is a question that in a trice returns Barthes and Baudrillard to their labours; and he forces himself to face in a more prolonged manner, via a reading of Heidegger triangulated by Freud and Levinas, the cultural, disciplinary and conceptual borders posed and surpassed by this limit-question. (It is obvious, of course, how this question is the aporia not just of this essay, but also of the collection that contains it and the collection of thought that contains this collection.) Recalling that for Heidegger, in contrast to certain theorists of the culture of death (whatever they may assume of their own positions), an existential analysis of death can *and must* precede *any* delimination of the subject (including the metaphysical), that, as established in the first action of *Being and Time*'s introduction, Dasein must provide 'the ontico-ontological condition for the possibility of any ontologies' (Heidegger 1962: 34), Derrida spells out just what this authoritative anticipation means in the context of transgressing borders:

it seems that from the start the organization of problems and limits in Heidegger's text frees itself from the problem of limit; in fact, though, this logic merely emphasizes the originary and undesirable character of death, as well as the finitude of the temporality in which death is rooted' (Derrida 1993: 55) that obliged this to be the starting point; the reaction of the first point above to the second point reveals precisely the prevalence in the phenomenological tradition *for prevalence*. There are also three corollories to this existential *préférance* for Derrida: death must have no border; there is no politics of death; existential analysis has no space or time in its determinations for mourning, spectrality and other figures of the non-desirable and non-reducible (it is here Freud and Levinas touch us) that holds us and is held within. It is at this moment that Derrida introduces the 'triple transitivity' of his verb 's'attendre' (Derrida 1993: 66), anticipating a conclusion that remains hostage to Heideggerian analysis while presenting it (*in order* to present it) with its own ghosts. Derrida firstly teases out the aporia at the heart of the logic governing *Dasein's* death. It is only Dasein for whom death can appear, and it must be resolutely assumed. But death is of course the impossibility of Dasein's continuing. So death is the possibility of the impossibility of Dasein; or, if resolutely assumed, the possibility of the appearing as such of the possibility (Derrida 1993: 75). But this is no different to the *im*possibility of appearing *as such* of the possibility, which means that the authentic and *in*authentic forms of existence of Dasein, the proper and *im*proper relations to death, must share common characteristics. The threshold between proper and improper, between first existential analysis and preceded anthropological/cultural/theological method, is breached. In fact, for Derrida, what is experienced and named in the syntagm 'my death' is fundamentally that which already precedes the 'first' analysis: the death of the other, the death of the other in 'me' (Derrida 1993: 76), and 'from the most originary inside of its possibility, the proper of *Dasein* becomes from then on contaminated, parasited, and divided by the most improper' (Derrida 1993: 77). In the final pages, Derrida outlines how part of this contamination involves the mutated presence within the Heideggerian resolution of the Judaic-Christian ontotheology which it obviously seeks to multiply and surpass; and suggests that this secretion has a complex temporality unmastered by existential determination. It is a time for change, *mutatis mutandis*, that conditions the work of the historian (Derrida 1993: 80–1). The point cannot be lost on this essay; and it has informed how I have accommodated my readings within the histographical demands of the task assumed.

In conclusion, my essay has given timorous voice, in a safe and staged way, to the stubborn foreigner's resistance to the singularity of a national(ist) affirmation or collection. In a gesture that solicits and subverts the ethnic, that is obviously one of cultural fidelity, but of fidelity to the culture of mutation, mimicry, frontiers and internal resistance, a whole *fort/da* of affect and affiliation, Derrida personifies this position as that of the Marrano. If I have strongly associated national(ist) affirmations in this essay with the subject handed down and the presumptions underlying the collection, in a gesture that is *of course* unfair to editors and readers alike, I defend myself desperately with the counter-affirmation that the tenacity and problematization of borders in Derrida's approach betray the same irritation, same prolonged *fury*. And it needs to be recognized that the desire to give voice in this way is every bit as violent as the belonging it refuses, for all its agony. For *any* shibboleth is violent; and even if it calls upon you merely to say your alphabet, the answer to that (which you must submit) either gives you a hand or adds you to the footnote. Moreover, while a demand such as this can always come from outside, in the normal social and political scene, in fact it is primarily a test imposed on *oneself*. The *fort/da* of such a threatening moment, far from repeating an absolute danger already encountered, is in *anticipation* of merely normal violence. All of this is another story, and like any other scene it has found its way mutated here into the *mise-en-scène* of French critical theory. For most of the time, of course, it has been kept within the originary inside of its possibility. But it may survive in spite of loss of faith, to speak, who knows, for itself, another time.

References

Barthes, Roland (1977) *Roland Barthes par Roland Barthes*, New York: Noonday Press.

Bataille, Georges (1973) 'Réponse à Jean-Paul Sartre', in *Sur Nietzsche: volonté de chance, Oeuvres complètes*, 6. Paris: Gallimard, pp. 197–205.

Baudillard, Jean (1976) L'échange symbolique et la mort. Paris: Gallimard.

—— (1979) *De la séduction*. Paris: Denoël-Gonthier.

—— (1987). *L'autre par lui-même*. Paris: Galilée.

Derrida, Jacques (1974) *Of Grammatology*. Baltimore, MD: Johns Hopkins University Press.

—— (1993) *Aporias*. Stanford, CA: Stanford University Press.

Heidegger, Martin (1962). *Being and Time*. Oxford Blackwell (trans. John Macquarrie and Edward Robinson).

Hollier, Denis (ed.) (1988) *The College of Sociology (1937–39)*. Minneapolis: University of Minnesota Press.

Kellner, Douglas (1989) *Jean Baudrillard. From Marxism to Postmodernism and Beyond*. Oxford: Polity.

Robbe-Grillet, Alain (1963) *Pour un nouveau roman*. Paris: Les Editions de Minuit.

Satre, Jean-Paul (1945) Présentation', *Les Temps modernes*, 1: 12–13.

——(1943/7) 'Un nouveau mystique', *Cahiers du Sud*, 262, December 1943; reprinted in *Situations I*. Paris: Gallimard, 1947, pp. 143–88 (references are to this later edition).

——(1948) *Qu'est ce que la littérature*, in *Situations II*. Paris: Gallimard, pp. 55–330; translated by Steven Ungar as *What is Literature? And Other Essays*. Cambridge, MA: Harvard University Press, 1988.

——(1949) 'Qu'est-ce qu'un collaborateur?', *Situations III*. Paris: Gallimard, pp. 43–61.

4
History Writing: from the *Annales* to the Institut d'Histoire du Temps Présent

Christopher Flood and Hugo Frey

Introduction

The national and international prestige gained by history writing in France since the Second World War has been largely due to what used to be called *la nouvelle histoire*, associated with the journal *Annales: Economies, Sociétés, Civilisations* (renamed *Annales: Histoire, Sciences Sociales* in 1994). The *Annales* had been launched in 1929 as a pioneering venture by Lucien Febvre and Marc Bloch while they were teaching at the University of Strasbourg. In the 1930s it had already begun to establish itself as a vehicle for historians attracted by its founders' innovative, interdisciplinary approach to historical research. There was a shared rejection of what they saw as the sterile, positivistic empiricism exhibited by the historiographical establishment of that period, as well as the latter's inordinate commitment to producing narrative histories of political events and the lives of political leaders.

Although Bloch did not survive the war to see it, Febvre was able to create an institutional base for himself and like-minded historians with the founding of the Sixth Section of the Ecole Pratique des Hautes Etudes in 1947 under his own direction, and with his disciples to assist him in the running of the Centre de Recherches Historiques within it. Following Febvre's death in 1956, Fernand Braudel oversaw the *Annales*. Already the holder of a chair at the Collège de France from 1950 onwards, Braudel also became president of the Sixth Section and in 1963 founded the Maison des Sciences de l'Homme as a centre for interdisciplinary research. By the end of the 1960s Braudel had brought in younger historians, including Jacques Le Goff, Emmanuel Le Roy Ladurie, Marc Ferro, André Burguière and Jacques Revel to share the running of the *Annales*. After Braudel's retirement in 1972, his place at the head of the Sixth Section was taken by Le Goff, who became president of the Ecole des Hautes Etudes en Sciences Sociales (EHESS) after an institutional reorganization three years later. He, in turn, was succeeded by François Furet from 1977 to 1985. By that time the former rebel group had long since become the establishment. In doing so, it had lost much of its distinctiveness. Nevertheless, the journal continues to be held in high esteem and old traditions have been maintained – at the time of writing, the director of the EHESS is Jacques Revel, a long-standing pillar of the *Annales*.

Much of the limelight which used to be concentrated on the *Annales* and its supporting institutions has shifted to the Institut d'Histoire du Temps Présent (IHTP), founded in 1978 to carry out work on the most recent of all historical periods – corresponding roughly to the span of a human lifetime up to the moment at which the historian is writing. The Institut, which subsumes the former Comité d'Histoire de la Deuxième Guerre Mondiale (CHDGM), has included distinguished historians such as François Bédarida, Jean-Pierre Azéma, Pierre Laborie, Pascal Ory, Jean-Pierre Rioux and Jean-François Sirinelli. But it has attracted particular attention through the work of its present director, Henry Rousso, whose conceptualization of the Vichy Syndrome has had enormous impact within France and abroad, providing a point of reference for other historians and for a number of researchers in French cultural studies.

The IHTP historians are not opposed to, or by, the *Annales*. From 1982 onwards the journal began to include an occasional section on *le temps présent*. From time to time it has opened its pages to IHTP historians: for example, in a special issue in 1993 devoted to the history and historical memory of the Occupation (Lévi-Valensi, 1993).[1] In Braudel's day, besides a massive level of scholarly work ranging from highly specialized monographs to broad-spanning textbooks and high-quality popularizations, the *Annales* historians had achieved considerable access to the media as contributors to newspapers, magazines or broadcasts on historical topics (Coutau-Bégarie, 1983; Rieffel, 1995). That has been no less true of the IHTP historians, whose field inevitably involves them with topics which are still highly controversial because of their recent date. Thus, some of the historians have found themselves at the crossroads between orthodox professional scholarship, expert consultancy and journalistic punditry.

Our purpose in this chapter is to give a brief overview of the distinctive characteristics of the *Annales* and to show how the development of particular lines of research fed into the work of a number of historians associated with the IHTP. We will use Henry Rousso's study of the Vichy

Syndrome to illustrate some of the virtues and the vices of the IHTP's work on collective memory of the Occupation. We then turn to the involvement of Rousso and other IHTP historians in recent public controversies relating to the wartime period.

From the *Annales* to the IHTP

The strategy of the *Annales* historians has always been to maintain a commanding position for history as a canonical but modern discipline which keeps abreast of the concepts and methods of the social sciences but retains its own autonomy. This has been a difficult line to tread. Notwithstanding his appeals for an end to border disputes as to what was or was not a social science, Braudel's frequent definitional discussions of the specific contribution which history made to the social sciences, alongside, but separate from, fields such as anthropology, sociology or economics, might be taken as signs of a perceived need for vigilance on this score. That was especially the case in relation to sociology, which Braudel (1969) considered the only other discipline with a right to an overview of every facet of human society. Similar concerns have been shared by later generations of *Annales* historians. The introduction to a major collection of essays edited by Jacques Le Goff and Pierre Nora in 1974 under the title *Faire de l'histoire* betrays a degree of anxiety that, amid the diversification of its subjects and methods, history might be exposing itself to the danger of losing its identity through fragmentation and absorption by upstart disciplines. Indeed, that concern is the theme underlying their whole presentation. Thus, after stressing the innovativeness and openness of historical scholarship, Le Goff and Nora nevertheless acknowledge the challenge to history at a time when, they say, 'the field which it occupied alone as a system for explaining societies in temporal terms is overrun by other disciplines with ill-defined borders, which threaten to absorb it or dissolve it' (1974: 11). This occupational hazard is inevitable. It has contributed to the recent perception among many historians that their discipline is in crisis, a victim of its own success (a theme in Boutier and Julia, 1995; Noiriel, 1996; and see above, Chapter 1 of this collection). The problem of disciplinary definition remains particularly acute for historians who cover the recent period up to the present day. For example, the IHTP organized a series of seminars in 1988–90 to bring together its historians with representatives of various social science disciplines to encourage mutual understanding and to show that the study of recent history was no less legitimate, rigorous or distinctive than other historical scholarship. The fact that the preface to the collection of selected proceedings refers to the outdatedness and undesirability of 'frontier disputes' with other disciplines suggests continuing anxiety on that score (Peschanski, Pollak and Rousso, 1991: 17).

Although it has been suggested that the *Annales* in its crowning years was the source of a historiographical paradigm (Dosse, 1994; Hunt, 1986; Stoianovich, 1976), it is important not to overstate the degree of uniformity among the *Annales* historians, nor to schematize their own history into a succession of periods characterized by the primacy of one approach or field of study at the expense of others. At any one time there was a broad range of approaches and objects of study, all of which had been more or less foreshadowed in the work of Bloch, Febvre and their early associates during the interwar years. The two main strands were economic and social history, on the one hand, and cultural history, including history of mentalities, on the other. Political history was given lesser prominence, though by the 1970s there were signs of a return of interest in this area (Burke, 1990). Economic and social history, often with heavy use of quantitative methods, developed rapidly from the 1940s to the 1960s, with the production of major works such as Braudel's (1966 [1949]) massive study of the Mediterranean world in the age of Philip II, Pierre Chaunu's (1975 [1959]) analysis of trade between Seville and the Americas from the mid-sixteenth to the mid-seventeenth centuries, Georges Duby's (1977 [1962]) study of the agricultural economy and rural life in the Middle Ages and Le Roy Ladurie's (1969 [1966]) work on the peasants of the Languedoc in the sixteenth and seventeenth centuries. By the 1960s, however, the history of mentalities was also developing strongly in parallel with increasing interest in cultural phenomena, and it continued to do so thereafter, with major works by Robert Mandrou, Jean Delumeau, Jacques Le Goff, Le Roy Ladurie, Michel Vovelle and others. More recently, since the 1980s, the history of collective memory (socially transmitted representations of the historical past) has been an important outgrowth of this current of interest. Its most acclaimed project has been the huge collection of essays edited by Pierre Nora under the title *Les Lieux de mémoire* (1984, 1986, 1992), including a massive chapter by Krysztof Pomian (1986) on the contribution made by the *Annales*. The study of collective memory has also become a central aspect of the work of the IHTP.

It is worth adding that the rise of interest in mentalities and cultural history did not mean the eclipse of economic and social history.[2] In any case, the borderlines between economic, social and cultural history were by no means rigid. On the contrary, besides the fact that some studies of mentalities used quantitative methods by analogy with those used in economic and social history, the economic and the social were often fused with history of mentalities in the spirit of totalizing explanation which was one of the characteristic features of the *Annales* approach. Thus, for example, Le Roy Ladurie's (1978) famous study of the Occitan village of Montaillou from 1294 to 1324 is divided into two parts. The first of these considers the socio-economic structures of the village community as an ecological system. The second presents itself as an archaeological exploration of their beliefs, their cultural practices and their ways of thought.

Over the course of the last five decades, in keeping with the claim to openness and interdisciplinarity, the *Annales* has absorbed the changing fashions of French intellectual life, while following the logic of its own internal development. There have certainly been Marxists among the *Annales* historians, including Ernest Labrousse, Pierre Vilar, Maurice Agulhon and Michel Vovelle, among others. But it was never a predominantly Marxist school of thought (Berger, 1996; Burke, 1990; Stoianovich, 1976). Take the case of Braudel. He certainly had an interest in Marx. Using an approach which was to become a hallmark of the *Annales*, he too gave particular attention to the analysis of slow-changing, long-term, infrastructural relationships between physical environment, technology, economic activity and social organization. He gave these factors a deterministic primacy over medium-term, faster-changing trends and over the rapid succession of short-term sets of occurrences. This was his famous tripartite distinction between the dimensions of *longue durée, conjoncture* and *événement*. But he did not consider himself a Marxist and did not apply the dialectical dynamics or the teleology of Marx's theory of history in his own work (Dosse, 1994, especially pp. 107–36).

Equally, some *Annales* historians showed at least a passing interest in early structuralism. For example, in his eclectic way Braudel had an interest in the work of Lévi-Strauss, as did Le Roy Ladurie, who also refers to Greimas in his *Carnaval de Romans* (1979). However, their own research was not shaped by structuralist models derived from Saussurean linguistics (see Clark, 1985 for comparisons). Rather, it was the filling out of the tradition passed down from Lucien Febvre and Marc Bloch. More generally, the high profile of anthropology in the 1960s and 1970s helped to encourage the expansion of the historians' work into areas such as history of kinship relations, history of cooking, or the history of myth and ritual (for definitional discussions of these fields, see essays collected in Le Goff and Nora, 1974a).

By the same token, the growth of interest in history of mentalities, cultural history, history of ideologies, history of collective memory, of discourse, of iconic forms and of other symbolic representations owed something to the kaleidoscopic, reflexive character of the later structuralism and poststructuralism represented by Barthes, Lacan, Althusser, Foucault or Bourdieu, among others. But, again, the work of the *Annales* historians continued to develop primarily on the basis of their own variegated tradition. The lines of research and the sources of methodological or conceptual reference were still an extension of paths opened up by Bloch and Febvre who had been interested in social psychology and had worked extensively in the areas of collective attitudes, beliefs and forms of representation. As *Annales* historians acknowledged (for example, Duby, 1961; Le Goff, 1974), the history of mentalities – the historical study of attitudes, assumptions and feelings, roughly corresponding to what we might nowadays call cognitive schemata which shape perceptions and underlie conscious beliefs – had been pioneered by Bloch in his study of belief in the healing power of monarchs (1983 [1924]) or in part of his work on feudal society (1986 [1939]). Likewise, Febvre, who favoured studying what he called 'historical psychology' of social groups through the lives of particular individuals, had produced path-breaking works on Luther (1968 [1928]) and Rabelais (1968 [1942]). Similarly, Pierre Nora's introduction to *Les Lieux de mémoire* (1984) refers back to the theories of the Durkheimian sociologist, Maurice Halbwachs, whose conception of collective memory had interested Marc Bloch. More recently, Henry Rousso (1990, 1991) and other IHTP historians have likewise followed Halbwachs on this subject.

The *Annales* historians have drawn on other disciplines to open up new fields or new angles on old topics. The importation of models and concepts has been extremely fruitful and has helped to give enormous vitality and diversity to their work. They have by no means been averse to theoretical discussion of their approaches. But in the main their research has not been theory-driven in the sense of being designed to test and develop the explanatory value of particular models of social reality. Their work remains historiographical in the traditional sense that it seeks to find out and make sense of *what happened*. For example, Pierre Nora's introductory chapter in the first volume of *Les Lieux de mémoire* (1984) contains very little discussion of Halbwachs's theory of collective memory and makes no reference to any other theoretical models. Instead, it offers a historical justification of the subject on the grounds that contemporary society has retained particular sites or objects of collective memory (in the form of commemorations, iconic representations, heritage sites, etc.) in compensation for the fact that memory no longer permeates the entire social environment in the way that it once did. That is to say, history, in the sense of acquiring and analysing information about the past, has replaced memory, in the sense of transmission of customs, traditions and shared values which sustain a sense that the past is alive and continuous with the present. Nora's discussion is interesting in its application of the anthropological distinction between traditional societies and historical societies, but it is impressionistic rather than systematic, and historical rather than theoretical. In the massive three volumes of essays which form the collection there is little further theorization of the concept of collective memory by other contributors.

As has been the case with some other canonical disciplines, such as literary criticism, which have been renewed by the eclectic application of theories derived from other disciplines, the historians are open to the charge that they are using, or misusing, theories which are outdated, or have been invalidated, or have a different meaning within the discipline from which they have been borrowed. A second danger is that the uncritical application of one or more theoretical models as a cognitive grid to shape the selection, the periodization and the interpetation of evidence can lead to significant distortions in the process of reducing what is known of the real to the historiographical. A third danger is that as a useful concept passes into wide circulation, it will be cut free from the theoretical framework to which it belonged and will become a loose, cover-all term used with different or even mutually contradictory meanings in different contexts. That was undoubtedly a problem with the notion of *mentalité*. Jacques Le Goff was already warning in 1974 that it must not be allowed to become a catch-all and 'an alibi for epistemological laziness' (p.90). Nine years later, François Furet (1983) was airing criticisms which suggested that Le Goff's warning had not been heeded. A similar vagueness surrounds the widespread historiographical use of the terms *mémoire collective* and *mémoire nationale*. All of these types of objection can be levelled at the work of historians of the IHTP on the memory of the Occupation, despite the justified interest and admiration aroused by their research.

The IHTP and the Vichy Syndrome

Although *Annales* historians such as Pierre Nora and Marc Ferro have focused on issues of historical memory, it is a field which has increasingly become associated with the IHTP, and more particularly with

François Bédarida, Jean-Pierre Azéma and Henry Rousso among its leading members. In the printed press, radio and television, they are called to comment on news stories which are directly related to the recent past (for example, the assassination of René Bousquet, or the Paul Touvier trial). They have been at the forefront of public responses to a series of ideologically motivated, revisionist interpretations of the Occupation.

The IHTP would not be able to play this role, were it not renowned for its research publications, which have made it the principal public voice of mainstream scholarship on the contemporary period (on the IHTP and on the notion of *temps présent*, see Azéma, 1986; Bédarida, 1995; IHTP, 1993, 1999; Rousso, 1998a). Since 1981 the pattern of international colloquia, initial in-house publication in the *Bulletin de l'IHTP* or the *Cahiers de l'IHTP* followed by wider public dissemination has produced a series of important works. These have included, for example, major edited collections on Vichy France (such as Azéma and Bédarida, 1992) and on French perceptions of the Algerian war (Rioux, 1990; Rioux and Sirinelli, 1991). Other IHTP historians specialize in a wide range of areas such as European immigration, the French penal system, May 1968, public opinion, local government and – as if acknowledging IHTP historians' profile in the media – television as a source and object of historical study. The historians also publish regularly in the journal *Vingtième Siècle*, produce reflective essays for *Esprit* and popularize their findings in the magazine *L'Histoire*. Outside France the IHTP's status has been assured through its work with the International Committee of Historical Sciences, which has been administratively based at the IHTP since 1990. The current director of the IHTP, Henry Rousso, has also held the post of Secretary-General of the International Committee for the History of the Second World War.

The IHTP has given prominence to political history, but has also continued CHDGM projects which included social and economic studies – for instance, on business life (Beltran, Frank and Rousso, 1994). There have also been interdisciplinary projects which introduced cultural history and the *mentalités* approach. Indeed, despite the broad range of work conducted in its name, the IHTP is best known for its research in the field of historical memory of the Occupation. The topic of war memory was already in the air by the early 1980s (for example, in Wahl, 1984). Amid the sequence of fortieth-anniversary commemorations of the Second World War, Gérard Namer, a sociologist with connections to the IHTP, where he collaborated with Jean-Pierre Rioux, also paved the way with *Batailles pour la mémoire. La commémoration en France de 1945 à nos jours* (1983). The IHTP's first major collective publication was entitled *La Mémoire des Français. Quarante ans de commémorations de la seconde guerre mondiale* (1986). The successive directors of the Institute, François Bédarida, Robert Franck and Henry Rousso have all devoted some of their work to this field. Rousso, in particular, is associated with the history of collective memory as author of *Le Syndrome de Vichy* (1990) and co-author of *Vichy, un passé qui ne passe pas* (Conan and Rousso, 1994), as well as numerous contributions to journals and edited collections.

Le Syndrome de Vichy is one of the most important studies to come from the IHTP. A detailed analysis of the historical memory of Vichy France, from 1944 to the late 1980s, it has been widely cited in France, Britain and the United States as an authoritative work. The aim of the book is to chart how the French have viewed collaboration from the Liberation to the present day. It analyses a spectrum of cultural products which have influenced how the past was reconstructed and represented. These include literary, filmic, journalistic, overtly political and other sources. Identified as 'vectors of memory', these texts are used to show that the nation has experienced a collective 'sickness' or syndrome in its attitude towards Vichy.

A sophisticated periodization, using the language of psychoanalysis, frames the interpretation. Rousso suggests that there have been five stages in the memory of Vichy. First, a period of incomplete mourning (1945–54) in which the nation was unable to come to terms with its record. Second, incapable of achieving unity or reconciliation on the subject of Vichy, the French nation 'repressed' the episode (1954–71), while memories of collaboration were replaced by selective recollections of the heroism of the Resistance. Third, in the language of the therapist, Rousso describes 'the broken mirror' (1971–4), the period in which the phase of repression was contested, then broken. Fourth, the topic of Vichy is shown to have become an obsessional reference point (from 1974 onwards). Thus, disproportionate repression is seen to have given way to an equally problematic and unstable fascination with the *années noires*. The argument is extended in *Vichy, un passé qui ne passe pas* to cover the events of the early 1990s, which are taken as evidence that, far from diminishing in intensity over that period, the collective obsession with Vichy has become even more intense.

Le Syndrome de Vichy is a highly original and interesting study which uses the sources and methods of traditional political history in combination with cultural analysis. Its overarching themes are drawn from social psychology and psychoanalysis. However, although it has been widely admired, it has also been criticized on theoretical and empirical grounds.

The theoretical problem lies with Rousso's use of the concept of collective memory. Invited to respond to arguments put forward by Rousso at an IHTP seminar, Marie-Claire Lavabre (1991), a political scientist from the Centre d'Etude de la Vie Politique Française (CEVIPOF), pointed, among other things, to the conceptual looseness of Rousso's use of a plethora of terms such as *mémoire collective, mémoire nationale, mémoire de groupe, mémoire officielle, mémoire dominante* and others. She remarked that Halbwachs's theory, though valuable, had been subject to criticism and that Rousso had not, in any case, analysed the Vichy Syndrome in a way that was faithful to Halbwachs. She also observed that there was a fundamental confusion in Rousso's account of collective memory. It blurred the distinction between two very different phenomena: on the one hand, the political, social and cultural symptoms of distorted behaviour allegedly revealing the persistent effects of the trauma of occupation and internal conflict during the war; on the other hand, the conscious and deliberate manipulation of the past for political and/or ideological motives. The first of these is based on assumptions concerning the weight of the past on the present, whereas the other assumes the selective, instrumental use of the past for present purposes. Most of Rousso's evidence illustrates the latter, but his framing of the subject is in terms of the former.

The point can be pushed further. Admittedly, Rousso explains that he is using the notion of neurosis only in a figurative sense, 'as the borrowings from psychoanalysis have only metaphorical, not explanatory value here' (1990: 19). But if a metaphor is used in a sufficiently extended way to frame an argument, it obviously is being used as a form of explanation, although the disclaimer as to its status allows it to be employed in a less rigorous way than if it was being applied systematically as a theoretical model. In the seminar at which Lavabre subsequently stated her criticisms Rousso (1991) appeared to have shifted his ground. Referring to his use of terms such as *refoulement* and *deuil* in *Le Syndrome de Vichy*, he asked rhetorically whether he should have retained these psychoanalytic concepts in the text rather than merely using them as an informal heuristic device in his research into the changing representations of Vichy since the Liberation. Rousso left his question without an explicit answer. Yet, the implication was that the concepts had indeed been intended as instruments of psychoanalytic explanation, although this appeared to contradict his statement in the introduction to *Le Syndrome de Vichy* itself.

Whatever the case, there is no clarification in his later writing along the same lines (see Rousso, 1998a: 17–18 for a similarly equivocal explanation). The reader is simply left to wonder as to the epistemological status being claimed for a term such as *obsession*. It can certainly be accepted that the equivocations, humiliations and squalid crimes of the Occupation or its aftermath did leave a deep imprint on contemporary French culture. But, as we have argued elsewhere (Flood and Frey, 1995), it is not clear that anything more than the most arbitrary, subjective judgement can be made as to when prolonged controversy over the interpretation of a divisive set of historical events becomes an unhealthy obsession, as opposed to a perfectly normal process of reinterpreting the past, subject also to factors such as ideological competition, personal rivalries for symbolic rewards and career advancement, vested interests, bandwagon effects and utilization by publishing houses or media companies for commercial reasons. In any case, it is not obvious how the pathology of the obsession should be measured. Is it more damaging than the Revolution Syndrome, the Dreyfus Syndrome or the Algeria Syndrome, for instance? Presumably the sickness must be curable – at least, Rousso (1998b) has appeared to assume that is the case. This is not to say that the study of psychohistory cannot be useful, however speculative it must necessarily be. But the invitation to interpret in terms of the irrational, and hence of the unverifiable, is too impressionistic to substitute for forms of historical explanation which do not require the presumption, or even the metaphor, of neurotic disorder.

A different type of criticism comes from the American historian of French collaboration, Bertram Gordon. In an issue of *French Historical Studies* devoted to the theme of the Vichy Syndrome, Gordon (1995) argues persuasively that while certain aspects of Rousso's research remain significant, an empirical study of publishing on Vichy France does not reflect the periodization which has been claimed. Studying directories of French publishing – *Biblio, Bibliographie de la France, Bibliographie nationale* and *Bibliographie annuelle de l'histoire de France* – Gordon seeks to show that interest in Vichy, Franco-German collaboration and French military history of the Occupation has been in relative decline since the late 1940s. There have been few significant 'troughs' or 'repressions' in which the subject has received proportionately low attention, whereas conversely, publishing in the 1970s and 1980s does not show evidence of massive circulation of Vichy-related texts which would categorically confirm the obsession stage of memory (see also Gordon, 1998).

Rousso's (1995) response was that Gordon's evidence relating to publishing cycles of non-fictional works did not disqualify the thesis with regard to patterns of political activity, literary and cultural debate, or filmic representation. Nevertheless, even if the rejoinder is valid, it still points to a revision of the original work. By arguing that different forms of representation operated through different periodizations of historical memory, Rousso weakens the totalizing thesis of the book. Instead, it might be more appropriate to make a series of genre-specific studies which chart different cycles of representation, such as film, the novel, autobiographical writing, scholarly writing, ideologically coloured writing, political journalism or private reflections. In fact, it seems probable that each type of product will have been created due to a variety of factors specific to the history of its particular genre, establishing sets of Vichy 'syndromes' (if the term is still appropriate), rather than a single one which pervades all forms of representation simultaneously and to the same degree.

Memory, the historians and the media

From 1990 to 1995 the series of fiftieth anniversaries of wartime events encouraged a great deal of public soul-searching on the subject of the Occupation, in parallel with ceremonies of commemoration and controversies over the appropriateness or otherwise of the responses of politicians, including the presidents, François Mitterrand and his successor Jacques Chirac. Public attention also focused on the judicial cases against Frenchmen indicted on charges of crimes against humanity – the long process involved in bringing Paul Touvier to trial in 1994, the political and legal manoeuvres surrounding René Bousquet until he was murdered in 1993 and the endless delays before Maurice Papon was brought to court in 1997 and convicted in 1998. These cases were widely expected not only to do justice but also to serve other functions. It was hoped that they would set the public record straight, make good the perceived inadequacies of the postwar purges, exorcise ghosts and instruct the younger generations born at a distance from the events of the Occupation.

Amid all of this, the Occupation became something of a boom industry for book and magazine publishers, producers of TV programmes, film-makers and novelists. The IHTP continued to play its part on the academic side, with numerous conferences and scholarly publications. Among its claims to distinctiveness within the discipline is the fact that the study of recent history allows the use of oral sources. Thus, the IHTP undoubtedly benefited from its ability to call on former leaders of the Resistance to take a prominent place at its conferences and lend them the particular authenticity associated with those who were really part of the events under discussion. IHTP historians were called to give their expert opinions on issues which remained controversial. For example, Jean-Pierre Azéma and François Bédarida were members of the commission chaired in 1992 by René Rémond to investigate the authenticity of the supposed *fichier juif* discovered by Serge Klarsfeld. Bédarida testified as an expert witness at Paul Touvier's trial for crimes against humanity and Azéma did the same at Maurice Papon's trial.[3] The widespread media interest in the Occupation also led to frequent invitations for the historians to give their expert opinions in the press, the weekly magazines and in broadcasts.

Nevertheless, it was a curious situation for the IHTP historians, given the fact that Rousso, Bédarida, Azéma and others not only wrote histories of wartime France, but also studied the different ways in which the Occupation had been represented in France since the war. They were in the complex position of being both contributors to the scholarly side of contemporary memory of the war and historical analysts of the phenomenon to which they themselves were contributing. Rousso accepted in *Le Syndrome de Vichy* that historians were only one vector of memory among others. He also acknowledged that historical works had no curative value as far as the syndrome was concerned (1990: 13). Still, the IHTP historians naturally considered that their research on the Vichy period and on subsequent representations of that period was rigorous and as accurate as the available evidence allowed. A mixture of professionalism, elitism and moral convictions made them see themselves as fighting for clarity and calm appraisal of the past amid the public hue and cry. François Bédarida referred to 'the dogged, tenacious struggle of historians against distortions and mythifications' (1997).

A particularly dramatic illustration of the dilemmas of the IHTP historians in relation to public interest in the Occupation was provided on the occasion of a round-table meeting held in the offices of the newspaper *Libération* on 17 May 1997 (published as a supplement on 9 July 1997, with articles by the participants following on 10–12 July – see *Libération*, 1997). The meeting was a consequence of the controversy stirred by a book published earlier in the year by Gérard Chauvy under the title *Aubrac, Lyon 1943*. The book had reproduced a number of documents, including a statement drawn up in 1990 on behalf of Klaus Barbie by his lawyer, Jacques Vergès. Chauvy compared these documents with successive statements made by the resistance heroes Raymond and Lucie Aubrac since the war to show that the latter contained inconsistencies. Chauvy did not explicitly endorse Barbie's claim that Raymond Aubrac had been 'turned' after his first arrest in March 1943 and had subsequently betrayed the timing and whereabouts of a meeting between Jean Moulin and leaders of the internal resistance, including Aubrac, in June of that year. Nevertheless, Chauvy did imply doubts. The round table had been called by the Aubracs on the advice of Daniel Cordier, himself a former secretary to Jean Moulin and more recently the author of a book which refuted the charge that Moulin had been working for the USSR. The Aubracs presumed that they would receive a quasi-official exoneration by exposing themselves to discussion with IHTP historians Bédarida, Azéma, Rousso, Dominique Veillon and Laurent Douzou, plus Daniel Cordier and two eminent historians of other periods, Maurice Agulhon and Jean-Pierre Vernant, who were there as friends of the Aubracs. Some staff of the newspaper were present to record the debate, but not to participate.

The details of the discussion need not concern us here. The important point is that the outcome was complex, equivocal and itself controversial. The Aubracs emerged feeling that they had been subjected to an unjustified level of interrogation and a presumption of guilt by Azéma, Bédarida, Rousso and Cordier. The historians had deplored Chauvy's methods and malicious intent. They had also rejected the specific charge that Aubrac had betrayed the meeting with Moulin after being 'turned' by Barbie earlier that year. But they had taken up other questions relating to Aubrac's period of interrogation and imprisonment from June to October 1943 in terms which implied suspicion that the inconsistencies in his subsequent statements pointed to a desire to conceal something discreditable. The Aubracs were particularly disgusted by suggestions that they might have been inadvertently responsible for the arrest and subsequent deaths of Raymond Aubrac's parents. They bitterly resented the way in which the historians had reproached them for allowing themselves to be given the status of legendary heroes by media appearances, and by Claude Berri's film, *Lucie Aubrac*, as well as by the inaccuracies in their own writings about their experiences. They remarked sourly that if they had been put on pedestals, the IHTP had been a party to the process by giving them prominence at its colloquia. If their memories of the period had been imperfect, that too should be understandable.

Vernant and Agulhon remained deeply sympathetic to the Aubracs and hostile to the way in which some of the IHTP historians had behaved. Vernant commented on what he saw as hostility towards the Aubracs and resentment towards those who had experienced the Resistance rather than studied it from a distance. He thought there had been an effort to cut the Aubracs down to size on the grounds that their celebrity was obscuring the wider movement. Daniel Cordier made it clear that he still felt Aubrac was concealing something which would explain the fact that he had not been interrogated in depth, even though Barbie had known he was one of the leaders of the Resistance. Bédarida, besides pointing to the unresolved questions raised by Chauvy's book, argued that the controversy would not have been so severe if the Aubracs had not allowed themselves to be represented as emblematic heroes. Both Bédarida and Rousso dwelt on the historians' duty to seek the truth behind the myths as impartially as possible, without hagiography or demonization (see also, Rousso, 1998a).

Some weeks later, Azéma (1997) replied to Serge Klarsfeld who had published an article in *Le Monde* pointing to local historical factors which could explain the obscurities surrounding Raymond Aubrac's period of imprisonment. Azéma reiterated the unresolved questions raised at the round table and stood firm on the ground that historians had a duty to investigate all of the different representations of the past without fear or favour. That did not prevent Klarsfeld from returning to his own interpretation, or from claiming unpleasantly that 'a fringe of historians who are perhaps frustrated by not having experienced a period as fascinating as the Second World War – when some people were making history rather than merely writing it – are intent on seizing power over the period by distributing good or bad marks to participants...' (1997). Meanwhile, a number of other historians had also protested individually or collectively at the tone and the procedures of the interrogation to which the Aubracs had been subjected: among them were Denis Peschanski and Pierre Laborie, both major figures linked to the IHTP, as well as Laurent Douzou who had participated in the round table itself (Delpla, 1997: 164–7; Guillon, 1999). There could be no finality about the findings of the round table because there was insufficient evidence to have real confidence on a number of key points. The Aubracs at least had the satisfaction of subsequently winning a lawsuit against Chauvy and his publisher for defamation. The argument over the real identity of Jean Moulin's betrayer has continued (Cordier, 1999; *L'Evénement du jeudi*, 1999)

Conclusion

The work of the IHTP on collective memory and representations is one of the most fascinating and fruitful aspects of the legacy of the *Annales*, but it is also highly contentious, even if one sets aside the conceptual and methodological questions which arise in the analysis of social phenomena taken to be evidence of collective memory. The IHTP histor-ians make much of their access to living witnesses, but they are mani-festly irritated when those witnesses hold to versions of events which do not fit comfortably with documentary evidence, even though the histor-ians acknowledge that documents too can be misleading. The IHTP historians consider themselves to be good researchers, and they are right to do so. They also see themselves as guardians of national memory, precisely because they do not serve any one current of it at the expense of others. They appear to imagine that if the national experience of the Second World War could be demythified and pinned down in the form of accurate historical analyses, it would lose its destructive force. But as we have suggested, no set of experts commands sufficient authority to put such matters definitively to rest. On the contrary, they can easily find themselves giving rise to further dispute and thereby produce the opposite effect from the one which they intend. In the case of the round table, the fact that the occasion was organized on the premises of a daily newspaper, which subsequently published the transcript and the retro-spective comments of the participants, testifies to the level of anticipated public interest. It also demonstrates the way in which this type of historical debate generates high drama for the media and propels the bandwagon forward. Furthermore, the historians are in the ironic posi-tion of deriving personal and institutional benefit from public interest in the subject. This, in turn, raises the danger that their legitimacy will be undermined.

Issues relating to the Occupation have been particularly delicate for the obvious reason that they refer to a comparatively recent period of suffering, humiliation and divisions within the French nation. Without fully accepting Rousso's quasi-psychoanalytic periodization of the Vichy Syndrome, one can certainly agree that it requires many decades to take stock of such an experience and come to terms with it. But there is every reason to suppose that there will be other matters which are scarcely less controversial. For example, the wars of decolonization are a potential case in point. Indeed, from outside the IHTP, Benjamin Stora (1992) has already applied the model of the Vichy Syndrome to the collective memory of the Algerian débâcle. The history of decolonization has not yet aroused the same intensity of interest and controversy as the Occu-pation, but it may do so. If that occurs before too long, some of those who participated in the events will still be alive. Residues of the ideolo-gical divisions and the moral dilemmas over colonialism and decoloni-zation remain present in contemporary French political life. They underlie debates concerning postcolonial relationships with developing countries. They feed anxieties connected with France's somewhat diminished role in the world today. Many old and new scores have still to be settled. Amid these or other debates, the IHTP will probably flourish, but the future is not without risks.

Notes

1   All references throughout the chapter are to French editions and all translations are our own, with the exception of references to Dosse (1994).
2   Lynn Hunt (1986) offers a classification of articles appearing in the *Annales* between 1965 and 1984. As Hunt acknowledges, the categorization is extremely approximate, given the diversity of subjects, and the fact that some articles are counted twice because they do not fit neatly into one category alone. On this basis, Hunt shows the distribution of articles between subdisciplines in percentages. We reproduce her figures below, as follows:

	Economic	*Social*	*Demographic*	*Political*	*Intellectual/ Cultural*
1965–74	18	22	13	14	34
1975–84	19	24	13	11	35

With no greater claim to scientific rigour, we propose an update covering the 1985 to mid-1997 period (534 articles, though rather than double count, we have left some unclassified), as follows: economic 20 per cent; social 25 per cent; demographic 1.5 per cent; political 20 per cent; intellectual/cultural 26 per cent; unclassifiable 7.5 per cent. This suggests that the proportion of articles on economic and social topics remained consistent with the periods covered by Hunt, while there was movement away from demographic history and to some extent from intellectual/cultural (including *mentalités*), but greater interest in political history, which had once been derided, though never entirely ignored, by Braudel and his circle. Hunt also emphasized the breadth of geographical focus, with 'less than a third' of the articles, as she puts it, being focused on France (213). Our figures suggest little change in that respect, with 34 per cent for France, 61 per cent for the rest of the world and 5 per cent unclassifiable. Of those dealing with France, Hunt points out that a large though diminishing majority covered periods before 1815 (the figure for 1965–74 was 74 per cent and for 1975–84 it was 65 per cent), reflecting the taste for long-term continuities over periods of upheaval. On that basis – and by inserting articles which straddle the divide into the category where their centre of chronological gravity appears to lie – our figures confirm the continuing, but still diminishing predominance of periods before 1815 (58 per cent) over post-1815 (42 per cent). However, it is not clear why Hunt chose 1815 as the chronological break for her figures, since 1789 would have fitted her argument better. If our own set had been broken at the start of the Revolution, the figures would have shown a fairly even balance between pre-1789 (45

per cent) and post-1789 (44 per cent), with a relatively significant number of other pieces (11 per cent), in pursuit of the *longue durée*, straddling both.
3 Some IHTP members, including Rousso, declined to do so on the grounds that the requirements of judicial processes – especially those of massively publicized trials pertaining to exceptionally serious crimes committed fifty years earlier – were incompatible with the provisional, highly nuanced judgements involved in historical interpretation (see Conan and Rousso, 1994: ch. 3, and Rousso, 1998a: 86–138 on the issues raised by the trials as Rousso saw them; and Jeanneney, 1998, for a valuable discussion which takes a different position from Rousso's).

References

Azéma, Jean-Pierre (1986) 'Temps présent', in André Burguière (ed.), *Dictionnaire des sciences historiques*. Paris: Presses Universitaires de France, pp. 653–6.
—— (1997) 'Affaire Aubrac: Les faits sont têtus', *Libération*, 28 August.
Bédarida, François (1995) 'La Dialectique passé/présent et la pratique historienne', in F. Bédarida (ed.), *L'Histoire et le métier d'historien en France 1945–1995*. Paris: Maison des Sciences de l'Homme, pp. 75–85.
—— (1997) 'Mémoire de la Résistance et devoir de vérité', *Libération*, 12 July.
Beltran, Alain, Robert Franck and Henry Rousso (1994) *La Vie des entreprises sous l'Occupation: Une enquête à l'échelle locale*. Paris: Belin
Berger, Stefan (1996) 'The rise and fall of "critical" historiography?', *European Review of History*, 3 (2): 213–31.
Bloch, Marc (1983 [1924]) *Les Rois thaumaturges: étude sur le caractère surnaturel attribué à la puissance royale particulièrement en France et en Angleterre*. Paris: Gallimard.
Boutier, Jean and Dominique Julia (eds) (1995) *Passés recomposés: Champs et chantiers de l'histoire*. Paris: Autrement.
Braudel, François (1966) *La Méditerranée et le monde méditerranéen à l'époque de Philippe II*, 2 vols, 2nd edn. Paris: Armand Colin.
—— (1969) *Ecrits sur l'histoire*. Paris: Flammarion.
Burke, Peter (1990) *The French Historical Revolution: The Annales School 1929–89*. Cambridge: Polity.
Chaunu, Pierre (1975 [1959]) *Séville et l'Atlantique, 1550–1650*. Paris: SEVPEN.
Clark, Stuart (1985) 'The *Annales* Historians', in Quentin Skinner (ed.), *The Return of Grand Theory in the Human Sciences*. Cambridge: Cambridge University Press.
Conan, Eric and Henry Rousso (1994) *Vichy: Un passé qui ne passe pas*. Paris: Fayard.
Cordier, Daniel (1999) *Jean Moulin, la République des catacombes*. Paris: Gallimard.
Coutau-Bégarie, Hervé (1983) *Le Phénomène 'Nouvelle Histoire': Stratégie et idéologie des nouveaux historiens*. Paris: Economica.
Delpla, François (1997) *Aubrac: Les faits et la calomnie*. Paris: Le Temps des Cerises.
Dosse, François (1994 [1987]) *The New History in France: The Triumph of the Annales*, trans. P. Conroy Jr. Urbana: University of Illinois Press.
Duby, Georges (1961) 'Histoire des mentalités', in C. Samaran (ed.), *L'Histoire et ses méthodes*. Paris: Gallimard/Pléiade, pp. 937–66.

—— (1977 [1962]) *L'Economie rurale et la vie des campagnes dans l'Occident médiéval*, 2 vols. Paris: Flammarion.

L'Evénement du jeudi (1999) Dossier '21 Juin 1943, qui a donné Jean Moulin?', 22–28 April: 52–9.

Febvre, Lucien (1968 [1928]) *Un destin. Martin Luther*. Paris: Presses Universitaires de France.

—— (1968 [1942]) *Le Problème de l'incroyance au XVIe siècle. La religion de Rabelais*. Paris: Albin Michel.

Flood, Christopher and Hugo Frey (1995) 'The Vichy Syndrome revisited', *Contemporary French Civilization*, 19 (2): 231–49.

Furet, François (1983) 'Beyond the *Annales*', *Journal of Modern History*, 55: 389–410.

Gordon, Bertram (1995) 'The "Vichy Syndrome" problem in history', *French Historical Studies*, 19 (2): 495–518.

—— (1998) 'World War II France half a century after', in Richard Golsan (ed.) *Fascism's Return: Scandal, Revision, and Ideology since 1980*. Lincoln: University of Nebraska Press, pp. 152–81.

Guillon, Jean-Marie (1999) 'L'Affaire Aubrac, ou la dérive d'une certaine façon de faire l'histoire', *Modern and Contemporary France*, 7 (1): 89–93.

Hunt, Lynn (1986) 'French history in the last twenty years: the rise and fall of the *Annales* paradigm', *Journal of Contemporary History*, 21: 209–24.

Iggers, George (1985) *New Directions in European Historiography*, revised edn. London: Methuen.

IHTP (1986) *La Mémoire des Français: Quarante ans de commémorations de la seconde guerre mondiale*. Paris: CNRS.

—— (1993) *Ecrire l'histoire du temps présent*. Paris: CNRS.

—— (1999) *IHTP-CNRS: Institut d'Histoire du Temps Présent*. http://www.ihtp-cnrs.ens-cachan.fr.

Jeanneney, Jean-Noël (1998) *Le Passé dans le prétoire: L'historien, le juge et le journaliste*. Paris: Seuil.

Klarsfeld, Serge (1997) 'Affaire Aubrac: Serge Klarsfeld répond à Jean-Pierre Azéma', *Libération*, 1 September.

Lavabre, Marie-Claire (1991) 'Du poids et du choix du passé. Lecture critique du "syndrome de Vichy"', in D. Peschanski, M. Pollak and H. Rousso (eds), *Histoire politique et sciences sociales*. Brussels: Complexe, pp. 265–78.

Le Goff, Jacques (1974) 'Les Mentalités: une histoire ambiguë', in Le Goff and Nora (1974a), vol. 3, pp. 76–94.

—— and P. Nora (eds) (1974a) *Faire de l'histoire*, 3 vols. Paris: Gallimard.

—— (1974b) 'Présentation', in Le Goff and Nora (1974a), pp. ix–xiii.

Le Roy Ladurie, Emmanuel (1969 [1966]) *Les Paysans de Languedoc*. Paris: Flammarion.

—— (1978) *Montaillou: village occitan de 1294 à 1324*. Paris: Gallimard.

—— (1979) *Le Carnaval de Romans*. Paris: Gallimard.

Lévi-Valensi, Lucette (ed.) (1993) *Présence du passé, lenteur de l'histoire*. Special issue of *Annales: ESC*, 48 (3).

Libération (1997) Dossier 'Les Aubrac et les historiens', http://www.liberation.fr/aubrac.

Namer, Gérard (1983) *Batailles pour la mémoire: La commémoration en France de 1945 à nos jours*. Paris: Papyrus.

Noiriel, Gérard (1996) *Sur la 'crise' de l'histoire*. Paris: Belin.

Nora, Pierre (1984) *Les Lieux de mémoire I: La République*. Paris: Gallimard.
—— (1986) *Les Lieux de mémoire II: La Nation*, 3 vols. Paris: Gallimard.
—— (1992) *Les Lieux de mémoire III: Les France*, 3 vols. Paris: Gallimard.
Peschanski, Denis, Michel Pollak and Henry Rousso (1991) 'Le Temps présent, une démarche historienne à l'épreuve des sciences sociales', in D. Peschanski, M. Pollak and H. Rousso (eds), *Histoire politique et sciences sociales*. Brussels: Complexe, pp. 13–36.
Pomian, Krysztof (1986) 'L'Heure des *Annales*: La terre – les hommes – le monde', in Nora (1986), pp. 377–429.
Rieffel, Rémy (1995) 'Les Historiens, l'édition et les médias', in François Bédarida (ed.) *L'Histoire et le métier d'historien en France 1945–1995*. Paris: Maison des Sciences de l'Homme, pp. 57–73.
Rioux, Jean-Pierre (ed.) (1990) *La Guerre d'Algérie et les Français*. Paris: Fayard.
—— and Jean-François Sirinelli (eds) (1991) *La Guerre d'Algérie et les intellectuels français*. Brussels: Complexe.
Rousso, Henry (1990) *Le Syndrome de Vichy de 1944 à nos jours*, 2nd edn. Paris: Seuil.
—— (1991) 'Pour une histoire de la mémoire collective: l'après-Vichy', in D. Peschanski, M. Pollak and H. Rousso (eds), *Histoire politique et sciences sociales*. Brussels: Complexe, pp. 243–64.
—— (1994) *Vichy, un passé qui ne passe pas*. Paris: Fayard.
—— (1995) 'Le Syndrome de l'historien', *French Historical Studies*, 19 (2): 519–26.
—— (1998a) *La Hantise du passé*, interviews with Philippe Petit. Paris: Textuel.
—— (1998b) 'Le Tribunal de l'histoire a jugé Vichy depuis longtemps', interview with Laurent Greilshamer and Nicolas Weill, *Le Monde*, 7 April.
Stoianovich, Traian (1976) *French Historical Method: The Annales Paradigm*. Ithaca, NY: Cornell University Press.
Stora, Benjamin (1992) *La Gangrène et l'oubli: la mémoire de la guerre d'Algérie*. Paris: La Découverte.
Wahl, Alfred (ed.) (1984) *Mémoire de la Seconde Guerre mondiale: Actes du colloque de Metz, 6–8 octobre 1983*. Metz: Université de Metz.

5

French Linguistics and *Enonciation*: Meanings, Utterances and Representational Gaps

Jacques Durand

In attempting to present, let alone evaluate, a particular field (in my case that of French linguistics), one runs the risk of being too general and perhaps unfocused, or, on the other hand, of being too selective and thus of misrepresenting the field in question. In this paper, I have deliberately taken the second option.[1] I have concentrated on a few ideas and intellectual figures, at the risk of giving a partial and biased view of modern French linguistics. I plead guilty in advance and can only encourage the reader to bear in mind that there is a great deal of valuable linguistic work going on in France under other banners than the ones mentioned here.

I think that, if there is a way of approaching the study of language which is typically French, it is surely to be found within the *énonciation* tradition. In speaking about a tradition, I do not wish to imply that there is a single set of assumptions shared by all French linguists who work on *énonciation*. But it is my claim that there are tendencies and constellations of features which recur from school to school and which unite the *énonciativistes* beyond the socio-political and personal divisions which characterize any domain of enquiry. What do I mean by *énonciation* in this context? I will take as a starting-point a few paraphrases or quotations borrowed from Benveniste's well-known article 'L'appareil formel de l'énonciation', as reprinted in the second volume of his *Problèmes de linguistique générale* (1974: 79–88).

In this article, Benveniste starts from the observation that much modern linguistics is devoted to the description of the use of forms (*l'emploi des formes*) – that is to say, in his terms, the set of rules which determine the morpho-syntactic conditions under which forms can or must appear. He points out that the use of forms, while central to the enterprise of linguistics, should not be confused with what he calls the use of language (*l'emploi de la langue*) – a phenomenon apparently so banal that its importance is often overlooked. This is where *énonciation* comes in, as the mobilization of language through an individual act of utterance. Benveniste points out that *énonciation*, in this sense, cannot be confused with Saussurean *parole* since the object of enquiry is the utterance as act and not the utterance as product (*l'énoncé*). What is therefore central to analysis, is the process of putting language to use and the linguistic markers of this relationship (cf. Benveniste, 1974: 80).

Enonciation so defined gives pride of place to the deictic system of person since the utterer (*l'énonciateur*) in any act of appropriating the linguistic system will set up the other (the *co-énonciateur*) as partner in the communicative exchange in order to participate in acts of reference. The pronouns *I* and *you*, therefore, are not semantically pro-forms, but indices of the basic coordinates of any speech-act which are opposed to the third person pronoun which designates the non-person. The term *co-énonciateur*, not used by Benveniste (who speaks of *destinataire*), is nowadays favoured by many French linguists for at least two reasons: first, the roles of speaker and addressee are mutually supporting and reversible in a typical act of communication; second, the utterance act, whether private or public, is itself structured in such a way that speakers are constantly modulating their own discourse and can indeed talk to themselves (cf. Lyons, 1994; O'Kelly, 1997; and the essays in Yaguello, 1994).

A second central example of a deictic category is that of the demonstratives (Eng. *this*, *that*; Fr. *ce*, *ici*, etc.) which are, as a first approximation, definable in terms of their relation to the speaker-addressee spatial coordinates. A third standard example is tense (in the technical sense of the grammaticalization of time-reference and by opposition to morphosyntactic tense). Tense, as has often been observed, can only be understood in terms of the time of speech which provides an anchor point to which the situation described will be related. But many other phenomena also need reference to the act of utterance. Thus, modality as manifested in predicates such as *pouvoir* or *devoir* is directly linked to *énonciation* since it reveals the speaker's attitude to the propositional content of what is being said – whether it is presented as being validated, questioned or merely entertained as a hypothesis. Moreover, the *co-énonciateur* must also be taken into account since certain values such as permission or obligation cannot be understood outside of the network of interpersonal relationships.

It seems worth pointing out at this stage that *énonciateur* in this sense is a rather abstract notion and is preferred by French linguists to *locuteur* (speaker) since it is quite possible to utter something without being the semantic source of it. One familiar example is that of the interpreter who proffers the translated message without being the locutionary agent. Another example familiar to literary criticism is that of the *style indirect libre* which often sets up an intricate relationship between the discourse of a narrator and other discourses. Benveniste himself gives the case of verbal jousting in certain cultures, such as the 'hain-teny' of the Merinas, where no dialogue is involved. The two protagonists try to outsmart each other in the quotation of proverbs and it is the one who has the largest stock of proverbs at his command who will win the day. Now what has just been said is not claimed to be totally new. Indeed, many of the central insights of *énonciation* theory have a venerable antiquity. John Lyons (1977b: 811, 821–2) has for instance drawn attention to the fact that the analysis of time-reference in terms of a zero NOW coordinate was already present in St Augustine. Indeed, take the following description by Benveniste (1974: 83):

> It might appear that temporality is innately part and parcel of thought. In reality, it is produced both within and through acts of utterance (*énonciation*). The act of utterance gives rise to the category of present, and the category of present engenders the category of time.... The formal present is only an explicitation of the present which is inherent in the act of utterance, and which is renewed within each production of discourse. It is on the basis of this continuous present, which is coextensive with our own presence, that there arises within our consciousness the feeling of a continuity which we call 'time'; continuity and temporality are the by-product of the unending present of acts of utterance, which is the present of being itself and which delimits itself by a process of internal reference between what is about to become present and what is already past.
>
> (my translation)

And compare it with what St Augustine says in his *Confessions*:

> What is now strikingly obvious to me is that neither the future nor the past exist. To say, 'Time exists in three modes: the past, the present and the future' is not to make a proper use of language. It would perhaps be more appropriate to say, 'Time exists in three modes: the present of the past, the present of the present, the present of the future. For these three kinds of time exist only in the mind and cannot be found anywhere else. The present of the past is memory;

the present of the present is direct intuition; the present of the future is expectation.

(St Augustine, *Confessions*, Livre XI, ch. 20, my translation)

On the basis of the pointers given above, it would be easy to conclude that *énonciation* is a mere re-enactment of traditional ideas. Old wine in new bottles! As I am a strong advocate of the need for linguistics to be cumulative if it is to qualify as a scientific enterprise – or less pompously as a rational enterprise – the fact that *énonciation* is rooted in classical work, and particularly in the rhetorical tradition, is in itself not an objection but a positive observation (see Durand and Laks, 1996). What seems to be worth stressing is that, although some of the basic tenets of *énonciation* are well known, they have not always been given the place they deserve in classical or modern work on language. For instance, Arnauld and Lancelot, the Port-Royal grammarians, whose work was insightful in so many respects, described pronouns as simple substitutes for nouns chosen for politeness and to avoid what we would nowadays call redundancy of information:

As men have frequently been obliged to speak of the same things within the same piece of discourse, and as it would have been irksome to keep repeating the same names, they invented some words to replace these names, and which they called *pronouns* for this very reason.

First of all, they recognized that it was often pointless and ungracious to name oneself; thus, they introduced the first person pronoun, to be used instead of the name of the person who speaks: *Ego, me, I, moi, je.*

To avoid being forced to name the person to whom one speaks, they also found it convenient to use in its place a word which they called second person pronoun: *you, tu, toi* or *vous.*

(Arnauld and Lancelot, 1969 [1660]: 43–4, my translation)

And so on for the third person pronouns. But, lest this should appear as the outdated thinking of another age, it is worth pointing out that the twentieth century has continued this venerable tradition. The vast number of major books on semantics published over the last hundred years which make no reference to the situation of utterance would be far too long to quote here. *Enonciation*, with its emphasis on deixis and on speech acts, does constitute an important research programme. Within this programme, which is partially shared by all linguists who have focused on deixis (cf. Lyons, 1977: ch. 15; Kleiber, 1992; Morel and Danon-Boileau, 1992), a number of fine-grained, and I believe new, observations have been made. The detailed examination of specific areas is out of the question here, but let us briefly consider time-reference. Expressions such as *then* in English and *alors* in French can both refer to the NOT-NOW preceding or following the time of reference since I can say equally felicitously:

1 Sarah opened the door of her house. She then saw the angel Gabriel.
1′ *Sarah ouvrit la porte de sa maison. Elle aperçut alors l'ange Gabriel.*
2 Sarah will open the door of her house. She will then see the angel Gabriel.
2′ *Sarah ouvrira la porte de sa maison. Elle apercevra alors l'ange Gabriel.*

Careful students of tense systems from a comparative perspective, such as Bernard Comrie (1985: 15), have, however, pointed out that no tense system has yet been found which grammaticalizes the reference to the NOT-NOW (as reference to non-continuous past and future) as a single tense. Equally, given the importance in many civilizations of cyclically recurring events which can be lexicalized (e.g. *every morning, every night*), we might have expected some tense systems to be based on a cyclic conception of time. Yet, whenever markers of cyclic time in the tense system are attested (as in some Australian languages such as Yandru-wandha), they appear to be optional, whereas reference to non-cyclic deictic centres is obligatory (Comrie, 1985: 17–18). Indeed, as the study of deictic systems has progressed, more and more observations have been made demonstrating that deictic location is not a simple matter of literal distance to the speaker or the hearer. If the difference between *ici* et *là* was simply 'at the speaker's location' vs. 'away from the speaker's location', it would be difficult to explain such natural dialogues as the following (see Adamczewski, 1991: 59–63):

3 A mini dialogue on the phone:
X: *Puis-je parler à Mme Dubois, si je suis au bon numéro?*
   'May I speak to Mrs Dubois if I am at the right number?'
Y: Je regrette, Mme Dubois est bien ici mais elle n'est pas là.
   (Literal translation: 'I'm sorry, Mrs Dubois is indeed here but she is not there', i.e. 'Mrs Dubois does live/work here but she is not here at the moment'.)

It is on the basis of observations of this kind that Benveniste stressed the need to go beyond mere inventories of structures and to consider language as an act and not as a product. In doing so, he made a number of observations which, nowadays, are often solely attributed to British postwar philosophy, and in particular to J. L. Austin (e.g. Benveniste, 1966: 258–66, 277–85). Benveniste's contribution was all the more interesting since at the time when he was publishing his seminal articles on *énonciation*, the leading French linguist was the structuralist André Martinet whose attitude to meaning was typical of post-Bloomfieldian linguistics.

Martinet had come back from the United States in 1955 as director of the international journal *Word* and was carrying a great deal of prestige for his work on phonology. His *Economie des changements phonétiques* (1955) remains one of the great publications of the century in this field. However, in the area of semantics, his position was quite typical of a certain brand of structuralism. While he saw no need to exclude, as some of the post-Bloomfieldians did, our intuitive knowledge of meaning differences from linguistic practice (e.g. in establishing phonemic distinctions), he was totally sceptical as to a possible analysis of meaning as mentally constituted, for methodological reasons. The argument went like this: since our only way of accessing this type of meaning would be via introspection, and since introspection is notoriously unreliable, the linguist should leave this study to others. In fact, in describing what should be a linguistic approach to meaning, he comes very close to the Bloomfield of *Language* since he sees it as dealing only with what is manifested in the form of linguistic or non-linguistic 'reactions' (i.e. responses) (cf. Martinet, 1960: 2.7–2.9).

As a result his famous 1960 textbook, *Eléments de linguistique générale*, which was the standard French introduction to linguistics in the 1960s, contained no sections on semantics (beside a few paragraphs expressing his reservations, cf. 2.7–2.9). Even later editions did not really correct this. The 1973 'postface' does acknowledge that semantics should be treated but on the analogy of the phonetics–phonology model and only once the treatment of morphology and syntax has been fully worked out (Martinet, 1973: 209).

It is against this backdrop that the modern *énonciation* tradition was established in France. While many linguists have contributed to this trend, I have chosen here to concentrate on one major exponent: Antoine Culioli, whose approach has become known as the *Théorie des Opérations Enonciatives* (TOE). In many respects, it seems to me that Culioli's enterprise can be interpreted as an attempt to extend and formalize Benveniste's insights. Benveniste's own work in theoretical linguistics was caught between two traditions: classical structuralism, of which he was an admirably clear exponent, and the *énonciation* approach, which he outlined and defended in his later work. The latter, however, remained unformalized and did not offer an overall model of language linking operations of reference and predication. This is where TOE makes its main contribution.

At the time Culioli was rising to fame in French linguistic circles (in the late 1960s and early 1970s), the major rival paradigm internationally was the work of Chomsky and his associates at MIT. Culioli, although he disagrees with a number of tenets in the generative-transformational school, has generally been careful not to confront Chomsky directly and recognizes the importance of Chomsky's work in the development of modern syntax beyond the strictures imposed by many post-Bloomfieldian linguists. Nevertheless, he has been critical of the separation between syntax and semantics advocated by Chomsky, and has seen the challenge of linguistics as devising formalisms for linguistic phenomena which are not captured by either algebraic systems or classical logical systems. To quote his influential 1968 article 'De la formalisation en linguistique':

> Anything would be preferable to the sharp separation of syntax and semantics which invariably brings us back to a syntax with a lexicon supplied with projective rules. In a nutshell, we will assume that a formal semantic approach is acceptable (since Frege and Husserl this will not come as a surprise); we will assume that there are utterances which are well-formed semantically but ill-formed syntactically; and we will recognize that the central difficulty for formalization in linguistics does not lie in the formalization of algebraic syntactic systems, nor in the distributional study of combinations of object-words in a one-to-one relationship with extra-linguistic reality, but in the halfway land characteristic of natural languages, where we must discover what entities we need to focus on, what new types of logical systems unknown to date must be devised, systems which probably do not function in a homogeneous way, and how to combine concepts, these 'burglary tools', which mathematics puts at our disposal and which must be adapted for our own goals.
>
> (Culioli, 1968, p. 113, my translation)

As a proper overview of Culioli's theory is out of the question here, I will organize my presentation under a few headings, which seem to me to be core notions in TOE and other *énonciativiste* work.

1. Utterances

At the centre of *énonciation* approaches is the utterance and the linguistic acts underlying its production. Although syntactic well-formedness is acknowledged, it is regularly stressed by Culiolians that a string can be a grammatical sentence but not an acceptable utterance. The standard example is:

4 *Un chien aboie* ('A dog is barking')

which, while grammatically well-formed, is a strange utterance in French (said out of the blue in spontaneous speech), whereas it is perfectly natural to say:

5 *Il y a un chien qui aboie* ('There is a dog barking')

If so, over and above grammatical well-formedness there are conditions which determine the well-formedness of utterances. And it cannot be an accident that an expression such as *il y a* ('there is'), which anchors (5) in a situation, is precisely what allows the sentence to become an appropriate utterance. But, of course, the utterance in the sense of utterance-signal only contains traces of the activity of the *énonciateur* and it is this latter which is the object of linguistic enquiry.

2. Meanings

(a) Notions

The activity of *énonciateurs* cannot be simulated or mirrored by a model which places syntax at its centre as in the Chomskyan tradition. On the contrary, it will be assumed that we start from notional structures which are 'complex representational systems of physico-cultural properties' and which are subjected to operations which will lead to well-formed utterances. There can be no clear separation between syntax, semantics and pragmatics within such a model. In TOE there are three types of notion: (a) notions belonging to the lexical domain such as the bundle of properties expressed by 'to read, reading, book, library, reader, etc.'; (b) grammatical categories in the European sense: e.g. mood, modality, polarity (positive/negative), diathesis, temporality, aspect and determination; (c) 'thought contents'. The latter are modelled by positing that complex notional (pre-linguistic) structures made up of several terms (e.g. <dog-eat-fish> are processed by working on the individual terms, by relating them in complex ways, by asking a question, rejecting a proposition, presenting it as a wish or by asserting it.

Two things are worth pointing out at this stage. First of all, the position on notions with its emphasis on physico-cultural domains is in clear opposition to 'mentalese' or 'markerese' as defended in the Chomskyan tradition (e.g. the works of Fodor, Katz and Postal in the 1960s, and more recently Pinker, 1994, for a non-technical overview and references). Secondly, the representation of notions adopted in TOE is clearly related to work which has initially gone on in the United States under the umbrella of 'prototype' theory (often associated with the name of Rosch) and which has been taken over in 'Cognitive Grammar' à la Langacker and Lakoff. The idea of core values of a notional domain (an interior), of boundaries and of complementary values (an exterior) is often mainly illustrated in the lexical domain. Whenever people indulge in statements such as 'She's a real woman' or 'He is a man alright', they are analysing a referent as a perfect representative of an ideal type. In TOE two interesting developments have taken place to deal with notions: the elaboration of a symbolic (topological) notation but also a systematic application of the concept of notional domain to grammatical categories and not simply lexical items (cf. the essays by Culioli, Joly and others in Rivière and Groussier, 1997).

(b) Lexis schemas

The processing of utterances cannot be simulated unless we move away from static notions belonging to the lexical or grammatical domain. Basically, this is formalized in TOE by (1) the mapping of complex notions onto predicative structures, (2) the anchoring of these predicative structures to the situation of utterance. In TOE, the basic schema is uniformly made up of a predicate variable and two argument variables. This schema is called a lexis. This is an unfortunate choice given that, in English linguistics, 'lexis' is often used to refer technically to the vocabulary of a language. Here we are not dealing with the lexicon but with something close to a propositional content or dictum for which the Stoics reserved the term *lekton*. The lexis is a pre-assertive entity which is not marked for mood, modality, polarity (positive/negative), diathesis, temporality, aspect and determination. Thus if we agree that:

6 (a)   The dog ate the fish
   (b)   The fish was eaten by the dog
   (c)   Did the dog eat the fish?
   (d)   Was the fish eaten by the dog?

share a common pre-linguistic notional content <dog-eat-fish>, the construction of an utterance will in part be the result of assigning this notional starting-point to a predicative schema made up, as we said, of a predicate variable and two argument-variables $<\xi_0 \pi \xi_1>$. The order in which these are written is immaterial, and the lexis-schema could just as well be symbolized as $<\xi_0 \xi_1 \pi>$. The reason is that ξ_0 represents the first argument or source, and ξ_1 the second argument or target. Incidentally, Culioli claims that every relation is oriented, including that between two argument terms of a predicative structure (here 'dog' and 'fish') separately from the connection that the predicate will establish between them.

(c) Operations

Whereas terms such as 'rules', 'conditions', 'constraints', 'principles' and 'parameters' have been widely used in the generative tradition, the *énonciation* tradition gives pride of place to the notion of operation (*opération*). The term 'operation' does not seem clearly different from that of 'relationship' from a formal point of view. Culioli himself in a 1992 interview stresses that the notion of 'operation' is fundamentally linked to the notion of localization (*repérage*), the mechanism through which we locate terms in relation to one another and which is central to his thinking. He further adds: 'it can be shown that we are dealing with *operations* in the sense that we are going to bring about a product through the application of an *operator* to a domain' (1992: 40–1, my translation). While Sylvain Auroux (1992) urges us not to adopt a realist interpretation of the concept of 'operation', the insistence on using this term seems to stem from a desire to move away from other models seen as too 'static' or too 'mechanical'. It is worth pointing out that in other *énonciativiste* works, the notion of operation is often given a 'realist' interpretation. This is, for example, the case in Lapaire and Rotgé (1993: 293) who assert:

> The production of an utterance necessarily implies some *mental work*. There is therefore a *deep, unconscious psychological activity*, a vast enterprise of *construction* which underlies each and every fragment of discourse. The various *cerebral manipulations* which are used by the enunciator are called *operations* [from the Latin operatio, 'work'].
>
> (emphasis in the original).

As part of the emphasis on operations, there is a definite move away from the tools provided by formal logic for the representation of meaning (e.g. propositional logic, predicate logic and various types of intensional logic). This is underlined at the end of Culioli's 1968 quotation given earlier and poses difficulties for many readers trained in the Anglo-American tradition. For instance, whereas in a logically-driven semantics one might say that, in the use of the specifier *the*, there is a presupposition of existence (which could be formalized by the use of the existential operator) or indeed an assertion of existence (as in the Russellian tradition), Culiolians will speak of operations of 'extraction' and 'pinpointing'. A perhaps more striking example is the devising of an operator of localization (*repérage*) which is partially based on the general observation that existence, identity, localization and possession are intimately related (cf. e.g. Anderson, 1971; Lyons, 1974, 1979). Thus, at its simplest, we can analyse the use of *être* and of the locative preposition *à* in constructions such as:

7   *Le livre est à Jean* ('The book is John's': literally, 'The book is to John')

as an instantiation of a general operator of identification-localization symbolized by $\subseteq$ (epsilon underlined). Leaving aside many complexities, we can therefore view the above utterance as corresponding, at some level of abstraction, to the predicative structure:

8   < 'livre' $\subseteq$ 'Jean' >

But, of course, it is well-known that *être* and *avoir* ('be' and 'have') share a number of properties and function as near converses in a number of constructions. Thus, if it is true that the book of which we are speaking is John's, then it is also true that John has a book. In other words, if (7) is true so is (9):

9   *Jean a un livre* ('John has a book')

Here Culiolians posit that the meaning of 'avoir' can be partially captured by positing a converse operator, symbolized by a mirror-epsilon (*epsilon-miroir*) $\supseteq$, a back-to-front epsilon underlined:

10   < 'livre' $\supseteq$ 'Jean' >

So far the reader is moving on grounds which are reasonably familiar, but then Culiolians go on to hypothesize the existence of other operators (or values of one single multi-operator, in another interpretation) – in particular, a third operator of 'disconnection' (Fr. *rupture*) which we shall presently mention with reference to the overarching concept of *énonciation*.

(d) Enonciation

If the model adumbrated here were limited to the above observations, it would not be very different from other semantically-based models which have been advocated during the course of this century. Indeed, the school of Generative Semantics in the late 1960s and 1970s shared at least with *énonciativistes* the claim that one should start from semantic representations and, in some versions, that syntax, semantics and pragmatics are intimately connected rather than modular. The specificity of the *énonciativiste* programme is to set up an account of utterance well-formedness via systematic processes of anchoring predicative structures to the basic coordinates of speech: the situation of utterance (Sit_0) which is the absolute origin of speech acts and which includes the *énonciateur* (S_0) and the time of utterance (T_0). (In Culioli's work, a distinction is made between the use of curly symbols and that of straight symbols. For convenience, this typographical distinction will be ignored here.) Clearly, Culioli is not the first linguist to assume such coordinates of speech acts. His approach, however, is original in that, first of all, he attempts to devise a notation which will allow him to derive certain categories instead of positing them as primitives. Pronouns, for example, are therefore the result ('the surface trace') of a simple calculus involving identification, differentiation and disconnection: *I* is the result of the identification of S_0 to the grammatical subject of the utterance, *you* is the result of a differentiation (mirror-epsilon) and *he/she/it* (the non-person) is the result of a disconnection between S_0 and the subject of the utterance.

The second respect in which this model is different from other frameworks is that Culioli builds one additional reference structure between Sit_0 and the coordinates of the event referred to by the utterance. This is the situation of locution, Sit_1 (i.e. (S_1, T_1)), which refers to the sources of the physical act of utterance. Finally, the coordinates of the event are Sit_2 (i.e. (S_2, T_2)). The distinction between S_0/T_0 and S_1/T_1 will not matter when the *énonciateur* endorses what s/he says as in an assertion. However, it is argued that yes/no interrogatives such as 'Has John met Mary?' should not be seen as the reflection of a primitive operation of 'questioning' but as the result of the operation of disconnection: standard yes/no questions set up an alternative p/not p or p/p' and it is up to the addressee (the *co-énonciateur*) to validate one of the alternatives.

Although the details must necessarily be skipped here, it is important to stress that the aim is to offer a unitary account of a range of phenomena which are usually treated as unconnected in the standard literature. To give the reader a flavour of Culioli's approach, here is a typical statement making use of some of the technical notions outlined so far:

> For there to be an assertion, there must be a notional domain. This is what $<\lambda>$ represents: a notion on which I shall construct a domain. If the notion is predicative: a notion of predicative relation, it is a *lexis*. $<\lambda>$ can be the value (p, p′), and can be set out as positive or as a negative for the sake of simplification. In an assertion, we can see that this notional domain, which represents a great number of possible representations, will be located with respect to Sit (i.e. S_2, S_1, S_0) with respect to the subjective system (locutor and enunciator) which endorses and guarantees, and with respect to a system of spatio-temporal coordinates, as well as S_2, the subject of the utterance. This will enable me to say that such and such a relation is validated for a specific moment, or in the case of the generic, for every occurrence that I can produce . . . *An utterance is a theoretical construct: it is produced by locating a predicative relation with respect to Sit.*
>
> (Culioli, 1995: 106, emphasis in the original)

Having sketched some aspects of Culioli's approach, I would now like to concentrate on what I consider problematic areas of the *énonciation* approach both in his work and in the work of the specialists I have consulted. I have called these 'weaknesses' representational gaps for reasons which should become obvious in what follows.

First of all, it seems to me that the lack of close dialogue with the generative tradition has contributed to isolating the Culiolian school and many of the French *énonciativistes* from an international point of view. In itself, isolationism is neither a good nor a bad thing, and I would rather be among the few if they are right than among the many if they are wrong. But in the area of scientific ideas isolation can be disadvantageous. The problem is that by putting theories to the test of translation into other languages and cultures, we allow for a closer examination of their core claims and we can often reduce the 'rhetorical' part which is unavoidable in any presentation.

At the risk of being more technical now, the lack of real dialogue with the Chomskyan generative tradition and closely related models (e.g. Lexical-Functional Grammar, Generalized Phrase Structure Grammar, Head-driven Phrase Structure Grammar, Categorial Grammars, and various types of unification systems) has meant that TOE is formally not as fully worked out as these models. It is quite possible that the extensional part of the early Chomskyan programme cannot be carried out (i.e. account for all and only the grammatical sentences of a language). For a while now, Chomsky has expressed reservations about this aspect of his early work (cf. Chomsky, 1986, 1993). But it should be noted that not all specialists agree and that some schools have gone on working towards this goal. In whatever form this programme is carried out, a great deal of precision in the treatment of natural languages has been gained and we understand processes such as complementation, relativization, long-distance dependencies, gapping, etc., a lot better than we did forty years ago when Chomsky published his *Syntactic Structures* (1957). By contrast, it does seem to me that many of the structures used in Culiolian work are not specified as precisely as one might wish (although the work done in collaboration with the mathematical linguist Desclés was a step in this direction but stopped before yielding all that it promised).

Consider, for instance, the structure of the lexis-schema as a two-place predicative structure which has been used from the early work onwards. I must confess that I have yet to see a full demonstration that this is really necessary for all utterances and in particular for intransitive verbs. I can remember already working on this problem some fifteen years ago and checking back early sources. Rouault (1971: 37) for instance tells us that 'The fixing of the number at three is presented from the linguistic viewpoint in (CULIOLI, FUCHS, PECHEUX – 1970 – pp. 19 sq)'. A glance at the work in question should convince the reader that no detailed justification has been given. Rouault (1971: 37ff.) himself considers two cases: that of verbs like *eat* used intransitively (where it is plausible to envisage a missing argument); and that of intransitive predicates such as *voler* in *L'oiseau vole*. Rouault additionally points out that there are variations across languages between intransitive structures and 'reflexive' structures: Fr. *l'oiseau vole*, Fr. *l'oiseau s'envole*, Fr. *l'horloge se déclencha*, Occitan *Lo relotge descroquet*. But this is hardly proof that universally we need to envisage the underlying structure of every propositional content as a two-place predicative structure. Even more problematic are structures like *Llueve* where even if we can envisage a dummy argument, there is certainly no reason to postulate two semantic arguments (on this question and others, see Durand and Kilby, 1983).

This is only an example which is perhaps not very damaging. More problematic seems to me the fact that the rules for building and combining structures and the like have never been fully articulated. We do not know whether the mechanisms are structure-building or structure-changing, or both. This point has recently been dealt with by Milner (1992) who, in a courteous, evaluative paper, points out that in the Culiolian theory a number of deletions of unrecoverable formal entities seem to be allowed. He proceeds to observe that since TOE rests fundamentally on a theory of possible operations, we would expect to see a list. But where is it? What are the properties of these operations? Can they be combined, and if so how? Are there any chaining and linking processes which are forbidden? If so, are they forbidden on a language-specific basis or across languages? My feeling is that this weakness in the nature of representation has been there since the beginning and is even more striking in many less formalized *énonciativiste* models.

The generative programme advocates a specification of well-formedness at all levels of representation (from the phonological to the semantic and pragmatic). And as a result work has been pursued in parallel on these various areas of structure within the generative school. Even semantics is not as badly off as claimed by French *énonciativistes*. The work of Jackendoff over a quarter of a century is a particularly inspiring example; in the area of tense the work of Hornstein also deserves mention; and Katz himself was not as unaware of the parameters of speech acts in his classical work as one might think from reading French critics (cf. his discussion of temporal specification in *Semantic Theory*, 1972: ch. 7). By contrast, whole areas of structure have been neglected in TOE. Despite the emphasis on notions, there seems to be no explicitly articulated theory of the lexicon. Morphological structures are hardly explored and I am not aware of any work in phonology (although there has been some thought-provoking work in the area of intonation, in particular by Marie-Annick Morel and Laurent Danon-Boileau). It is quite possible that the Chomskyan thesis of the autonomy of syntax will prove to be untenable in the long run. But it does not follow that the thesis that semantics drives all linguistic levels can be maintained. In any case, if this latter thesis is to be validated, it needs to be made formally much more precise. It also needs to be put to the test of psycholinguistic experimentation on a much wider scale than has been the case so far. It is worth pointing out that there is now a vast literature on first and second language acquisition, on the production and perception of language and on language disorders which has put generative grammar through its paces with often intriguing results (for further references, see Durand, 1990; Pinker, 1994; Gleitman and Liberman, 1995; Smith and Tsimpli, 1995). Nor is it the case that the broad Chomskyan approach is as unrewarding in terms of language and society as is often claimed in French linguistics (cf. Durand, 1993, 1996).

To conclude, I have focused here on the *énonciation* tradition in French linguistics. Rather than starting with a historical summary and series of lines of descent, I have based my presentation on Benveniste and Culioli as a means of making my overview more concrete. I have stressed that this approach has a long historical background with roots in the rhetorical tradition. Within France, this century, linguists like Bally and Guillaume, long before Benveniste, emphasized the need to take into account the subjective operations which underlie the construction of utterances (see Joly, 1987). Moreover, outside the Culiolian school, there are many linguists who have contributed to an *énonciation* approach (To limit ourselves to some survey works, cf. Kerbrat-Orecchioni, 1980; Fuchs and Le Goffic, 1992; López-Alonso and Séré de Olmos, 1992; Maingueneau, 1994; Viel, 1993). There are also strong parallels between *énonciation* and other approaches – a great deal of work carried out on pragmatics within France has broached themes closely related to *énonciation* (cf. the 1994 *Dictionnaire encyclopédique de pragmatique* by Jacques Moeschler and Anne Reboul). In this context, the work of Ducrot and his associates certainly deserves a special mention (cf. Ducrot, 1970, 1980, 1984, 1986). The tradition of discourse analysis has also had preoccupations closely linked to the above (see the survey work by Maingueneau, 1991).

I have argued that some of the insights of *énonciation* must be incorporated into a modern linguistic theory which believes in the possibility of characterizing linguistic meaning. More controversially, I have stressed some weaknesses in this tradition. The representational gaps, which I had provocatively thought of calling black holes, are the distance between utterances and their putative meanings. If generative representations are often seen as hugging the ground too closely, the *énonciation* tradition definitely runs the risk of hanging in the air too much.

Placing the work I have just discussed within the French intellectual scene from the 1950s onwards would take far more space and far more competence than I have (the two volumes *Le Champ du signe* et *Le Chant du cygne* by the French historian Dosse go some way towards providing a description of this kind). The distance, indeed the chasm, between much *énonciativiste* work and the modern North American (particularly the generative) tradition and the relative isolation which has resulted need explaining. Part of the explanation lies, I believe, in the fact that France has always had a strong intellectual tradition proud of its roots and of its specificity. An example of this is the link between *énonciation* and the French psychoanalytic tradition – a link practically absent from technical work on linguistics in the Anglo-American tradition (cf. Danon-Boileau, 1987). The two volumes by Dosse mentioned above provide a fascinating description of the many concerns which unite French intellectuals despite their numerous skirmishes. The power of *maîtres à penser* in the old and prestigious universities is also no doubt a factor not to be neglected. Another important parameter is the existence of *concours* (national competitive exams such as the *Agrégation*). These have maintained a certain literary tradition of textual commentary and given linguistics a subservient role since whole areas of description (e.g. phonology, morphology) have not typically been included and theoretical questions (e.g. the formal power of grammars, the nature of phonological primes, or whatever) have little real place. No doubt the indifference of many North American linguists to European work is also responsible for the lack of dialogue. Sadly, this indifference is also found in much work in Cognitive Grammar which can be argued to be rediscovering intuitions in the *énonciativiste* paradigm but rarely acknowledges its existence. Perhaps, in the end, it all has to do with cultural relativism. If I may be frivolous, it could be that our intellectual approaches are as different as our approaches to the sexual life of our presidents and, indeed, our presidents' attitudes to their own sexual life. If we believe the press over the past few years, the Americans seem to care a great deal, the French far less or not at all. If this is true, my claim that the French *énonciativiste* tradition is an important research programme will no doubt be ignored by many American linguists. As for my French *énonciativiste* colleagues, when presented with my assertion that generative grammar has changed the field and introduced major advances in general linguistics, I suspect that they will react like Mitterrand when confronted with the first journalist who had the audacity to ask: 'Mr President, is it true that you have an illegitimate daughter?' The answer was the unequivocal and unanswerable riposte: 'Et alors?' ('So what?').

Note

1 *Acknowledgements*. A number of colleagues and friends have helped me in the preparation of this article. I have received useful comments from Philip Carr, Marie-Hélène Clavères, Francis Cornish, Chris Flood, Nick Hewlett, Anne Judge, Chantal Lyche, Hélène Miguet, Dairine O'Kelly Dennis Philps, Marc Plénat, Henri Le Prieult, Jean-Rémi Lapaire, Wilfrid Rotgé, Paul Rowlett and Carol Sanders. Needless to say, they are not responsible for the statements made here and, in some cases, they disagree quite fundamentally with some

of the claims I defend. Previous versions of this paper have been presented at the Institute for Romance Studies (University of London), the University of Surrey and the Université de Toulouse-Le Mirail (séminaire ELAN, CAS). I am extremely grateful for the various comments I received from the audiences in these institutions and which cannot all be acknowledged here.

References

Adamczewski, Henri (1991) *Le Français déchiffré. Clé du langage et des langues*. Paris: Armand Colin.

Anderson, John (1971) *The Grammar of Case. Towards a Localistic Theory*. Cambridge: Cambridge University Press.

Arnauld, Antoine and Lancelot, Claude (1969) *Grammaire générale et raisonnée*. Paris: Paulet.

Auroux, Sylvain (1992) 'La Philosophie linguistique d'Antoine Culioli', in Culioli et al. (1992), pp. 39–59.

Benveniste, Emile (1966) *Problèmes de linguistique générale*, vol. 1. Paris: Gallimard.

—— (1974) *Problèmes de linguistique générale*, vol. 2. Paris: Gallimard.

Chomsky, Noam (1957) *Syntactic Structures*. The Hague: Mouton.

—— (1965) *Aspects of the Theory of Syntax*. Cambridge, MA: MIT Press.

—— (1986) *Knowledge of Language: Its Nature, Origin, and Use*. New York: Praeger.

—— (1993) *Language and Thought*. Wakefield, RI: Moyer Bell.

Comrie, Bernard (1985) *Tense*. Cambridge: Cambridge University Press.

Culioli, Antoine (1968) 'La Formalisation en linguistique', *Cahiers pour l'analyse*, 9: 106–17.

—— (1973) 'Sur quelques contradictions en linguistique', *Communications*, 20: 83–91.

—— (1976) Séminaire de D.E.A. Transcription. Département de recherches linguistiques. Université de Paris 7.

—— (1990) *Pour une linguistique de l'énonciation. Opérations et représentations*. Paris: Ophrys.

—— (1995) *Cognition and Representations in Linguistic Theory*. Amsterdam: John Benjamins.

—— (1997) 'A propos de la notion', in Claude Rivière and Marie-Line Groussier (eds), (1997) *La Notion*. Paris: Ophrys, pp. 9–24.

——, Fuchs, Catherine and Michel Pêcheux (1970) 'Considérations théoriques à propos du traitement formel du langage', *Documents de linguistique quantitative de la faculté des sciences de l'Université de Paris*.

—— et al. (1992) *La Théorie d'Antoine Culioli. Ouvertures et incidences*. Actes de la table ronde 'Opérations de repérage et domaines notionnels', Université de Paris 7, May–June 1991. Paris: Ophrys.

Danon-Boileau, Laurent (1987) *Le Sujet de l'énonciation. Psychanalyse et linguistique*. Paris: Ophrys.

Dosse, François (1991) *Histoire du structuralisme. I. Le Champ du signe, 1945–1966*. Paris: Editions La Découverte.

—— (1993). *Histoire du structuralisme. II. Le Chant du cygne, 1967 à nos jours*. Paris: Editions La Découverte.

Ducrot, Oswald (1970) 'Les Indéfinis et l'énonciation', *Langages*, 17: 91–107.

—— (1980) 'Analyses pragmatiques', *Communications*, 32: 11–60.

—— (1984) *Le Dire et le dit*. Paris: Editions de Minuit.

—— (1986) 'Les Plans d'énonciation', *Langages*, 73.

Durand, Jacques (1990) 'Language: is it all in the mind?' Inaugural Professorial Lecture. Manchester: University of Salford.

—— (1993) 'Sociolinguistic variation and the linguist', in Carol Sanders (ed.), *French Today. Language in Its Social Context*. Cambridge: Cambridge University Press, pp. 257–81.

—— (1996) 'Linguistic purification, the French nation-state and the linguist', in Charlotte Hoffmann (ed.), *Language, Culture and Communication in Contemporary Europe*. Clevedon: Multilingual Matters, pp. 75–92.

—— and Kilby, David (1983) 'Réflexions critiques sur *Opérations énonciatives et apprentissage de l'anglais en milieu scolaire* d'André Gauthier', in Jacques Durand (ed.), *A Festschrift for Peter Wexler*. Colchester: University of Essex, Department of Language and Linguistics (Occasional Paper 27), pp. 57–89.

—— and Bernard Laks (1996) 'Why phonology is one', in Jacques Durand and Bernard Laks (eds), *Current Trends in Phonology: Models and Methods*. Manchester: European Studies Research Institute, University of Salford, pp. 3–13.

—— and David Robinson (eds) (1974) *La Linguistique en Grande-Bretagne dans les années soixante*. Special issue of *Langages*, 34.

Fuchs, Catherine (1994) *Paraphrase et énonciation*. Paris: Ophrys.

—— and Pierre Le Goffic (1992) *Les Linguistiques contemporaines. Repères théoriques*. Paris: Hachette.

Gleitman, R. Lila and Mark Liberman (eds) (1995) *Language. An Invitation to Cognitive Science*. Cambridge, MA: MIT Press.

Guillaume, Gustave (1964) *Langage et science du langage*. Paris: Librairie A. G. Nizet/ Québec: Presses de l'Université Laval.

Jakobson, Roman (1963) *Essais de linguistique générale*. Paris: Editions de Minuit.

Joly, André (1987) *Essais de systématique énonciative*. Lille: Presses Universitaires de Lille.

—— (1997) 'La Longue Marche de "la notion" du percevoir au dire: remarques sur la chaîne des causations du langage', in Claude Rivière and Marie-Line Groussier (eds), *La Notion*. Paris: Ophrys, pp. 27–50.

Kerbrat-Orecchioni, Catherine (1980) *L'Enonciation*. Paris: Armand Colin.

—— (1986) *L'Implicite*. Paris: Armand Colin.

Kleiber, Georges (1992) 'Anaphore-deixis: deux approches concurrentes', in Morel and Danon-Boileau (eds), pp. 613–26.

Lapaire, Jean-Rémi and Wilfrid Rotgé (eds) (1993) *Séminaire pratique de linguistique anglaise*. Toulouse: Presses Universitaires du Mirail.

López-Alonso, Cavadonga and Arlette Séré de Olmos (1992) *Où en est la linguistique? Entretiens avec des linguistes*. [A. Culioli, O. Ducrot, P. Charaudeau, F. Rastier, J.-P. Bronckart, M. Molho, I. Tamba, S. Fisher.] Paris: Didier.

Lyons, John (1974) 'Remarques sur les phrases possessives, existentielles et locatives', in Durand and Robinson (eds), pp. 47–53.

—— (1977a and b) *Semantics*, 2 vols. Cambridge: Cambridge University Press.

—— (1978) *Eléments de sémantique*. Paris: Larousse. Translation by Jacques Durand of Lyons (1977a).

—— (1979) 'Knowledge and truth: a localistic approach', in D. J. Allerton et al. (eds), *Function and Context in Linguistic Analysis. A Festschrift for William Haas.* Cambridge: Cambridge University Press, pp. 111–41.

—— (1980) *Sémantique linguistique.* Paris: Larousse. Translation by Jacques Durand and Dominique Boulonnais of Lyons (1977b).

—— (1994) 'Subjecthood and subjectivity', in M. Yaguello, (ed.), pp. 9–17.

Maingueneau, Dominique (1991) *L'Analyse du discours. Introduction aux lectures de l'archive.* Paris: Hachette.

—— (1994) *L'Enonciation en linguistique française.* Paris: Hachette.

Martinet, André (1955) *Economie des changements phonétiques. Traité de phonologie diachronique.* Berne: A. Francke.

—— (1960) *Eléments de linguistique générale.* Paris: Armand Colin.

Milner, Jean-Claude (1992) 'De quelques aspects de la théorie d'Antoine Culioli projetées dans un espace non-énonciatif', in Antoine Culioli et al. [ouvrage collectif] (1992) *La Théorie d'Antoine Culioli. Ouvertures et incidences.* Actes de la table ronde 'Opérations de repérage et domaines notionnels', Université de Paris 7, May–June 1991. Paris: Ophrys, pp. 17–38.

Moeschler, Jacques and Anne Reboul (1994) *Dictionnaire encyclopédique de pragmatique.* Paris: Seuil.

Morel, Mary-Annick (1995) 'Valeur énonciative des variations de hauteur mélodique en français', *Journal of French Language Studies,* 5 (2): 189–202.

—— and Laurent Danon-Boileau (1992) *La Déixis.* Paris: PUF.

O'Kelly, Dairine (1997) 'Autour de la notion de personne', in Rivière and Groussier (eds), pp. 297–307.

Pinker, Steven (1994) *The Language Instinct: the New Science of Language and Mind.* London: Allen Lane.

Rivière, Claude and Marie-Line Groussier (eds) (1997) *La Notion.* Paris: Ophrys.

Rouault, Jacques (1971) 'Approche formelle de problèmes liés à la sémantique des langues naturelles'. Thèse de Doctorat d'Etat, Université scientifique et médicale de Grenoble, Institut de Recherches en Mathématiques Avancées, November 1971.

Smith, N. and Tsimpli, I. (1995) *The Mind of a Savant: Language Learning and Modularity.* Oxford: Blackwell.

Viel, M. (ed.) (1993) *Les Théories de la grammaire anglaise en France.* Paris: Hachette.

Yaguello, Marina (ed.) (1994) *Subjecthood and Subjectivity.* Paris: Ophrys.

6

Social Anthropological Perspectives in French Intellectual Life

Lieve Spaas

If critical observers of recent developments in social anthropology could agree on anything, it would be that present-day French anthropology has fragmented into a myriad of activities, research interests, beliefs, political issues, debates on gender and a variety of even more disparate movements.[1] Nowadays, to speak of 'anthropology' as a single discipline, or an activity practised with different emphases, would be misleading. Moreover, social anthropology has not remained isolated but, instead, has served as a catalyst in other disciplines from which, in turn, it has itself borrowed conceptual models.

To investigate the role of social anthropology in French intellectual life is, I suggest, a twofold process. Firstly, it implies tracing its intellectual roots, and secondly, gauging its impact on other disciplines and on French intellectual life in general. In the course of this investigation I shall map the most decisive landmarks of French anthropology to illustrate how it has been marked by, and in turn marks, France's intellectual tradition.

A brief history of French social anthropology begins with philosophers, rather than anthropologists, and includes authors such as Montaigne, Montesquieu, Rousseau and Condorcet, whose writings were deductively argued from principles implicit in their own culture. These writers regarded societies as legitimate objects of study and looked critically at social inequalities. The early nineteenth-century philosopher Auguste Comte asserted more directly, like his predecessor and teacher Saint-Simon, that societies are systems and not just aggregates of individuals. Although the nineteenth century heralded early anthropological documents in the Anglo-Saxon world, little activity took place in France. Travellers, missionaries and colonizers reported on exotic peoples, but 'ethnology' as such did not emerge until the 1920s, when Emile

Durkheim was the first to define the discipline and the method of 'sociology'. Durkheim was to use ethnographic sources extensively and referred systematically to the anthropological fieldwork of others, as may be seen in the many volumes of *Année sociologique*, the journal he founded. The work of his disciple and nephew, Marcel Mauss, became more specifically ethnological. Mauss's work dominates the first half of the twentieth century, a period which was seriously affected by two world wars, in the course of which many promising young social scientists were killed or emigrated to the United States.

Let us briefly compare the different developments in France with those in early British anthropology. An early interest in primitive culture coincided with Darwin's *Origin of Species* (1859). The publication of Darwin's work helped to arouse an interest in the theoretical aspect of cultural differences. The first anthropologists adhered to the idea that socio-cultural institutions progressed in a predetermined way. The early anthropologist, E. B. Tylor, showed a strong interest in cultural and religious phenomena. His *Primitive Culture* (1871) inspired J. G. Frazer whose monumental fresco *The Golden Bough* became a catalyst for anthropological research. A. R. Radcliffe-Brown, influenced by both Durkheim and Mauss, offered valuable studies on Australian kinship structures. But it was not until B. Malinowski undertook intensive research in the Trobriand Islands that the great British tradition of fieldwork commenced which was to become the main method in anthropological research. These anthropologists perceived social phenomena 'functionally', namely in terms of their interrelationship. A genuine British tradition of 'participant observation' was created and produced such eminent scholars as Fortes and Evans-Pritchard.

British as well as French social anthropology had to contend with the fact that it was associated from its beginnings as an academic discipline with colonial expansion. From the fifteenth century onwards all the great European powers were involved in colonizing non-European parts of the world, following the Portuguese example. These self-proclaimed legitimate colonizing ventures involved the exploitation of all local resources (including human ones) mainly, if not exclusively, for the benefit of the colonizing country, and there was a total failure to conceive of the indigenous people as having any rights whatsoever. Indeed, these 'civilizing' processes gave the colonizers the 'right' to kill or force out the indigenous people, to evangelize them and to assimilate them culturally and linguistically.

What can be described as early ethnological documents, from the sixteenth century onwards, are mainly reports from navigators, missionaries, administrators and health workers; these provided the West with information on so-called exotic peoples. In the mid-nineteenth century colonizers came to realize that anthropological knowledge could facilitate their travels and invasions and it thus became an integral part of further colonial activities. Early ethnographic researchers were sent out to collect ethnographic data, including peoples' mores, customs and social behaviour, essentially to serve the interests of the colonizers. In France, as in other Western empires, ethnology is rooted in the creation of a colonial empire. Since anthropology's past cannot be dissociated from Western colonialism and missionary activities, we must ask to what extent the discipline remains steeped in colonial politics or, alternatively, has freed itself from its colonial past.

Writing in the 1950s, the French author, Michel Leiris, was one of the first to draw attention to the suspect alliance between colonialism and anthropology and to denounce the inevitable conflict and moral dilemma which anthropology faces. In his 'L'Ethnographie devant le colonialisme' Leiris demystifies the anthropologist's dream of studying primitive societies (1950, 1969). According to him the 'integrity' of a society does not exist. The societies studied by anthropologists have all been subjected to colonial rule or at least exposed to the economic, political and cultural domination of European society. Georges Balandier, philosopher and ethnologist, who in the 1950s studied postwar developments in Africa, expressed concern over the abuse of power by colonizers and became the first Africanist to reflect upon the colonial situation. His early denunciation of the colonial impasse led to a critical investigation of western modernity (Balandier, 1957, 1967, 1974). It may seem paradoxical that, at the time when anthropology was most severely criticized for being rooted and steeped in colonialism, structuralist anthropology developed and was marked by overwhelming success. This was especially the case in the late 1950s and early 1960s when the colonial period was coming to an end.

The second half of the twentieth century was dominated by the advent of structuralism, which revolutionized anthropology in the 1950s and 1960s. This new intellectual current coincided with profound social changes. In the post-1968 period and throughout the 1970s, when it had to contend with the social realities of ethnic violence, mass migration, media manipulation and the proliferation of urban ghettoes, it became the target of criticism. In the 1980s and 1990s its relevance came into question.

This brief survey may be concluded with the observation that 'anthropology', originally referring to a 'system of interpretation accounting for the aspects of all modes of behaviour simultaneously, physical, physiological and sociological' (Lévi-Strauss, 1987: 26), has become an inadequate omnibus concept for dealing with what Christian Bromberger calls: 'the hesitant and multiform evolution and theoretical changes which have affected the whole discipline and led to the scattering of methods and paradigms' (Bromberger, 1997: 313). It now seems possible to apply the word 'anthropology' to any academic activity which deals with cultural phenomena. It is not surprising that in the latter part of the twentieth century anthropology developed into the study of specialized areas, giving rise to urban anthropology, medical anthropology, the anthropology of cyberculture and ethnopolitics.

Let us now briefly examine the success of structuralist anthropology as developed by Lévi-Strauss. The term 'structuralist' was not new, since it was coined and used in linguistics by Hjelmslev. Linguistics played an important role in the formation of Lévi-Strauss's structuralist programme. Early influence came from the Swiss linguist Ferdinand de Saussure and from the German anthropologist, Franz Boas, who had emigrated to the United States. The work of Saussure implied that the laws of language operate on an unconscious level and are outside the control of the speaking subject. According to Lévi-Strauss, Boas stated this more explicitly and also concluded that these laws can thus be studied as objective phenomena and are, therefore, social facts (Lévi-Strauss and Eribon, 1996: 59). But it was phonology which was to become the cornerstone for the development of structuralism.

Phonology created order out of an apparent chaos of sounds, and since the speaker of a language distinguishes between sounds without being conscious of it, there must be an unconscious system of oppositions. Lévi-Strauss, fascinated by the possibility of applying linguistic methods to social structures and inspired by Trubetzkoy and especially by Roman Jakobson, heralded structuralism in France. His intuition had already led him earlier to adopt a structuralist perspective. This developed from his fascination with geology, which had preceded his interest in linguistics. In *Tristes tropiques* he reports how, while hiking in his youth over the mountains, he came to the insight that in order to understand phenomena one must reconstruct the system of which they are manifestations. It is, then, not surprising that he was to feel intuitively attracted to structuralism. 'I was', he states, 'a sort of simple structuralist. I was a structuralist without knowing it' (Lévi-Strauss and Eribon, 1996: 63).

Lévi-Strauss was to be responsible, more than anyone else, for the development of structuralism as an intellectual movement. While linguistics laid the main theoretical foundation of Lévi-Strauss's structuralist anthropology, it is clear that influences from other fields contributed considerably to the formulation of his structuralist programme. Marx and Freud exercised a decisive influence upon him. 'Marx followed Rousseau in saying', he writes in *Tristes tropiques*, '– and saying once and for all, as far as I can see – that social science is no more based upon events than physics is based on sense-perceptions. Our object is to construct a model.' Lévi-Strauss saw a similarity between geology, Marxism and psychoanalysis: 'All three showed that understanding consists in the reduction of one type of reality to another' (1961: 61).

In 1945 Lévi-Strauss published his first structuralist piece: 'L'Analyse structurale en linguistique et en anthropologie', in which he formulated the basic principles of structuralism: firstly, that of concentrating on the unconscious infrastructure rather than on conscious phenomena, and secondly, that of regarding the elements of a system as interdependent and interrelated.

The two main areas where Lévi-Strauss applies the structuralist method are the study of kinship systems and the study of primitive myths. His 1948 thesis on kinship systems, *Les Structures élémentaires de la parenté*, and his four volumes on the study of myth, *Mythologiques* (1964–71), are landmarks in structural anthropology. In his study of kinship systems Lévi-Strauss explores the so-called 'elementary' kinship relationships, that is to say those for which specific rules apply for the choice of a spouse. The phenomenon which Lévi-Strauss attempts to elucidate is the dichotomy between cross-cousins and parallel cousins (cross-cousins are daughters of a father's sister or mother's brother; parallel cousins are daughters of a father's brother or mother's sister). Some kinship systems allow marriage with cross-cousins but not with parallel cousins, who are considered sisters. On the simplest level, but by no means general, society would thus be divided into two parts or, to use the anthropological term, moieties. The analysis operates on two levels, on the level of structures and on the level of alliances. The law of alliance is not considered in itself structural although, as Nick Allen stresses, it implies necessarily three terms, the two entities plus the relationship they constitute. The law explains why certain structures are organized in a specific way. As Jean Ladrière puts it, 'the law of alliance . . . finalises the auto-structuring of systems' (1971: 74).

While there is thus a functional aspect to the structures underlying kinship systems, in *Mythologiques* there is no functional link between the structure and a different kind of reality. Yet analogies may be perceived between the different registers which Lévi-Strauss identifies, such as the culinary, the cosmological, the sociological or the zoological registers. In each register there is a similar developmental scheme. What is at stake in the two domains studied by Lévi-Strauss, kinship and marriage systems and myths, is how culture is at the core of what is under consideration. The laws of alliance implement rules which are specifically human and cannot be reduced to nature. If alliance rules are often seen as 'natural', that is as serving the reproduction of the species, they belong to the realm of culture, in that they guarantee reciprocity and introduce an incest taboo.

With Lévi-Strauss French social anthropology became an academic discipline. His appointment as Professor of Social Anthropology at the Collège de France in 1959 firmly established the new discipline in French academic life. It allowed him to to set up a laboratory of social anthropology. In 1961 he founded *L'Homme*, the French journal of anthropology. In founding *L'Homme*, Lévi-Strauss's aim was to set up a journal comparable to the *American Anthropologist* and the British journal *Man*, which would be the organ of French social anthropology.

Structuralism was to unite major intellectuals from different fields. Its unequalled success resided in its theoretical promise to offer a rigorous method for advances in different sciences. It marks a significant moment of critical consciousness at the heart of the emerging social sciences. It was also a reaction against the hegemony of traditional academia, represented mainly by the Sorbonne, and it questioned established intellectual tradition. The well-known dispute between Lévi-Strauss and Jean-Paul Sartre is a case in point. Even in 1955 Lévi-Strauss remarked on existentialism as a promotion of 'private occupations to the rank of philosophical problems' (1961: 62).

In 1962 *La Pensée sauvage* turned the dispute into a major event in the history of French intellectual thought. The publication of this remarkable book was a major event for two reasons. Firstly, it transformed our vision and understanding of primitive 'logic' which, according to Lévi-Strauss, differs little from our own. Primitive people, Lévi-Strauss argues, also refer to codes composed of things outside themselves to make sense of the events of daily life. Secondly, the work provoked a major dispute between historicism and structuralism which brought the dispute with Sartre to a climax. In the final chapter, entitled 'Histoire et Dialectique', Lévi-Strauss argues that there is little difference between the study of history diachronically in time and that of anthropology synchronically in space. In history, as in myth, Lévi-Strauss claims we are dealing with the same thing, namely recollected experience, which is inevitably contemporaneous. In fact, Lévi-Strauss equated the study of history to that of myth. Lévi-Strauss's reaction has been considered as too extreme but it was, nevertheless, a serious blow to Sartre's historicism and a success for structuralism, which became a turning point in many disciplines. Lévi-Strauss was the undisputed father of the group whose main protagonists included Louis Althusser, Roland Barthes, Michel Foucault and Jacques Lacan. Ironically, the 'father' survived the sons, who all died in dramatic circumstances. (Roland Barthes died in 1980 and, according to his friends, he 'let himself die' after being hit by a car; Louis Althusser strangled his wife in the same year and remained interned until his death; Jacques Lacan, suffering from aphasia, died in 1981; and finally, Michel Foucault, suffering from AIDS, committed suicide in 1984. Only Lévi-Strauss remains and continues his work.)

Structuralism had a major impact on French intellectual life yet it did not remain unassailed. Let us look at how Lévi-Strauss's work was received by younger intellectuals in the 1960s and 1970s, especially in the light of the events of 1968. Georges Balandier emphasized the importance of history and believed in the inseparability of diachrony and synchrony. For Balandier, anthropology is inevitably also political. In his *Anthropologie politique* (1967) he conceptualized the colonial situation by shifting the emphasis to the relationship between colonizer and colonized and pleaded for the political emancipation of his anthropological field, Africa. His political convictions excluded an adherence to structuralism although for some time he was close to Lévi-Strauss. From 1961 until 1966 he taught a seminar on Africa in the Ecole Normale, Rue d'Ulm. In an interview with François Dosse, referring to these seminars, he states: 'The Africanism that I exposed did not concede anything to the structuralist world' (1992b: 314). He will remain convinced of the need to develop a 'dynamic' anthropology and to break free from a static type of structuralism.

A second reaction came from the philosopher Jacques Derrida at the famous 1966 Johns Hopkins colloquium on structuralism where the main structuralists were present, with the exception of Claude Lévi-Strauss, and included, besides Derrida, Roland Barthes, Jacques Lacan, Gérard Genette, Lucien Goldmann, Tzvetan Todorov, Nicolas Ruwet and Jean-Pierre Venant. Jacques Derrida's intervention, 'La structure, le signe et le jeu dans le discours des sciences humaines', constituted an attack against structuralism. Derrida's criticism of Lévi-Strauss was directed at the application of the phonological model to the social sciences and not at *Mythologiques*, whose importance he recognized. In his *De la grammatologie* (1967) Derrida criticized Lévi-Strauss's naive Rousseauist view of the Nambikwara and accused him of reverse ethnocentrism by idealizing societies without written language.

Although the deconstruction proposed by Derrida was seen by American academics as the advent of poststructuralism, it would be wrong to see it as the end of structuralism. In fact, a renewed current emerged in social anthropology which attemped to reconcile Marxism and structuralism, as represented by Marxist anthropologists such as Claude Meillassoux, Emmanuel Terray, Maurice Godelier and Marc Augé. It was not a matter of destroying structuralism but of giving it new impetus ('to dynamise and not dynamite' – *dynamiser et non dynamiter* – is Terray's formula). Although Marxist structuralism never formed a school, it sustained an impetus for more than two decades. Emphasis was placed on the material aspects of the modes of production, as in Meillassoux's *Anthropologie économique des Gourou de Côte d'Ivoire* (1964) and Terray's Althusserian rereading of it. Terray's *Le Marxisme devant les sociétés primitives* (1979) and Maurice Godelier's *Sur les sociétés précapitalistes* (1970) or *L'Idéel et le matériel* (1984) are not rejections of structuralism but, as Godelier writes: '[We take over] when it is necessary to move into areas not covered by Lévi-Strauss' (1984: 35). In the main, however, structuralism continued to inspire scholars who embraced the structuralist method or attempted to reconcile it with the new ideologies of the 1960s and 1970s.

The events of 1968 appeared at first to constitute a serious blow to structuralism and also structural anthropology, but Lévi-Strauss saw this as the decline of a 'fashion' and not the death of a method. As Maurice Godelier was to formulate much later: 'We continue to use the structural analysis on myths and kinship terminologies without being ashamed, but without being structuralists' (1997: 5). Scholars whose reputations remained untouched in the events of 1968 included Louis Dumont and Georges Dumézil, whose work on Indo-European material had become very influential. Dumézil, together with Lévi-Strauss, inspired Jean-Pierre Vernant, who produced an anthropological analysis of the Greek myths and reconciled two rival disciplines, namely history and anthropology. Vernant entered the Collège de France in 1975 adding a new field to structuralism: historical anthropology.

A discipline can be gauged mainly through its journals. I have already mentioned *L'Homme*, founded shortly after the discipline was academically recognized. Through the troubled years of the 1960s and 1970s the journal *L'Homme* reflected the main trends in social anthropology. A survey of its main activities will throw light on the development of anthropology since 1961. The nature of *L'Homme* may well seem to confirm the criticism that anthropology failed to deal with man as a subject. The editorial board comprised Lévi-Strauss himself, a linguist,

Emile Benveniste, and a geographer, Pierre Gourou. There was no opening statement to the first issue, no philosophy, no specific direction given. The opening article by André G. Haudricourt, 'Richesse en phonèmes et richesse en locuteurs', firmly established the link between linguistics and social phenomena. *L'Homme* reflects three main developments. The first concerns the expansion of the notion of anthropology, the second the strengthening of collaboration with other disciplines, especially linguistics, history and mathematics, and the third the expansion of the areas studied. If we compare the years 1961–83 with the years 1984–96, new fields such as acculturation, zoological anthropology, economics and ecology, information technology, illness, *métissage*, politics, labour representations, modernity and nomadism are seen to emerge. The old friction between history and anthropology is resolved, a long list of articles is devoted to 'anthropology and history' and it is now possible to speak of 'historical anthropology'. Interestingly, the number of articles on France and other European countries has increased considerably over this period.

The appointment of Jean Pouillon as *secrétaire général* of *L'Homme* is significant. Pouillon's varied interests, his membership of the editorial board of *Les Temps modernes* and later also of *La Nouvelle revue de psychanalyse*, reveal the widening of the anthropological horizon, the presence of a humanities dimension and collaboration with other disciplines. Lévi-Strauss describes Pouillon's approach as follows: 'Pouillon is less concerned with the relationship between the work and the author as a person... than with interrelationships between the works themselves.' The survival of structuralism is thus guaranteed. Yet from the mid-1970s onwards structuralism had begun to be questioned, as new cross-disciplinary programmes such as cultural studies and semiotics emerged. We shall return to these later.

L'Homme has attempted to keep abreast of theoretical and other developments. Lévi-Strauss is no longer involved in the journal although he still publishes articles in it. He stresses that since it was founded in 1961, two generations of anthropologists have emerged. In an interview in 1985, given by Lévi-Strauss and Pouillon to two editors of the psychoanalytical monthly, *L'Ane*, the importance of the link with the human sciences was emphasized. It is striking that, at about the same time that *L'Homme* was founded, two other journals, *Cahiers d'études africaines* and *Etudes rurales*, were also founded. Like *L'Homme*, both aimed to keep an interdisciplinary approach and appointed historians, linguists and geographers to their editorial boards.

Another journal, entitled *Ethnologie française,* was founded in 1971, which replaced *Arts et traditions populaires.* This changeover revealed a shift from the study of primitive or exotic societies to the study of European societies. The title of the first issue established the journal's aim: '*Construire son objet: l'ethnologie du domaine français*'. The publication heralded the transition from the study of folklore to that of the social anthropology of France. Shortly before the new journal appeared, *Arts et traditions populaires* published its last issue. Jean Cuisenier, its director, stated that the new journal would deal with the same corpus as that of the closing one, but that the research would be carried out according to ethnological methods. There is no doubt that these methods are inspired by structuralism, as may be illustrated by an example taken from the first issue. One of the articles, written by a mathematician, Alain Charraud, presents an analysis of the representation of age in human life in popular engravings of the nineteenth century. The article used a corpus of engravings kept in museum collections. But the aim was not, Cuisenier writes, to give the history of the engravings or to study the various influences upon the engravings. Instead, 'it aimed to reveal the structures underlying the way oppositions can be seen to function between different specimens' (1997: 278).

The survey of these journals confirms that one scholar continues to tower over all the above outlined changes of social anthropology: Lévi-Strauss. His life's work is rooted firmly in a multiplicity of intellectual explorations from philosophy to psychoanalysis and linguistics (Lévi-Strauss, 1955: 42–52). *Structures élémentaires* and *Mythologiques* constitute Lévi-Strauss's most influential oeuvre from a structuralist point of view, yet his other contributions to the field of anthropology and to French intellectual life are no less remarkable. *Tristes tropiques* (1955) was written when he had been twice turned down for a post at the Collège de France. In it he devotes a chapter to the question: 'How does one become an anthropologist?' One passage in this chapter reveals a powerful similarity between many ordinary human beings and the anthropologist (1961: 58):

[H]e himself acquires a kind of chronic uprootedness from the sheer brutality of the environmental changes to which he is exposed. Never can he feel himself 'at home' anywhere: he will always be, psychologically speaking, an amputated man. Anthropology is, with music and mathematics, one of the few true vocations; and the anthropologist may become aware of it within himself before ever he has been taught it.

If the tropics are sad, it is because primitive societies are on the wane, locked between conservation and disappearance.

What then, one may ask, is the future of social anthropology? *Ethnologie française* proposes the study of France's own culture. This raises the question of the relationship between anthropology and the emerging field of cultural studies. The discipline of 'cultural studies' is absent in this volume because the practice of cultural studies does not in fact claim the status of a discipline. Yet when discussing the future of social anthropology one must inevitably look into the growing field of 'cultural studies' whose aim, like that of social anthropology, is the study of 'culture'. When defining culture in 1988, Lévi-Strauss does not hesitate to return to Sir Edward Tylor's 1871 definition of culture as 'that complex whole which includes knowledge, belief, art, morals, law, custom, and any other capabilities and habits acquired by man as a member of society' (1871: 1). But Lévi-Strauss postulates a second meaning to this definition of culture, a meaning in which everything constitutes an object of study: that which 'in the first sense one might value the least or the most' (Lévi-Strauss and Eribon, 1996: 229).

There is a similarity between this notion of 'culture' and that proposed by narratologist and cultural analyst Mieke Bal, in her book *Double Exposures: The Subject of Cultural Analysis*. For Bal, 'cultural analysis has developed as a new approach to a new subject matter; an integrative, interdisciplinary analysis of objects from everyday culture, the rejects of the official disciplines'. In this venture, Bal argues, there is a 'foregrounding of the active presence of the object, or text, in the same historical space as inhabited by the subject, *me* [the cultural analyst]' (Bal, 1996: 11). This last comment may help us to understand the distinction between social anthropologist and cultural analyst. Whereas Bal reduces the distance between cultural object studied and cultural analyst, Claude Lévi-Strauss argues that, in order to observe 'one must be outside' ('il faut être en dehors'). In social anthropology knowledge is obtained, in the first instance, through the distance between subject and object, and only in the second instance should an attempt be made to bridge that distance. The originality of social anthropological research lies in this incessant to and fro movement (Lévi-Strauss and Eribon, 1996: 214–15). Whatever the developments in cultural studies, there is little doubt that they are rooted in anthropology and that it is not always clear where the distinction actually lies. The development of a concept of culture, according to Edward LiPuma, is 'the key contribution of anthropology to the human sciences' (1993: 14).

Yet it cannot be denied that both semiotics and cultural studies are indebted to social anthropology or more precisely to French structuralism, which is itself a movement encompassing a variety of disciplines. Semiotics and cultural studies are founded on two distinct premises. Semiotics is based on the dissolution of the subject, as Culler argues: 'As the self is broken down into component systems, deprived of its status as source and master of meaning, it comes to seem more and more like a construct: a result of systems of convention' (Culler, 1981: 33). Cultural studies, on the other hand, more a British development than a French one, has gone through three phases according to Antony Easthope, Professor of Cultural Studies at Manchester University: the Culturalist phase of the 1960s, the Structuralist phase of the 1970s, and the Post-Structural-Cultural Materialist phase of the past twenty years (1997: 3–18 *passim*). The overwhelming interest in the concept of culture has remained vivid, and whether studied as a system of signs or as a validation of all forms of culture, it is clear that social anthropology lies at the heart of these developments but has also become the target of criticism.

The idea that cultures are 'bounded wholes which can be treated as discrete units of study and analyzed "holistically" and in relative isolation from other more global influences, has become more and more questionable' (Ahmed and Shore, 1995: 30). Increasingly, the notion of a holistic 'culture' has to be replaced by that of a 'multicultural society' (*pluri-cultures* in France or *métissage culturel*). It may seem that 'cultural' has become a screen which veils the fragmentation of society and its myriad problems and that the word 'culture' may no longer be sufficiently discriminating to show society's complexity, especially since 'culture' is sometimes used as an ideological justification for ethnic violence.

A displacement seems to have emerged between what constitutes the primitive and the exotic. The legacy of the colonial past has created a multicultural France characterized by fractured social identities. In the case of Algeria this is particularly significant; ethnologists who explored possibilities of integration soon had to contend with the million Algerians who sought asylum in France. The postcolonial migrations seem to have created, within Western society itself, a fertile area for fieldwork. Travelling to 'primitive' societies might well seem unnecessary since there are Kurds in Paris and North Africans in Aix. The French cities have themselves become the 'elsewhere'; the Barbès market in Paris and the 'Goutte d'or' have become anthropological fields. But who is now the anthropologist? And how does he or she deal with this situation where large groups of people are prey to economic polarization, where there is arguably a new division between primitive and civilized? In his *Lettres persanes* Montesquieu reversed the anthropological situation and put forward the Western world as the object for 'otherness' and 'ethnographia'; now the postcolonial débâcle leads us to question the notion of fieldwork since it has created a vast anthropological shambles in the shanty towns all over France. It is perhaps this new reality which has thrown doubt on the structuralist enterprise because structuralism appears to dispose of subjectivity and fails to deal with man as a subject. Moreover, the momentous developments in media, communications and information technology over the past decade have had major implications for culture. On the one hand culture has become global; on the other it has become 'ethnic' and local. The fall of Communism in 1989 has created a new Europe in which ethnicity and geopolitical conflicts have become central. Moreover, the media explore and exploit the ever-increasing ethnic conflicts, claims for national identity, fundamentalism and genocide. 'Exotic' societies have become spectacles of violence on Western television. The notion of 'culture' and the task of cultural analysts and anthropologists is increasingly brought into question.

How then can one assess anthropology, the very social science which earlier aimed at studying and recording 'primitive culture'? It is clear that during the last twenty-five years social anthropology has changed considerably and that its 'subject', namely the study of culture, has not remained social anthropology's prerogative. According to Christian Bromberger 'the study of past or residual rural practice has been progressively replaced by the analysis of present-day situations which are no longer restricted to small village communities' (1997: 313). Global development confronts anthropology as well as cultural studies with a constantly shifting agenda. In anthropology the biggest change has perhaps not occurred in the methodology but in the objects it studies.

Lévi-Strauss's longevity has undoubtedly contributed to maintaining stability in social anthropology's prestige in the social sciences in France and beyond, and looking back at his earlier work, it appears that many of the developments outlined here were perceived by him. This is particularly apparent in his 1955 travel account, *Tristes tropiques*. This spontaneous book which intermingles the account of his travels, an intellectual autobiography, reflections on philosophical and anthropological issues, and also the plot of a play he wrote in the jungle is a seminal text. It is an anthropological testimony which reveals the intellectual and emotional constitution of an astonishing mind and a searching human being. There is a pessimism concerning the survival of cultural diversity:

'humanity has taken to monoculture, once and for all, and is preparing to produce civilization in bulk, as if it were sugar beet. The same dish will be served to us every day' (1961: 39); there is also bewilderment at the realization of the absurdity of the human predicament, i.e. humanity's transient presence in the world ('The world began without the human race and it will end without it', 1961: 397).

There seems to be no answer to the many contradictions the anthropologist uncovers. Yet in this 1955 book Lévi-Strauss finds an answer in Jean-Jacques Rousseau. 'He it is who showed us how', he writes, 'after we have destroyed every existing order, we can still discover the principles which allow us to erect a new order in their stead' (1961: 389). Marx, Freud and Jakobson were instrumental in the formulation of structuralist anthropology, but Rousseau, Lévi-Strauss's master, is the mentor who enables him to be a social anthropologist. At a moment where social problems call for new visions and new models, and where anthropology's agenda is questioned, Rousseau's modernity, which Lévi-Strauss emphasized in 1955, calls for renewed interest.

There is a second master, namely Marcel Mauss (1872–1950), without whom Lévi-Strauss's work cannot be understood, and whose writings, like Rousseau's, offer insights into the fragmentation which characterizes society at the end of the century. Mauss represents the foundation of French anthropology. 'The first thing that strikes us about Mauss's thought', wrote Lévi-Strauss in 1950, 'is what I would call its modernity.' The essay on *The Gift* is Mauss's most celebrated text, which continues to inspire scholars from different disciplines: anthropologists, sociologists, philosophers, linguists, historians and economists. The relevance and renewed importance of the essay calls for more than a brief note. Lévi-Strauss records the emotions experienced when first reading this seminal text: 'Few have managed to read the *Essai sur le don* without feeling the whole gamut of . . . emotions . . . : the pounding of the heart, the throbbing head, the mind flooded with the imperious, though not yet definable, certainty of being present at a decisive event in the evolution of science' (1987: 38). *The Gift* is Mauss's main illustration of the concept of 'total social phenomena' ('fait social total'). It reveals that the social phenomenon is a reality, a 'concrete fact'. The gift, founded on reciprocity, is a structure consisting of three obligations: giving, receiving, returning. These three obligations may be seen as isolated parts but, as Lévi-Strauss puts it, Mauss attempts to locate a 'source of energy to synthesize them'.

The importance and modernity of this essay lie also in its belonging to a French philosophical tradition while at the same time breaking new ground. Mauss continues and expands a line of thought which runs from Montaigne, Descartes, Montesquieu and Rousseau and paves the way for Lévi-Strauss's structural anthropology. In a recent book on Mauss, Bruno Karsenti distinguishes three modes of knowledge which evolved mainly in the eighteenth century: the sociological mode, the anthropological mode and the philosophical mode. All three modes are interrelated, yet in the eighteenth century they begin to find a specificity which will eventually lead to separate autonomous disciplines. While philosophy is concerned with the knowledge of man in the abstract (mankind), sociology and anthropology concern themselves with the understanding of man as a social being. This question, Bruno Karsenti argues, 'amounts to treating the human as a privileged philosophical object' (1997: 4).

However, Jacques Derrida's recent philosophical reading of Mauss's concept of the gift (i.e. giving, receiving and returning) is founded on a unilateral understanding of the gift. For there to be a real gift, the receiver must not be indebted and must not return a gift. Derrida goes so far as to remark:

> It could even be said that such a monumental book as Marcel Mauss's *Essai sur le don* speaks of everything but the gift. It deals with economics, trade, contract (*do ut des*), auction, sacrifice of the gift and the return gift, in fact everything in the thing itself which both encourages and annuls the gift.
>
> (1991: 39)

Current intellectual developments explore the paradoxical aspect of the gift: the gift can only be a gift if it does *not* involve exchange. Pierre Bourdieu, who began as an anthropologist but, in direct contrast with Mauss, turned from anthropology to sociology, also examines the concept and warns against projecting the reciprocity retroactively in the gift-giving. In other words, it is important to understand the real nature of the gift at the moment when it is given. The symbolic development ('le travail symbolique') corresponds to a temporalization of the phenomenon. The reciprocated gift must be deferred and be different. To return an identical gift immediately would be tantamount to a refusal (Bourdieu, 1980: 179; also Karsenti, 1997: 347, n. 1). This is no different from Mauss if read carefully.

Mauss's theory on the gift continues to inspire and fuel current intellectual debate in France. Using Mauss's name as an acronym, a movement has been created: MAUSS–Mouvement anti-utilitariste dans les sciences sociales. Their publications include a study of the gift, *Ce que donner veut dire: don et intérêt* ('What giving means: gift and interest'), in which Alain Caillé urges caution in using the concept 'don'. In what kind of theoretical framework do we place it? Should it be idealized or demystified? In order to actualize the analyses of Mauss for contemporary society, it is important to keep the anthropological dimension of the concept in mind and to determine to what extent the gift is in fact a pure gift or carries with it obligations of reciprocity. Questions which arise are, what is the function of the gift in economics and the issue of the gift of human organs (Bertoud, 1993: 257–74).

Furthermore, the question raised by the late British anthropologist, Evans-Pritchard, concerning the relevance of the gift for Western society seems to gain new significance with the economic imbalances which increasingly characterize the world. In the introduction to *The Gift*, Evans-Pritchard writes:

> Mauss is telling us, quite pointedly, in case we should not reach the conclusion for ourselves, how much we have lost, whatever we may have otherwise gained, by the substitution of a rational economic system for a system in which exchange of goods was not a mechanical but a moral transaction, bringing about and maintaining human, personal, relationships between individuals and groups.
>
> (Mauss, 1954: ix)

More and more business and organizational systems reveal 'delayed' reciprocities.

The Gift, undoubtedly Mauss's major contribution to the social sciences, is a 'modern' text. Yet Mauss's modernity lies in his versatility. If he closes the first half of the century, his work gains renewed relevance in his being a scholar whose work encompasses and unifies preoccupations from various disciplines. Moreover, unlike Dumézil and Lévi-Strauss who remained apolitical, Mauss had a strong political commitment. The recent publication of Mauss's *Ecrits politiques* gives access to a corpus of political writings which reveal an author who remains one of the most important theoreticians in the social sciences. Like Rousseau, Mauss succeeds in offering a unified perspective of what has become, at the end of the century, a myriad of disciplines and subjects.

There is no doubt that in French intellectual life social anthropology's success and importance have been considerable. This is due to several factors. First, it is founded on France's specific cultural and intellectual heritage which penetrates all intellectual activity. Anthropology, initially a philosophical tradition rooted in antiquity, developed into a more specific discourse in the eighteenth century. Although it was still part of the general philosophical tradition, a new emphasis emerged in the eighteenth century and was to develop into 'the science of man'. Its major innovative method, as represented in structuralism, is due not only to the solidity of that tradition but also to concurrent intellectual developments in linguistics. Structuralism may no longer be fashionable but the success of the father of structuralism, Claude Lévi-Strauss, remains unqualified. His longevity, undoubtedly, contributes to this continued success. However, whereas Lévi-Strauss abandoned philosophy and embraced anthropology, in a paradoxical development anthropology now generates philosophical debates. Such debates cannot remain isolated from the specific social problems which characterize present-day society; it seems that the 'anthropologists' whose work proves to be of particular relevance, as current research reveals, are two founders of social anthropology: Jean-Jacques Rousseau and Marcel Mauss. They are founders in different ways but share a vision in which the study of society is part of a philosophical enquiry, of a political commitment and of an intellectual dialogue. It is this intersection which explains their renewed relevance at the end of this century.

Note

1   I am grateful to Nick Allen, Alex Gunasekara, Jacqueline Page and Jacqueline Waldren for their comments.

References

Ahmed, Akbar and Shore, Cris (1995) *The Future of Anthropology: Its Relevance to the Contemporary World*. London and Atlantic Highlands, NJ: Athlone Press.
Bal, Mieke (1996) *Double Exposures: The Subject of Cultural Analysis*. London: Routledge.
Balandier, Georges (1957) *Afrique ambiguë*. Paris: Plon.
—— (1967) *Anthropologie politique*, Paris: PUF.
—— (1974) *Anthropo-logiques*, Paris: PUF.
Bassnett, Susan (1997) *Studying British Cultures*. London and New York: Routledge.
Bertoud, Gérard (1993) 'La Société contre le don. Corps humain et technologies biomédicales', in MAUSS (1993), pp. 257–74.
Bertoud, G. and Busino, G. (1996) *Mauss: hier et aujourd'hui* (Actes du XIIe Colloque Annuel du Groupe d'Etudes 'Pratiques Sociales et Théories', *Revue européenne des sciences sociales*, 34). Geneva: Droz.
Bromberger, Christian (1997) 'L'Ethnologie de la France et ses nouveaux objets', *Ethnologie française*, 3: 224–313; English summary, p. 313.

Bourdieu, Pierre (1980) *Le Sens pratique*. Paris: Minuit.

Cuisenier, Jean (1997) 'Quelles ethnologies, pour quels domaines?', *Ethnologie française*, 3: 277–80.

Culler, Jonathan (1981) *The Pursuit of Signs: Semiotics, Literature, Deconstruction*. London: RKP.

Derrida, Jacques (1991) *Donner le temps, la fausse monnaie*. Paris: Galilée.

Dosse, François (1992a/b) *Histoire du structuralisme*, 2 vols. Paris: La Découverte.

Easthope, Antony (1997) 'But what *is* cultural studies?', in Bassnett (1997).

Godelier, Maurice (1984) *L'Idéel et le matériel*. Paris: Fayard.

—— (1996) *L'Enigme du don*. Paris: Fayard.

—— (1997) 'American anthropology as seen from France', *Anthropology Today*, 13 (1): 3–5.

James, Wendy and Allen, Nick (1998) *Marcel Mauss: A Centenary Tribute*. Providence, RI and Oxford: Berghahn Books.

Karsenti, Bruno (1997) *L'Homme total: sociologie, anthropologie et philosophie chez Marcel Mauss*. Paris: PUF.

Ladrière, Jean (1971) 'Le Structuralisme entre la science et la philosophie', *Tijdschrift voor filosofie*, 33 (1): 66–111.

Leiris, Michel (1969) *Cinq Etudes d'ethnologie: le racisme et le tiers monde*. Paris: Denoël/Gonthier.

Lévi-Strauss, Claude (1945) 'L'Analyse structurale en anthropologie', *Word*, 1 (1): 33–53.

—— (1952): *Les Structures élémentaires de la parenté*. Paris: Presses Universitaires de France.

—— (1955) *Tristes tropiques*. Paris: Union générale d'éditions. Translated as: *World on the Wane*.

—— (1961) *World on the Wane*, trans. J. Russell. London: John Murray.

—— (1964) *Le Cru et le cuit*. Paris: Plon.

—— (1966) *Du Miel aux cendres*. Paris: Plon.

—— (1968) *L'Origine des manières de table*. Paris: Plon.

—— (1971) *L'homme nu*. Paris: Plon.

—— (1987) *Introduction to the Work of Marcel Mauss*, trans. F. Baker. London: RKP.

—— (1997) 'L'Homme de *L'Homme*', *L'Homme*, 143 (3): 13–15.

Lévi-Strauss, Claude and Eribon, Didier (1996) *De Près et de loin*. Paris: Odile Jacob.

LiPuma, Edward (1993) 'Culture and the concept of culture in a theory of practice', in Craig Calhoun, Edward LiPuma and Moishe Postone (eds), *Bourdieu: A Critical Perspective*. London: Polity Press, pp. 14–34.

MAUSS (1993) *Ce que donner veut dire: don et intérêt*. Paris: La Découverte.

Mauss, Marcel (1925) *Essai sur le don*, in Mauss (1950).

—— (1950) *Sociologie et anthropologie*, ed. G. Gurvitch. Paris: PUF.

—— (1954) *The Gift*, trans. I. Cunnison. London: Cohen & West.

—— (1998): *Ecrits politiques*. Paris: PUF.

Tylor, Edward B. (1871) *Primitive Culture*. London: John Murray.

7
Sociology: Four Players in the Field

Laurence Bell

Rather than attempting to provide a comprehensive account of how sociology has developed as an academic discipline in France, this chapter focuses on salient aspects of the work of four sociologists who have influenced the field in recent decades and contributed to shaping French intellectual discourse. There is little attempt here to do a 'sociology of sociology'. Rather, the four authors considered here – Pierre Bourdieu, Raymond Boudon, Michel Crozier and Alain Touraine – are viewed as exponents of modern French social thought. Nevertheless, it will be useful to begin by considering the development of the institutional field in which their work has been formulated.

It is perhaps paradoxical that in the country in which social science first achieved a degree of intellectual independence (thanks largely to Comte and Durkheim), it should, in the period following the Second World War, have had such difficulty in establishing itself institutionally as a distinct academic discipline (see Karady, 1981: 33–47). While, after considerable difficulty, Durkheimism succeeded in the early twentieth century in establishing its influence in the university system, it became to a large extent fossilized, in the form of the doctrines of *organicisme* and *solidarisme*, whose role was to provide the Republic with a theory of social integration and moral consensus. The generation of young Durkheimians of the beginning of the twentieth century was to a large extent decimated in the First World War, and Durkheim's presumptive intellectual heir, his nephew Marcel Mauss, turned away from sociology, properly speaking, to ethnology. This discontinuity was prolonged in the post-Second World War period by the widespread intellectual influence of phenomenology and its more visible partner, existentialism. On the other hand, France's most striking innovator in the social sciences in this period, Lévi-Strauss, made his name in the field of structural anthropology and considered sociology as a method rather than a specific field (cited in Lemert, 1981: 11). The institutional weakness of sociology in France therefore led, in the period 1945–54, to a marked degree of dependence on the example of American sociology with its emphasis on empirical methods (the introduction of public opinion polls, for example). However, by the beginning of the 1960s postwar economic growth and the development of planning offered a new role to the social sciences: to instrumentalize themselves in the service of a new technocracy (Bourdieu and Passeron, 1967). This again weakened the academic basis of sociology and the autonomy of the discipline.

To the above must be added a number of more general cultural factors such as the philosophical and encyclopedic nature of the culture associated with the Ecole Normale Supérieure (ENS), the alma mater of many of the social scientists of the postwar decades. This tendency was doubtless amplified by the French model of the committed intellectual, who had to be able to pronounce on any given subject, the result being, as Bourdieu has pointed out (1967), that French sociologists and philosophers often became specialists of the general. This leads us to the *tout Paris* effect: because of the concentration of intellectual activity in Paris, because of the relative weakness of the symbolic rewards available within universities and because of the proximity of academic life to broader intellectual circles and the media (publishing and, more recently, broadcasting), sociologists have often been tempted to address themselves principally to a broad audience (Boudon, 1977). This of course influences their choice of subjects and the way in which they approach them.

Finally, French intellectual life in general in the period from the end of the war until approximately the mid-1970s was marked by the influence of Marxism. The relatively late popularization of theoretical Marxism in France in the postwar period coincided with the antagonisms of the Cold War and was followed fairly shortly by the fracturing of Marxist thought in the wake of the crushing of the 1956 Budapest revolution. This produced a considerable degree of ideological effervescence, which had a marked effect on intellectual life in general.

The factors mentioned above have in many respects set French sociology apart from its Anglo-American cousin and it was in this context that the four sociologists considered here began to make their mark from the late 1950s onwards. Through their espousal or rejection of this or that aspect of the 'field', or through their attempt to retrieve elements they feel to have been misguidedly lost from it, or, yet again, through innovations they feel to be vital for its advancement, each of them has struggled to define and defend his own intellectual enterprise. However, none of them began his academic career in sociology properly speaking: Crozier graduated from the Ecole des Hautes Etudes Commerciales and Touraine studied history at the ENS, while both Bourdieu and Boudon studied philosophy there. Their initial academic training undoubtedly influenced their subsequent orientation in sociology: Crozier's concern with the functioning of organizations; Touraine's with social movements and the explanation of broad historical change; and Bourdieu's and Boudon's with epistemological and methodological questions. However, in contrast to the prevalent Anglo-American tradition, none is a sociologist of any one narrow field: Crozier's analysis of dysfunctional organizations extends outward to broad macroscopic cultural phenomena; Touraine's concern with social movements leads to a consideration of 'historicity' and society's 'production of itself'; Bourdieu's investigations in the fields of education, social mobility and culture are more fundamentally about power, class and the construction of social reality; Boudon's methodological probing is so wide-ranging, both in terms of its philosophical references and the empirical work he discusses, as to be impossible to reduce to one field.

Each of the four has had ample exposure to the USA and American sociology. Broadly speaking, we can say that while the general tenor of the latter (if not all of its achievements) is more or less germane to the liberal outlook of Crozier and Boudon, it is much less so to that of Touraine and Bourdieu, who can be more readily situated within the French tradition of the left-wing intellectual and whose work has clearly been influenced by varieties of neo-Marxism (although it would be entirely misleading to pin such a label on either of them). However, although Boudon may be considered the most 'American' of the four, his concern to construct concepts which will serve as the proper objects of sociology is a far cry from the empirical or sociographical approach often seen as prevalent in American sociology.

Pierre Bourdieu

The work of Bourdieu is as good a point as any at which to begin an examination of French sociology, since he, among others, has been particularly concerned to define what doing sociology is about and is concerned by the heteronomy of the discipline – particularly in France, where its 'porous' nature leads to it being easily affected by Parisian intellectual fashions and the agenda of non-specialists, who feel they are sufficiently qualified to do what Bourdieu disdainfully calls 'spontaneous sociology'.

However, Bourdieu's early work (on the Kabyle tribespeople of Algeria) was of an ethnological nature and he has sought to bring an ethnological focus to bear in his sociology of his own society. Indeed, he has argued (1967) that Lévi-Strauss's structural anthropology should be seen as the resurrection of the Durkheimian tradition, with its emphasis on identifying the objective relations which, within a given social formation, structure the behaviour and experience of individual subjects who are not conscious of these objective relations and their functions. For Bourdieu, just as the social world of the Kabyle tribespeople is structured by determining factors whose functions they are not aware of, in contemporary urban societies individuals generally 'misrecognize' the forces at work which structure their lives and their perceptions of them.

If the distance of ethnologists from the 'exotic' cultures they study (with the risk of ethnocentrism that their external viewpoint implies) enables them to reconstruct the 'real' system of relations operating in them, then sociologists must likewise achieve a similar intellectual distance from the mentality generated by their own social environment. Not to do so would be to fall prey to the unconscious assumptions into which they, like everyone else, are socialized. So the caveat that applies to ethnologists concerning ethnocentrism also applies to sociologists studying their own society. However, the predispositions and assumptions which affect sociologists are so unconsciously pervasive that mere well-intentioned attempts at neutrality are insufficient to guard against them. What is required therefore is constant epistemological vigilance and, since these assumptions are socially produced and situated, this means constantly practising a sociology of sociological knowledge (Bourdieu, Chamboredon and Passeron, 1983: 102).

In examining Bourdieu's approach to the 'craft' of the sociologist we can already see anticipations of some of his conclusions regarding the nature of the phenomena analysed in his work: put crudely, the main-spring of the behaviour and attitudes of individuals is not to be found in their conscious intentions, but in social forces beyond them (which they fail to see). These forces are actuated within particular, structured social situations, that is, relatively autonomous fields (such as workplace relations, education, the legal system, and literary or artistic life), which are fields of struggle, the main thing at stake being the achievement or maintenance of dominant positions within the field. The effect or *function* of the forces structuring each field is, according to Bourdieu, to perpetuate the positions of those who dominate within that field. There is therefore a strong functionalist element in Bourdieu's thought.

However, Bourdieu is not a mere 'objectivist'. If he were, his work would probably not have attracted the attention that it has. For the notion of the 'field' as a site of struggle to be effective, individuals cannot be seen as mere automata or carriers of functions, but must be endowed with properties which enable them to be seen as actors. But neither can an interactionist version of the field (one in which the field would consist merely of subjective personal interaction) suffice. Clearly, the subject cannot be 'rescued' in this way since it ignores the role of structures and their functions.

One of the features of Bourdieu's thought is to view the above opposition between structures and human agency (or between objectivism and subjectivism) as a false problem, or at least as a problem falsely resolved in the past. His solution is to recommend a 'science of dialectical relations between the objective structures . . . and the structured dispositions within which those structures are actualized and which tend to reproduce them' (1977: 3). The name Bourdieu gives to the locus of this process of interplay between the objective and the subjective is the 'habitus', which is a set of structured dispositions which individuals derive from their socialization and which evolve according to the conjunction of objective structures and personal history. The habitus supposes a subjective adjustment to one's (usually inherited) social position within a field (the 'internalization of the external') and plays a role in reinforcing the objective conditions associated with that position (the 'externalization of the internal'). However, Bourdieu's insistence that the habitus operates at an unconscious level, beyond the reach of introspection and the control of the will (1984: 466), sits uneasily with his assertion that it also includes a person's knowledge of the world and that this knowledge is not simply a passive imprint but has constitutive power. His solution to this dilemma is to argue that the habitus has a generative capacity analogous to Chomsky's generative grammar, which enables him to replace Durkheim's idea of rules of behaviour with the more flexible one of strategies.

Habitus is not all, however, for inherent in the different social positions of individuals is the possession of different kinds of capital: material capital, obviously, but also social capital (being well connected), cultural capital (having certain types of performative competence and culturally valued taste and consumption patterns) and symbolic capital (having prestige, status and authority). These different kinds of capital are mutually convertible, but the most important kind is symbolic capital, since it legitimizes possession of the other kinds and enables its holders to impose the 'correct' version of the social world.

To summarize then, Bourdieu replaces the structure/human agency dichotomy with the following formula: (Habitus × Capital) + Field = Practice. He has applied this method to the study of a wide variety of cultural practices and it is undoubtedly its combination of the subjective and the objective and his insistence that analysable structural properties are embedded in the details of everyday life which account for a good part of its appeal – particularly to those working in the area of Cultural Studies.

Let us return briefly to Bourdieu's idea of the 'craft' of the sociologist and the types of assumptions sociologists must avoid in their work. Sociologists, even more than ethnologists, must guard against the illusion of immediate, that is empirical, evidence because the code they use to 'read' the behaviour of social subjects is itself constituted through a socially conditioned learning process and is part of the cultural code of the groups that sociologists belong to. Of all of these codes *class ethos* exerts its effects in the most systematic and latent way, since it is the 'principle' upon which the acquisition of the other unconscious models is organized. An example he gives of this effect is that while it may be widely accepted that the language of the working classes concerning their likely opportunities in life reflects the high degree of social and economic determination which bears on their experience, the assertion that the choices most apparently symbolic of personal freedom (in the areas of artistic taste or religious experience, for example) are likewise determined provokes disbelief and indignation on the part of the cultivated classes (Bourdieu, Chamboredon and Passeron, 1983: 101).

Most insidious of all for Bourdieu, however, is 'intellectual ethnocentrism', because the 'spontaneous sociology' of the intellectual class (practised in the media, for example) is less easy to denounce as prescientific than more working-class expressions of the same banalities. It generates unexamined assumptions and imposes its agenda. The highly integrated nature of the field of French (Parisian) intellectual life imposes on those who occupy positions within it and on those trying to get into it (students) a system of constraints which take on the appearance of the rules of good taste and good 'form'. One must therefore take all fashionable *idées reçues* to task, says Bourdieu, and '. . . turn annoyance with prevailing fashions into a rule for guiding sociological enquiry' (Bourdieu, Chamboredon and Passeron, 1983: 102). Part of Bourdieu's attraction doubtless lies in the polemical nature of his work and in this 'declaration of war' on received opinion and the world of intellectual fashion. Much of his work suggests that a hidden truth can be revealed in the field of cultural production and the behaviour of everyday life and that, while this does not get rid of the constraints of structures, it can lead to a liberating awareness and a more authentic life. His concern is not limited to the health of sociology, but embraces the whole field of cultural production. This is illustrated, for example, in his analysis of television and journalism (Bourdieu, 1994, 1996).

For Bourdieu, journalism is a field with its own structure. Through the pressures of audience ratings the economy exerts commercial pressure on television which makes itself felt in turn on journalism and on all other fields of cultural production (Bourdieu, 1996: 65). In every field there are those who dominate and those who are dominated according to the internal values of the field. A 'good historian', for example, is someone whom other good historians think good (Bourdieu accepts the circularity of such statements). However, heteronomy begins when someone who is not a historian or a mathematician, for example, can judge a historian or a mathematician with the 'authority' which television lends to such criticism, whether it is informed or not. Here Bourdieu talks of a 'law' (1996: 72–3) according to which the more producers of culture are autonomous, rich in specific capital (that is, specific to a particular field) and orientated towards the other producers in that same field (in other words, their competitors), the more they are inclined to resist external pressures. On the other hand, the more their production is aimed at the mass market, the more they are inclined to submit to the demands of external powers, such as (in the past) the State, the Church, the Party and (today) journalism and television. Indeed, Bourdieu insists that 'heteronomous intellectuals' must be opposed, because it is through them that the laws of commerce and the economy invade the fields of cultural production. Against the criticism of cultural elitism which this position might suggest, Bourdieu argues that it is imperative both to defend the conditions of production which will advance universal culture, and to enable more people to fulfil the conditions which will enable them to appropriate it (1996: 77). Bourdieu, thus, has a particular idea of the democratization of culture in mind – one which is redolent of a certain French republican tradition.

One of the results of the distance Bourdieu's sociology maintains from the phenomena it observes, and of his reflexive approach, is, of course, the legendary difficulty of his language, since his expositions constantly seek reflexively to take account of the conditions under which they have themselves been produced. However, there is also a conscious strategy at play: in order to promote the autonomy of sociology as a discipline, Bourdieu consciously makes access to his texts difficult. He argues that if his language is complex, that is because society is complex. A much less charitable view has been voiced by Raymond Boudon, who argues that Bourdieu's language and tautologies are merely a smokescreen which enables him to claim he has been misunderstood by his critics (Boudon, 1989: 157).

Raymond Boudon

Boudon too has devoted a great deal of attention to what the proper business of sociology should be. Indeed, in spite of the fact that Bourdieu probably views him as an empiricist (or 'worse', as a positivist), much of his work is of a methodological and epistemological nature rather than being devoted to original empirical studies. And yet, Boudon does belong to a certain empirical tradition. His examination of the epistemology of sociology, for example, does not begin, as with Bourdieu, with a socially situated sociologist confronted by a socially situated subject, but with an analysis of some of the main elements of the vocabulary of the social sciences ('theory', 'function', 'structure', etc.), which he shows to be polysemic. Thus, he points to the confusion which arises when the same word is used in different ways within the same argument. However, his method here is not empiricist in that he does not establish these different meanings (and their implications) normatively, but in terms of categories of meaning with distinct logical properties (Boudon, 1980: 135–48; Boudon, 1986: 90–4).

Boudon is critical of system-building and of sociologists whose 'realism' mistakes structures for real aspects of societies, whereas they should, he argues, be viewed as conceptual models. Likewise, he tends to describe concepts, constructs or paradigms which he accepts as 'useful', 'fruitful' or having 'creative capacity'. In general, he invites sociologists to take a modest view of the scope of their discipline and of its potential for apprehending the real world. He is particularly critical of macro-sociological representations, attempts to predict social change (or reproduction) and systems based on intuitive inference, rather than logical constructs which produce verifiable propositions.

Boudon makes no bones about where he himself stands regarding his fundamental choices. He describes his central argument as 'methodological individualism' (1989: 7–9). In this he follows Max Weber's suggestion that sociological analysis should treat individuals' behaviour and choices as rational and meaningful for them. However, rationality is to be understood in a broad sense: the utilitarian idea of a 'rational choice model' (where rational actors are those who pursue objectives which accord with their immediate interests) is, he says, useful, but too limited and narrow to explain many forms of behaviour, attitudes and beliefs. Rather, proceeding on the basis of the behaviour of actors being rational implies identifying the *good reasons* which have led them to adopt such behaviour. And these may be utilitarian, teleological or other. Therefore Boudon excludes the possibility of explaining actors' behaviour by anything other than the reasons which they themselves would give if they had the time to reflect introspectively on the matter. His approach thus excludes hypotheses which assume that actors can be unwittingly manipulated by forces outside themselves – such as 'false consciousness' or the subconscious (or, indeed, the habitus). Boudon doubts the usefulness of such ideas for explaining behaviour, since the irrational motivation they posit is a construct which is inaccessible both to internal experience and to external observation. Since it can only be inferred, it is not amenable to sociological explanation.

In Boudon's scheme of things the macro-social is simply the aggregation of a host of individual behaviours which happen at the micro-social level and he refers to their unforseen outcomes as 'aggregation effects', or, when the outcomes are unfortunate and particularly contrary to the intentions of individuals, as 'counter-intuitive effects' or *effets pervers* (1986: 56–60).

So Boudon follows Weber's recommendation that sociology should seek to comprehend the individual actor. This means establishing the kind of relationships between the actor's situation and motivation and action which enable the observer to conclude that, in the same situation, he or she would have acted in a like manner. He argues that this approach is not atomistic (that is, does not suppose a society made up of totally isolated individuals), since it does not rule out the phenomena of relationships (such as influence or authority) and stresses the need to understand an actor's behaviour with reference to a situation, which may be partly determined by macro-social variables. However, it is clear from this that Boudon cannot accept Bourdieu's notion of the individual as the locus of a dialectical process or Alain Touraine's that the individual is merely an intersection point of particular social relations. In contrast to Touraine's earlier work, Boudon is hostile to the idea of making collective entities actors. He accepts that individuals may be 'class conscious' (that is, feel that they belong to a class) but, for him, 'collective consciousness' is a doubtful idea, and the idea that the low level of educational ambition of children from underprivileged backgrounds is due to the 'weight of tradition' or 'class ethos' is, he says, based on the 'society-centred' illusions of the sociological observer.

Indeed, Boudon does not accept that the use of a deterministic frame-work is a prerequisite in sociology. He argues that many social scientists have derived this postulate from a particular image of the natural sciences. In his words, 'the constant refusal to treat social phenomena as the result of the aggregation of individual actions can also probably be seen as the effect of a certain image of "science" as a discipline in which there is no room for subjective phenomena' (1986: 216). Chance and subjectivity are therefore often rejected by the social sciences. However, Boudon argues that it is only if they are given their proper place that the social sciences can have any claim to objectivity. This implies identifying and rejecting questions to which there is no answer.

One kind of determinism which Boudon particularly takes to task is functionalism. However, this concerns not so much its use as its abuse. Functionalist analyses can, he says, explain why particular institutions come into existence and why they are accepted and regarded as legit-imate by the members of a given society. In the examples which he examines (voting systems, systems of deliberation and the way the American Democratic Party became rooted) there is no mystery in the notion of function (1989: 155). Functional analysis shows that a particu-lar institution makes sense for a set of individuals, either because it meets demands and needs which they see as justified, or because it means that they can solve a problem facing the group in conditions acceptable to the members of the group. However, he argues, the functionalist *para-digm* also gives rise to distortions which gain their legitimacy from the paradigm's creative capacity. As a result, certain sociologists adhered to the idea that *everything* in society has a function and this led them to change a paradigm into a vision of the world. This was especially misguided when combined with a particular version of neo-Marxism, since it led to the attempt to explain any institution by its presumed macro-social effects. The various writers of this movement made their main question

'what purpose is served by...?': prison (Foucault), education (Althus-ser, Bourdieu), culture (Bourdieu), cities (Castells), the State (Mili-band). The answer to the question *'whose* purpose is served by...?' is of course known in advance: that of the ruling class.

(1989: 226)

However, Boudon does not regard the existence of ideology as a false problem and has tried to square its existence and nature with his own approach. Briefly put, he argues that ideologies can emerge normally in the subject's mind, rather than being the result of arbitrary or unclear forces over which the subject has no control. In contrast to Bourdieu he argues that adherence to received ideas is not a result of delusion in the habitus, but can be analysed as a meaningful act. While Boudon accepts that the perception of subjects is influenced by their social position and dispositions (the latter he understands in a much more voluntarist way than Bourdieu) he agrees with Mannheim, the originator of the sociology of ideologies, that ideas cannot be understood without reference to the social and historical context in which they appear. But this, he says, also implies that ideas have to be *understood* (that is, by subjects) and that they cannot be interpreted as mechanical reflections of historical and social situations. In other words, they cannot be derived from some sort of collective consciousness, but must be capable of being imputed to rational actors (1989: 73–4).

Michel Crozier

Like Boudon, Crozier rejects determinism, particularly of the functionalist variety (Crozier, 1977: 25), and holds that the consciousness and experience of individuals is the necessary starting point of analysis. However, Crozier's central concern is collective behaviour, particularly within organizations. The latter are systems of human interaction which necessarily involve very specific patterns of constraint. The perceptions of actors must therefore be understood in terms of the context of the system they are acting in. While Crozier holds that systems are not pre-established structures, he also rejects purely interactionist and intersubjective approaches, since they fail to grasp the existence of objective 'rules of the game' specific to any system of human interaction (Crozier, 1977: 83). Steering a path between determinism and subjectivism, he argues that while all structures or systems entail constraints on human action, no system is entirely regulated and it is precisely the element of uncertainty in the 'game' (internal dynamics) of a system which allows individuals to exercise freedom of action in the form of strategies.

The aim of Crozier's strategic analysis is to reconstruct the nature and game rules of the power structure which regulate the interaction of actors and condition their behaviour in particular organizational systems (1977: 410). He postulates that the strategies of actors are rational in that they have a rationality (an intended purpose) which analysis must find, but he adds that this postulate is part of a *heuristic* approach. In other words, it provides a yardstick for behaviours which might equally be irrational. However, it is not the rationality or independence of actors, but relations of dependence and power which interest Crozier, since he holds that power is an integral part of all processes of social integration and that the latter is the central concern of sociological enquiry (Crozier, 1970: 29).

It is worth noting here Crozier's observation that while deterministic structuralist theories often seem to place power at the centre of their analysis, their assertion that all the elements of a given social formation or system are absolutely determined by the structure of that system leaves no room for the concept of power, since, for example, it implies that even a dominant group has no choice as to its action. While he made this criticism of Althusser and Poulantzas (Crozier, 1977: 23), he might equally well have made it of Bourdieu.

At all events, the principal characteristic of power as a factor of integration, for Crozier, is that it involves confrontation, transfer and exchange. Power must be understood, not as a substance or the attribute of an actor, but as a set of relations between individuals or groups. Power relationships in organizations are, therefore, specific and imply a degree of (albeit skewed) reciprocity and negotiation (Crozier, 1970: 34; 1977: 59). For Crozier the important word here is negotiation and he emphasizes that alongside the formal rules of organizations (their official structures) there are informal power relations, without which no organization can function effectively, and which are subject to negotiation. Indeed he argues that the imperative for organizations to regulate themselves, adapt to their environment and innovate requires that the official, legitimate and 'noble' aspect of power, which, because it represents cohesion and collective leadership, has traditionally been endowed with a high moral value, has to accommodate the other aspect: that of bargaining, which has traditionally been viewed as morally suspect (Crozier, 1970: 38–41)

Can such insights, derived from the study of power in organizations, be applied to whole societies? While Boudon rejects such an approach (Boudon, 1980: 20–1; 1986: 164),Crozier argues that such extrapolation is possible, in large part because certain developments have narrowed the gap between organizations and society. While organizations have become more open and tolerant, integrating informal negotiations into their formal decision-making in a way which makes them resemble political entities, in society control is increasingly regulated so that the pursuit of self-interest, which might in the past have operated in a hidden way with no regard for its consequences for others, is subject to organized systems which facilitate conscious decisions. So, while in organizations there has been a relaxation of moral imperatives, broader social relationships have become increasingly transparent and moralized. Moralization, tolerance and rationalization are therefore part of the same process (1970: 41–6) and this makes the development of a culture of negotiation vital for modern societies, in which the rapid pace of change requires constant institutional adjustment and innovation. Failure to recognize and accept this, argues Crozier, has been the main source of organizational or *bureaucratic* blockage, especially in France. Indeed, it is his application of the idea of bureaucratic blockage to the problems of French society which has attracted a broad audience to his work.

However, Crozier's critique of the French 'style of action' predates his explicit formulation of the theory of bureaucracy and, from the 1950s, drew on his observations of a set of typically French cultural traits. He argued that the French model of relations of authority, which was marked by the considerable distance between the different strata of society, an absolutist conception of authority, a preference for impersonal rules rather than face-to-face relations and the transposition of social questions into the political arena, meant that the standard solution to the problems of collective action was centralization and recourse to the state (Crozier, 1957). If France had, since the Second World War, experienced a deep malaise, it was because of the maladjustment of its dominant cultural model to the demands of the modern world, in which change had become an important factor in itself. The militancy of advocates of revolution and the penchant of intellectuals for abstraction merely served to reinforce the inherently conservative nature of the system, which could therefore only change through crisis. On the other hand, the real problem was innovation and this could only be achieved by the participation of citizens in face-to-face relations involving dialogue and compromise (Crozier, 1961).

So many of the key elements of Crozier's later formulation were already present in his earlier work that it is reasonable to ask whether the notion of 'extrapolation' from organization theory to the macrosocial level is accurate, or whether his theory of bureaucratic blockage is a formalization of his culturalist observations. At all events, his de Tocqueville-like critique was taken up in the early years of the Fifth Republic by a modernizing liberal left, preoccupied by the question of how to democratize technocracy. Crozier himself felt that his theory of bureaucratic blockage and change through crisis, as he formulated it in *Le Phénomène bureaucratique* (1963: 275–95, 307–42) was vindicated by the explosion of May 1968, which led him shortly afterwards to reiterate the same diagnosis in a more pointed and didactic fashion in *La Société bloquée* (1970). In both of these works he argued, firstly, that while the French system of centralized administration was considered omnipotent, it was in fact crippled by its bureaucratic functioning and, secondly, that for entrenched historical reasons, public administration was able to impose its mode of organization on French society as a whole.

In Crozier's model, French administrative centralization entails a marked separation between deciders and actors: between those at the top, who have the formal right to take decisions (but are badly informed about the concrete realities which they are attempting to act upon) and those who are affected by such decisions (operatives). The system has advantages, in that the deciders do not have to bear the consequences of their decisions, while the operatives are free from the intrusion of their hierarchical superiors. Secondly, the system is highly stratified and each stratum protects its own members according to an egalitarian rule, but at the cost of considerable group pressure on the individual.

Communication between strata is difficult and this reinforces reliance on abstract rules. However, while the system can only function in practice by tolerating arbitrary exceptions and personal privileges, the struggle to eradicate these merely reinforces centralization. Since local adjustments to the system are considered as temporary rule-bending rather than precedents to be learned from, change can only come through crisis, that is when a build-up of mistakes and maladjustments threatens the survival of the system. However, this mode of change preserves the principles of the system and its rigidity (1970: 95–6).

According to Crozier, this mode of administration is at the heart of all French models of action and organization and is closely connected to a number of specific cultural traits (1970: 129–35). Again, here, he points to a generalized fear of face-to-face relations: because of the risk of conflict or dependency which these entail, individuals prefer to safeguard their autonomy by conducting their social relationships in a markedly formalized manner. The second cultural trait is an adherence to an absolutist conception of authority. However, while absolute authority is viewed as necessary to solve any problem, the burden and risk of humiliation it implies are considered intolerable. The solution to this quandary is to preserve the absolute and arbitrary nature of authority, but to render it 'inoffensive' by keeping it at a distance by means of centralization, stratification and the adherence to impersonal rules. In this way face-to-face relations, conflict and dependency are avoided, and individual autonomy protected, without the social system falling into anarchy and disorder. It is, says Crozier, because such a solution was available to them that the French were able to cultivate that sense of the autonomy of the personality and the critical intellectual freedom and sense of internal security which so typify French civilization (1970: 103–4). However, while individuals are critical and innovative *as individuals*, as members of a group they become conservative, and their reluctance to engage in face-to-face relations of negotiation makes discussion and progress by trial and error difficult. As a result, any collective activity is likely to require the intervention of the state, making public life congested at the centre and atrophied on the periphery (1970: 132–3).

Clearly, then, while the problematic of power is a central concern in Crozier's work, it is closely linked to the problematic of change. In later works he continued to identify France's principal problems as the bureaucratic blockage of its system of public administration, the rigidity and resistance to reform of its centralized national education system and the caste-like nature of its elites, which are selected and moulded by the *grandes écoles*, dominate both the public and private sectors and reproduce the bureaucratic model (1979: 67–74). He insisted that modern societies are characterized by their complexity and by the immense volume of exchange which takes place in them, and, rather like Boudon, argued that such complexity means that great reforms introduced from above in accordance with some grand design are almost bound to produce counter-intuitive effects (Crozier, 1979: 11). His criticism was increasingly directed at the role of the centralized state and the pretensions of politicians and technocrats which perpetuate rigid decision-making structures and institutions which, in turn, stifle the dynamism of civil society (1987: 47–65, 96–102).

Alain Touraine

Touraine's work, too, is marked by the theme of the autonomy of civil society. However, he does not approach it from a Tocquevillean liberal perspective. His central concern is social movements and his analyses suggest, firstly, that it is the struggles of social movements which are the motor force of historical change and, secondly, that economic factors and economic class are no longer their defining features.

While Touraine's overall framework is inspired by Max Weber's idea of the opposition between the rationalization of the technical world and the meaning of the moral and religious world, it is also influenced by certain aspects of Marx's historicism. Indeed, the major thrust of Touraine's work has always been to try to identify the historical 'subject', the essential harbinger of the future. While Touraine uses the term 'sociology of action', by this he means, not individual subjectivity, motivation or intentionality, but the collective action of society on itself, or society's 'self-production'. Since all meaning is arbitrary and therefore shaped by convention, the constructed meaning of our social lives has necessarily been produced by a collective, historical process. He calls the active part of this process 'historicity' and insists that the motor force of change in post-industrial society is the struggle for the control of the 'production' of such meaning.

This sounds like a far cry from the field of *sociologie du travail* in which Touraine began his career. However, this branch of sociology in France was from the start much less concerned with microscopic studies of industrial relations than with broad analyses of the development of industrial society, and Touraine lent a historical perspective to that endeavour (on *sociologie du travail* see Rose, 1979: chs 2 and 7).

Touraine's early work was concerned with the effects of changes in the organization of industrial production on workers' 'consciousness' and on the orientation of the labour movement (Touraine, 1955). In the mid-to-late 1950s, for example, he argued that, with the advent of rationalized mass production (of the 'Fordist' type), the development of mass consumption (in particular of cultural products, with the growth of the mass media) and the increasing interdependence of production and consumption, the economy and social organization in general were increasingly subject to the political decision-making process (Touraine, 1956, 1959). The demands of workers would therefore be increasingly orientated towards the control of that decision-making process, and Touraine did not seem to doubt that the labour movement would be victorious in this respect. However, he was already concerned about the totalitarian implications of such a trend, since the rationalizing drive of the planned economy tended to impose certain social and cultural models. It was, indeed, in this area, rather than in that of championing the cause of workers' control, that his work developed. It may be characterized as a critique of 'programmed' or post-industrial society.

Setting out his position in the 1960s, Touraine argued that, just as early industrialism was marked by the primacy of the economic (because of the upheavals it had brought about and because poverty was the most important social fact of the nineteenth century) and just as the period of industrial rationalization was marked by the primacy of the political and shaken more by totalitarianism than by economic conflicts, 'programmed' society would – because of the antagonistic relationship between mass culture and private life – be marked by the primacy of moral problems (Touraine, 1965: 460–3). This may seem to suggest a move away from a social perspective towards an individualistic one, but, for Touraine, individual identity is a particular intersection point in a complex of human relations and the social embeddedness of individual consciousness offers individuals a point of leverage, through collective action in 'social movements', to act on society.

Touraine viewed certain aspects of the May '68 events as a confirmation of his analysis. While he agreed with Crozier that the events could be qualified as a crisis which exposed the dysfunctional nature of France's institutional structures, he also held that the student revolt presaged a new kind of conflict, which would pit the future 'professionals' of programmed society against the integrative drive and manipulation of culture practised by technocratic organizations (Touraine, 1968: 37–40). However, while this was a collective struggle, the reappropriation of meaning would come about at the level of the individual subject's resistance, and would be expressed not only at work but also in education, in leisure activities and in interpersonal relationships.

Much of Touraine's work in the 1970s focused on the social significance of the post-68 social movements, in particular the anti-nuclear movement (see, for example, Touraine, 1980). He went against the grain of the resurgent socialist left in arguing that the labour movement was no longer a social movement. That is, although it engaged in the defence of workers' interests, it was no longer the carrier of a universal message or project capable of challenging the existing social order, because industrial workers were no longer the least well-off in society and, more importantly, because the central social conflict had changed (Touraine and Wieviorka, 1979: 39–64). At the heart of this conflict lay the resistance of social movements to the logic of control of big organizations (whether public or private) and their struggle to escape such integration by defining an alternative model of society.

In the late 1990s, however, Touraine no longer expressed the same confidence concerning the potential of social movements to change society. Once again, the context had changed and so, therefore, had the nature of social movements and the 'task' they had to fulfil (Touraine, 1997: 117–24). As most observers agreed, the contemporary context was marked by the globalization of trade, the dominance of international financial markets, the spread of a globalized mass culture, the growth of social exclusion, the weakening of social cohesion, the collapse of communism, the rise of religious fundamentalism, the reappearance of ethnic and identitarian movements and the crisis of the nation state. In short, the context was characterized by a crisis of modernity, whose most important aspects for Touraine were, on the one hand, the weakening of the link between the social roles of individuals in institutions and the 'instrumental' logic of the globalized economy and, on the other, the weakening of the link between the 'inner person' of private life and a globalized mass culture which was everywhere, but from nowhere in particular. Culture no longer ordered social organization, which in turn no longer ordered economic activity (Touraine, 1997: 14). The cultural (the sphere of meaning and, therefore, identity) and the economic (the sphere of rationalized, instrumental activity) had become separate to such a degree that the greatest danger was no longer the kind of manipulative integration he had denounced in the 1970s but, rather, the fragmentation of society and of the self.

While Touraine accepts this 'postmodernist' analysis, he rejects the conclusion of postmodernist theorists that it puts an end to any kind of historical vision of the human condition and argues that postmodernism is unable to take on board the consequences of the separation between these two halves of our experience (Touraine, 1997: 40–1, 114). The consequences of this separation for Touraine are, on the one hand, that the involvement of individuals in economic life is reduced to an instrumentalized function in the global economy and equally meaningless, imitative consumerist behaviour and, on the other, that the search for identity pushes people towards a sense of community, defined in closed, exclusive, essentialist and probably ethnic terms. The major contemporary problem for Touraine is, therefore, how individuals can both define an identity and live in society with individuals with other identities.

Against the facile confidence of liberalism in free-market individualism (1997: 356) and the postmodernist thesis that the dissociation of the economic and the cultural simply creates an infinitely relative void, Touraine argues that this process of dissociation is in itself a structuring factor and can be understood and acted upon. The source of such action is what he calls the 'Subject'. Understanding the role he assigns to the 'Subject' is perhaps easier than understanding what it actually is. The role of the 'Subject' is to remedy the fragmentation of each individual's personality by relinking the dissociated spheres of the economic and cultural (1997: 28, 125, 143). However, the 'Subject' is not a concrete actor, nor indeed a person of any sort. Nor is it a moral conscience, an individual's immediate experience of self or the private image individuals may have of themselves (1997: 102, 123). Rather it is the search of individuals for the conditions which enable them to become the actors of their own story. 'Subjectivation' is therefore a desire for individuation, a process which can only develop if there is a sufficient interface between the sphere of 'instrumentality' and the sphere of communitarian identity (1997: 78–9). However, this is not an individualistic quest, since the 'transformation from individual to Subject' is only possible through recognition of the Other as a Subject also working in his/her own particular way to combine 'cultural memory' and an 'instrumental project' without being reduced to either of these poles. This, says Touraine, is the very definition of multicultural society. The idea of the 'Subject' therefore links the recomposition of individual personality to intercultural communication and is, he claims, the principle which ensures the unity of social life in 'late modernity' (1997: 28, 162–3, 178–9).

What, then, is the place of social movements in this perspective? Touraine argues that social movements are now less about the creation of a new social order than about the defence of personal liberty, security and dignity (1997: 94). There may be other forms of collective action in civil society (such as those which pursue the defence of particular interests), but only those which incorporate a moral dimension and relate to what Touraine sees as the central conflict of programmed or post-industrial society (that is, the defence of the 'Subject') can properly be called social (or as he now prefers) *societal* movements. Such 'movements' may therefore not be physical groupings of people but involve, rather, an interplay between debates, shifts in public opinion and cultural behaviour (1997: 117–24). The women's movement is exemplary in this respect in that, freeing themselves from the imposed definitions of men, and struggling to attain the status of 'Subject', women strive more actively than men towards the articulation of the two separate halves of human experience – working life and personal life. Thus it is the dominated actor rather than the dominant actor who plays the principal role in the 'recomposition of the world', and men who seek to combine the two sides of their existence look to the model created by women, since there is no available masculine model, men having traditionally defined themselves, predominantly, in terms of their work (1997: 226–31).

In conclusion then, Touraine argues not only that a historical representation of society is still valid, but also that what defines contemporary society is the acceleration of 'historicity', that is the increase in society's capacity to act on itself, both through the nature of the relationships of domination which characterize particular societies and through the social movements which oppose such domination (1997: 185). He also argues that the situation within which this takes place, marked as it is by the fragmentation we have seen above and the 'desocialization' of identity, means that the central theme of sociology has become social decomposition (1997: 191).

Conclusion

One might well ask, on the basis of what we have seen above, whether there is a sociology which is specific to France. Certainly the works of French sociologists are characterized by a style of exposition which differs from that of their Anglo-American counterparts. However, this has more to do with the specificity of French intellectual discourse in general than with that of a particular subset, such as sociologists. It has been argued that the characteristics of the institutional field of French sociology produce a Parisian 'hothouse' effect whereby sociologists, like other intellectuals, are constantly looking over their shoulders at each other and devoting much of their energies to a more or less veiled argument with their proximate rivals (Lemert, 1981: 7–22). This chapter suggests, however, that the four sociologists examined have been more concerned to labour in their separate vineyards and more preoccupied with mapping out and defending their own intellectual territory. There are, of course, themes and concerns which are common to them – for example, the desire to see a more democratic form of communication in France (Crozier, Touraine and Bourdieu), the autonomy of culture and of the individual (Touraine and Bourdieu), the importance of the idea of strategy (Bourdieu and Crozier), change and modernization (Crozier and Touraine), the status of sociology (Boudon and Bourdieu). But each approaches such themes in terms of his own very particular (and consistently followed) problematic. Indeed, French culture is much less a culture of debate than the importance traditionally accorded to intellectuals in France might suggest. But that is another story.

References

Boudon, Raymond (1977) 'The French university system since 1968', *Comparative Politics*, 10 (1): 89–119.
—— (1980) *The Crisis in Sociology*. London: Macmillan.
—— (1986) *Theories of Social Change*. Cambridge: Polity Press.
—— (1989) *The Analysis of Ideology*. Cambridge: Polity Press.
Bourdieu, Pierre (1977) *Outline of a Theory of Practice*. Cambridge: Cambridge University Press.
—— (1984) *Distinction*. Cambridge, MA: Harvard University Press.
—— (1994) 'L'emprise du journalisme', *Actes de la recherche en science sociales*, 101–2 (March): 3–9.
—— (1996) *Sur la télévision*. Paris: Liber.
—— and Jean-Claude Passeron (1967) 'French sociology and philosophy: death and resurrection of a philosophy without subject', *Social Research*, 34 (1): 162–212.

——, Jean-Claude Chamboredon and Jean-Claude Passeron (1983) *Le Métier de sociologue*, 4th edn. Paris: Mouton.

Crozier, Michel (1957) 'France: terre de commandement', *Esprit*, 256 (December): 779–98.

—— (1961) 'Le citoyen'. *Esprit*, 292 (February): 195–213.

—— (1963) *Le Phénomène bureaucratique*. Paris: Seuil.

—— (1970) *La Société bloquée*. Paris: Seuil

—— (1977) *L'Acteur et le système*. Paris: Seuil.

—— (1979) *On ne change pas la société par décret*. Paris: Grasset.

—— (1987) *Etat modeste, Etat moderne*. Paris: Fayard.

Karady, Victor (1981) 'The prehistory of present-day French sociology (1917–57)', in Lemert (1981), pp. 33–47.

Lemert, Charles (1981) *French Sociology: Rupture and Renewal since 1968*. New York: Columbia University Press.

Rose, Michael (1979) *Servants of Post-Industrial Power?* London: Macmillan.

Touraine, Alain (1955) *L'Evolution du travail ouvrier aux usines Renault*. Paris: CNRS.

—— (1956) 'L'Evolution professionnelle du travail ouvrier', *Cahiers de la République*, 1: 91–103.

—— (1959) 'Problèmes actuels du mouvement ouvrier', *Cahiers de la République*, 21: 22–36.

—— (1965) *Sociologie de l'action*. Paris: Seuil.

—— (1968) *Le Mouvement de mai ou le communisme utopique*. Paris: Seuil.

—— (1980) *La Prophétie antinucléaire*. Paris: Seuil.

—— (1997) *Pourrons-nous vivre ensemble?* Paris: Fayard.

—— and Michel Wieviorka (1979) 'Mouvement ouvrier et nouveaux mouvements sociaux', in *Faire, Crise et avenir de la classe ouvrière*, pp. 39–64. Paris: Seuil.

8
Between Conformity and Heterodoxy: Market, State and Society in French Economics

François Nectoux

During the years 1983 and 1984, momentous changes were forced upon economic policy in France. These ended nearly four decades of a particular mode of economic development, which had been successfully presiding over thirty years of nearly uninterrupted growth. Variously described as 'state Fordism', 'administratively funded economy' or 'state monopoly capitalism', it had not survived for long during the global crisis which from 1973 forced upon the industrialized world a reassessment of economic practices and policies. Economics as a social science also went through a period of upheaval, which is not in any way surprising; since the early 1970s in North America, mainstream neo-Keynesian economics had been challenged in the policy-making area by a resurgence of the neoclassical school of thought in anticipation of the Reaganite and Thatcherite conservative revolutions.

The context in which economic policy and practices shifted in the early 1980s is quite unique. A Socialist government, brought to power in 1981 in the aftermath of the election of François Mitterrand as President, had been implementing an economic strategy based on a blend of neo-Keynesian macro-economics and a relatively radical programme of structural reforms of the economy. Although far more forcefully slanted towards state interventionism and towards objectives of social progress and equality, it was not very different from the traditional French mix of public sector intervention in the management of the economy (the 'mixed economy') and social-democratic redistributive strategies. These had successfully structured the long period of economic growth and modernization of the French capitalist economy after the Second World War, the so-called 'thirty glorious years' (Fourastié, 1979).

But in 1983 the international economic crisis had pushed the trade deficit to new depths; internal inflation pressures and an increased public budget deficit, largely brought about by government policies of demand-led growth, provoked a fall of the franc and three successive devaluations. With added pressure from European partners within the EMS, the authorities concluded that the country could no longer implement economic strategies running counter to trends in international financial markets and counter to the policies of the other main economic powers in Europe, especially Germany (Fonteneau and Muet, 1984).

In a few months the discourse of political and business elites changed dramatically, as well as economic practices. Young socialist politicians, such as Laurent Fabius, soon to be appointed Prime Minister by Mitterrand, were invoking the importance of the enterprise spirit and the primacy of the market as the main mechanism for modernization and economic progress. This reversal was perhaps not the first attempt at steering economic policies away from strategic interventionism and Keynesianism. Indeed, when in 1976 Raymond Barre replaced Jacques Chirac as Prime Minister, his conservative administration attempted for a while to implement monetarist, supply-side economic policies. But Mitterrand in 1981 had been elected on the promise to restore the primacy of demand-side economics in a bid to combat the social consequences of the economic crisis. The reversal of 1983–4 suddenly promoted liberal values in a way that could not have been foreseen a few years before, let alone in the previous forty years of economic development in France. A new economic orthodoxy, based on neoclassical theories and liberal ideology, had finally taken over.

Since then, France has been in search of a new economic model, without much success. Every government since 1983 has extolled the virtues of market deregulation, reliance on open markets as a way to improve the competitiveness of the French economy and its integration into the European Union, in order ultimately to improve growth and job creation. Such has been the unanimity of decision-makers in this respect that the intellectual framework behind these policies has been dubbed by its opponents *la pensée unique*, comparable to Thatcher's TINA ('There is no alternative') of the 1980s.

The hegemony of this liberal orthodoxy, pervading the official discourse as well as the economic policies of governments of all complexions, has meant the adoption of various policy buzzwords. The best known ones have been the 'competitive disinflation' and the 'strong franc' of the 1980s and the 'reduction of public deficits' (in view of achieving the Maastricht criteria for the adoption of the single European currency) in the 1990s. In terms of theory, this has been the result of the adoption, stage by stage, of supply-side economics largely derived from updated forms of neoclassical theories. However, deep tensions are at work in the policy-making arena, and this is reflected in the diversity of positions held by economists and the numerous public debates in which they are now involved.

The economic policy debate in France has obviously been focusing on the labour market, as in 1998 the official unemployment figure was 11.8 per cent; should working life be made more 'flexible', or should jobs be shared through an organized reduction of working time? Another debate has developed around the Euro and the prospects for further economic integration within the European Union. In the background, the recurrent question of the role of the state and the future of public services is crucial. Other questions appear on business governance, market regulation and the financing of the welfare state.

Two important points need to be made for a proper understanding of contemporary developments in French economics. First, economic theory (and therefore economists as a professional group) has been deeply influenced by North American thinking. The debates between neoclassical and neo-Keynesian ideas have been as heated, and have moved in the same broad directions, as in the US and Britain, with the same turning point around the mid-1970s. Second, there are variations specific to France on these two main schools of thought, as well as alternative sets of theories, that one could call 'heterodox', the importance of which comes from the specific approach to the socio-economic and political framework. The originality of much of French economics is to attempt integrating within the realm of economics various forms of social categories other than the market, and not analysing these forms as 'imperfect' or hidden markets. Social and institutional categories are often given a central and autonomous role, as operative structures and/or substantive to economic categories. A typical example would be the analysis of money by Michel Aglietta (Aglietta and Orléan, 1984; Aglietta, 1986). He defines money as a complex social relationship which can only be properly understood within specific systems of social interaction, not simply as an economic instrument defined by its functions within an immanent market structure. Similarly, the state is seen as a specific socio-political construct, not as an abstract, neutral category or agent.

In this context, the complexity of the debates and the multiplicity of areas in which economics has specialized make it difficult to appraise the whole evolution and impact of economics in contemporary French society. Rather, this chapter will focus on the macro-economic developments and debates which in the last few decades had the most influence for societal choices in France. First, the context in which economics have been operating will be presented, focusing on developments both before the Second World War and since 1945. This will include the impact of the specific French development model, as well as the ways in which the professional status of economists has evolved. Some heterodox developments in French economics in this period will then briefly be examined.

A third part will focus on the emergence of the consensual *pensée unique* orthodoxy which since the mid-1980s has confirmed the abandonment of the modernization economics of the Thirty Glorious Years and its brand of Keynesian economics now largely perceived as impotent. But it will also describe how the recurrence and the deepening of the social crisis that accompanied the implementation of policies derived from the new hegemonic liberal economics soon brought a reaction from alternative perspectives. These mostly emerged from the ashes of the neo-Keynesian framework and the impact of those alternative analyses on economic debates in France has been quite noticeable in the 1990s. New types of heterodox economics, influenced by intellectual traditions such as structuralism and neo-Marxism, also contribute to these debates. The best known and most important development in this respect is the Regulation School but it is certainly not the only one. The conclusions will come back to the idea that the ways in which social and public parameters feature in much of French economic analysis differentiate it from the dominant North American traditions.

Economics in French society: the context

French economics has a long tradition of originality, if not idiosyncrasy, right from the origins of the discipline. Antoine de Montchrétien coined the concept of political economy in the seventeenth century. Turgot and Quesnay, the best known of the eighteenth-century physiocrats, were celebrated by the first classical economists such as Ricardo and Smith, and after them by Marx, as the true founders of the discipline. Jean-Baptiste Say, similarly, conceptualized some of the dynamics of the economy. During the first half of the nineteenth century, a few thinkers participated in the development of mainstream economics, such as Dupuit, who established the basis for the major micro-economic concept of marginal utility.[1] Alternative thinking on the economy was particularly rich, either in the anarchist tradition (Proudhon) or within the Marxist movement (Lafarge), although those thinkers and activists, for obvious reasons, did not claim a place in the professional world nor in the pantheon of economists.

The birth of modern mainstream economics can be dated in France to the creation in 1887 of its first academic journal, the *Revue d'Economie Politique*. This signalled the start of the current of so-called 'professors', who over three generations, marked by the epistemological tradition of 'eclecticism', mostly described institutions and collected tools in various theoretical frameworks, especially in the emergent marginalist school and in economic sociology. Apart from a few figures, this tradition had relatively little intellectual legacy. It is slightly later and in another context that the roots of the most important developments in economics in the post-1945 era can be found.

The aftermath of the First World War was in Europe a period of deep uncertainties, marked by social conflict, recurrent financial and monetary crisis and an inability to engage in an efficient reconstruction programme. Peace could well be perceived as a failure. In this context, a new generation of industrial managers and public administrators, who had often been engaged in the management of the war economy, came to the conclusion that modern society in its complexity required new forms of 'scientific' management in order to operate efficiently. These were often taught in scientific and engineering *grandes écoles* such as the Ecole Polytechnique or the Ecole Centrale, hence the name 'engineers' sometimes given to graduates later (Baslé et al., 1988). It was also frequently thought in these circles that the strategic components of the national economy could be better controlled by the public sector (but not in a collectivist way). Basically, the market was no longer seen as the most efficient tool for the social allocation of strategic resources. An important influence at the time was that of Fayol, an industry management specialist. In some ways, Fayol played a role in France comparable to Taylor in the USA. Interestingly, alongside this generation of public sector administrators, Fayol's ideas also found some favour in left-wing trade unions such as the CGT, which saw in these ideas possible ways for the scientific management of a future socialist society (Rosanvallon, 1990).

This generation of engineers came to the helm in the public sector, either as managers or researchers, or both, after 1945. The postwar reconstruction of the country was not only understood then as an economic and engineering project, but also as a socio-political overhaul of the very fabric of the nation. The ideas and ideologies that presided over this process were varied, mostly coming out of the main branches of the Resistance. Most agreed on the need for vigorous state intervention in the realm of the economy, as well as on the idea of collective responsibility.[2]

New, autonomous institutions were created in order to provide the necessary research and policy tools, and these were filled with the new breed of technicians of the economy. These people also took important posts in newly nationalized utilities, such as Electricité de France (EDF), where some of the most prestigious economists of the day conducted their research. Particularly relevant was the creation of the national statistics and economic research agency, the INSEE (and later of a *grande école* attached to it, to train statisticians). Even more important, the *Commissariat général du plan* was set up by Jean Monnet, its first director, as an independent elite think-tank that had a considerable influence on structural policies and economic policies of the state up to the late 1960s.[3] The political and intellectual importance of these bodies was also due to the need for building social consensus in a period of intense ideological and social conflicts between the two sides of industry. For instance, planning commissions were established in order to provide consensus-building material for the *Commissariat général* to establish the five-year plans. This was a rare instance in which civil servants, trade unionists, employers and representatives of other social lobbies debated together on economic and social issues. Deliberations needed to be backed by economic research, hence the development of a corpus of studies at INSEE and the *Commissariat général du plan*.

During the 1950s and the 1960s the position of INSEE, the Treasury and the *Commissariat général du plan* allowed for the development of applied economics, strategic studies, econometrics and economic modelling which had not been seen in France before. Interestingly, much of the conceptual development and economic policy framework came from the US, but one cannot say that Keynesian ideas were always hegemonic, despite their undeniable popularity. Although many tools from the new Keynesian approach were used, there were no qualms about reverting to neoclassical theory. Some neoclassicists, such as Jacques Rueff, an unreconstructed liberal monetarist in contact with Hayek, had criticized the New Deal and other demand-led types of policies since the prewar period. Rueff was a well-known international monetary advisor from the 1930s onwards, and a fierce defender of the Gold Standard. At the end of his life he became a monetary advisor to de Gaulle, devising the anti-inflation Rueff Plan in 1958–9 (Rueff, 1961).

Some of the most important names have now acquired an international stature. Maurice Allais, awarded the Nobel Prize for Economics in

1988, developed aspects of the theory of rational choice within a neo-classical theoretical framework (Allais, 1984). However, Allais, working in an age and in a society that put emphasis on collective economic mechanisms in market economies, contributed to the analysis of public sector choices based on the development of the concept of surplus. His theory of social yield (Allais, 1945) helped develop marginal cost tariff-setting in non-competitive markets (used for instance by public services and utilities). More recently Allais made the front pages by opposing the form taken by the Single European Currency.

Paul Massé, Marcel Boiteux and Claude Gruson are three other well-known figures of this important group of technocratic economists. The first two developed further the theory of marginal costing in non-competitive markets and the intricacies of peak-load pricing, and studied the economics of public sector investments (Massé, 1959). They were not only economists, but also managers in the public sector. Massé was *Commissaire Général au Plan* in the early 1960s (Massé, 1965) and Boiteux became the executive director of Electricité de France (EDF) when the electricity generating utility implemented its first nuclear investment programme in the mid-1960s. Gruson, a true Keynesian, worked in the 1950s at the Treasury where he created the Department of Economic and Financial Studies (soon to become the Forecasting Department) which became an important centre for research in econometrics. He then became head of INSEE for most of the 1960s, at a time when not only techniques of national accounting were progressing fast (Gruson, 1968), but also when the statistical agency was developing its economic studies which since 1970 have been published in its high-profile *Economie et statistique* journal.

Edmond Malinvaud and Jean Pascal Benassy, from a younger generation, proposed a rereading of Keynes, and developed further the theory of disequilibrium (Benassy, 1984). Malinvaud is well known for his participation in the now classic study of growth factors in the economy during the 1950s and 1960s (Carré, Dubois and Malinvaud, 1972), which demonstrates the importance of the role of human capital and social investment patterns in accelerated growth. More recently Malinvaud, who was Director of Forecasting at the Treasury and director of INSEE in the late 1960s before occupying a chair at the prestigious Collège de France, applied the theory of disequilibrium to the labour market and conducted a number of research projects on unemployment (Malinvaud, 1980, 1983, 1984). Also interested in epistemology and the methodology of economics (Malinvaud, 1991), he is now France's best prospect for another Nobel prize in economics.

It would be easy to see the postwar era as a schizophrenic period for the sociology and epistemology of economics. On the one hand, as noted above, the economics of public decision-making developed enormously. On the other hand, few developments occurred in the 1950s and 1960s within the two professional environments which in other countries often constituted the hotbeds of economic creativity – that is the academic and the corporate worlds. In universities, professors such as Jean Marchal and Jean Lecaillon, specialists of national income analysis, Jean Weiller and Maurice Byé, who were working on international economic institutions and exchanges, or Alain Barrère, continued a long analytical tradition based on descriptive statistics and an institutionalist approach. Raymond Barre, professor of economics but also EEC commissioner and then Prime Minister and Finance Minister in the second half of the 1970s, is an emblematic figure of the theoretical eclecticism of many university economists of this time, expounding a cautious and comfortable mix of neo-Keynesianism and neoclassical synthesis on which generations of students were trained (Barre, 1966).[4] However, there were bridges between the engineers on one side and the academic world on the other. Specialized research institutions, such as the economic laboratories of the Ecole Pratique des Hautes Etudes en Sciences Sociales (where Gruson was Director of Studies) and the Ecole Normale Supérieure, and other centres such as François Perroux's Institut de Sciences Mathématiques et Économiques Appliquées (SMEA), were able to connect the two worlds.

By contrast with the US, where economists for a long time had a recognized status within large firms and financial institutions, there were relatively few economists in the private sector in France before the 1970s. There were few large private concerns – those which did exist were often under-capitalized and family-controlled – and the financial markets were quite narrow with their role largely carried out by public financial institutions. It was only in the 1980s that private capital really started developing in France, through concentration of capital, privatization programmes and the creation of proper financial markets: the professional economists then appeared on the corporate scene.

A tradition of heterodoxies

The mainstream economic currents that dominated the period of the Thirty Glorious Years, namely Keynesian or neoclassical, were accompanied – or more exactly, opposed – by 'heterodox' economics, proposing alternative theoretical frameworks and analytical methods, and often advocating radical changes in economic structure. This is not surprising. The relentless process of modernization of the industrial economy, in a society with especially deep inequalities, was creating considerable social conflicts, to which mainstream economics were not able, or were not seen to be able, to respond. Furthermore, both social science and political life in France have always been strongly influenced by various forms of radical intellectual currents, such as Marxism, socialism or anarchism. This was especially the case during the 1960s, when there were large-scale protests, including the celebrated May 1968 student revolt and workers' general strike, which drew on and would feed these currents.

Heterodox economics were particularly diverse. In the case of Marxist economics, for instance, the whole spectrum of ideological differentiation that had developed since the beginning of the century was represented in France, and the various shades of Trotskyism were an extreme case of subdivisions. Of the currents of Marxism which counted intellectually during the Thirty Glorious Years, only two were relevant.[5] The first was made up of groups attempting to regenerate Marxism out of the Stalinist mould, often made up of ex-members of the Communist Party who had left or had been excluded in 1956 or at other times. Many wrote in the journals *Socialisme ou Barbarie* and *Arguments*. Particularly relevant is the renewal of social class analysis by Nicos Poulanzas (1974) and by Cornelius Castoriadis, or the analysis of bureaucracy by Claude Lefort.

On the other hand, the French Communist Party, which was still a considerable force to be reckoned with, was redeveloping its economic framework after the Stalinist period and other changes such as the end of the decolonization process marked by the independence of Algeria in 1962. Communist economists, such as Herzog, Boccara or Delaunay, grouped around the journal *Economie et Politique*, developed the concept of state monopoly capitalism (Boccara, 1973) in order to account for the specificity of the French economic system. This was the basis for a considerable amount of analysis at the time including the peculiarities of the mode of development of French socio-economic structures, with particular attention given to the role of the state apparatus in coordinating, funding and managing the economy: 'In the current period, capitalist exploitation is by no means confined to the framework of the firm. It is a global phenomenon. Intervention of the state in state monopoly capitalism constitutes the decisive element in the continuation of exploitation' (Dufour et al., 1970). This theory was used in order to define the parameters of an 'anti-monopolistic alliance' (a kind of updated Popular Front) that would manage the capitalist system in a transition period towards socialism. The signature of the *Programme Commun de Gouvernement* between the Communist Party and Socialist Party, in 1972 was the first step in this direction. The theory, however, was widely criticized for its lack of rigour and unresolved contradictions, as well as its heavy-handedness. It had few followers after the end of the 1970s.

Another branch of economics which was strongly influenced by neo-Marxism was the study of the world economy and especially relations between South and North. The critique of imperialism and neo-imperialism, by people such as Palloix, Castells or Bettelheim, was deeply influenced by the Latin-American Desarollo school (Cardoso, Furtado and so on) and others such as Frank, Baran and Sweezy especially. The most celebrated member of this group was Samir Amin (Amin, 1970, 1973), an Egyptian economist working mostly from France, who developed concepts such as the center/periphery dichotomy.

Another author, who is impossible to classify but who has wielded a considerable influence, is François Perroux. Unattached to any school but often described as 'structuralist' (Baslé et al., 1988), he played in France a similar role to the one Schumpeter played in the Anglo-American world. Far from being a Marxist but interested in many of its aspects, Perroux was a Christian humanist (Perroux, 1961) and also a technocrat who worked intensively on national accounts and econometrics, and was also critical of Keynesianism. He attempted to build analytical bridges between social, political and economic structures (Perroux, 1960). He also researched the dynamics of economic power, especially at an international level, in the context of developing nations (Perroux, 1969). Perroux did not in fact leave a coherent school behind him, but he influenced several generations of economists, both within and outside of the institute he created and then directed for a long time, the ISMEA; his influence was particularly important for the Regulation School. He was typical of independent economists, who were both planners close to public institutions and academics attempting an eclectic synthesis, but not fully part of either world. His enduring legacy is that, although a specialist of econometric modelling, he put much effort into reinserting social considerations into economic analysis.

The originality of French economics during the postwar period is therefore twofold. Under the hegemonic consensus of Keynesian and neoclassical systems of analysis and their derived policy systems, economics has focused upon the role of the state and the public sector. The downside of this is that the analysis of the firm and of international markets was left largely untouched, but economists have written extensively on the interaction between economic and social spheres, drawn in this direction by heterodox currents.

The emergence of the *pensée unique* and the return of ism

Neither the 'engineers' nor the eclectic academics really managed to get to grips with the economic crisis which erupted in 1973–4. However, this provoked a radical realignment of mainstream economics, the consequences of which have been felt ever since. The change of strategy of socialist governments in the early 1980s (Fonteneau and Muet, 1984), and the conversion of the whole political right to economic liberalism (including the Gaullist party, previously attached to an interventionist approach) signalled the emergence of a consensual economic strategy firmly based on liberal principles, the *pensée unique* outlined above.

In the medium term, the proponents of this strategy could rightly claim that it had been a success. Inflation has fallen to among the lowest world-wide for a number of years and the deregulation and privatization programme has largely been implemented. But, as noted earlier, these gains were at the cost of growing unemployment, from one million jobless in 1981 to more than three million in 1996. This was accompanied by a resurgence of poverty (named *nouvelle pauvreté* in the 1970s, before the extent of multidimensional deprivation brought to the fore the concept of *exclusion*) and, from 1985 onwards, a marked increase in inequality of income and wealth distribution.

In terms of economics as a social science, a dual movement characterizes the period from the early 1970s to the late 1990s. First, neoclassical theories supporting the dominant liberal policies gained a wider acceptance; second, the backlash against the *pensée unique* brought a resurgence of neo-Keynesian theories and research. This upheaval was accompanied by changes in the status of economists.

Claims about the sclerosis of Keynesianism and the inefficiency of French interventionism started quite early. After all, it was during the 1960s that French society was said to be 'blocked' by bureaucratic administration and interventionism (Crozier, 1963, 1970), and the American model of free enterprise was both proposed and perceived as a threat for France (Servan-Schreiber, 1967). In the late 1960s and early 1970s much work was done, away from the limelight, in research groups such as the *Cercle Aftalion*, which developed neoliberal theories inspired by the North American neoliberal revival. However, it was only in the late 1970s that liberal economists started to have a real impact. In 1977 the debate on the Gulag and the Stalinist terror had erupted in France, with the

Nouveaux philosophes making the front pages. An important collective book on liberal economics was published (Rosa and Aftalion, 1977) and the question of economic and social individualism was attracting new interest (Dumont, 1977). In 1978, liberal intellectuals, from the elderly liberal philosopher Raymond Aron to economists such as Jean-Claude Casanova, created the CIEL (Comité des Intellectuels pour l'Europe des Libertés) in order to promote liberal values with the motto 'Freedom cannot be negotiated'. The same year, the influential journal *Commentaires* was launched, edited by Casanova. Henri Lepage, an economic journalist who had published extensively on the free market, introduced ultra-liberal US economists in a best-seller (Lepage, 1978) and with a number of articles and some media publicity, the *Nouveaux économistes*, dubbing themselves 'new' as a reference to the new philosophers who were then at the peak of their fame, took on the task of breaking up the traditional neo-Keynesian and interventionist consensus. In fact, the mood had already changed, and the new economists were simply importing from the Anglo-American world the neoclassical and liberal economic philosophy and policy prescriptions that they needed. The sociologist René Boudon brought in the theory of 'sociological individualism' (Boudon, 1979), explaining collective phenomena by rational calculations and anticipations of autonomous individuals, therefore reinforcing the liberal analysis of markets. In terms of political economy, liberal economists were denouncing 'institutional blockage' in France in favour of state interventionism and the 'prejudice against business' (Lévy-Leboyer and Casanova, 1991), and advocating rolling back the frontiers of the state (Crozier, 1987), the deregulation of markets (especially labour) and so on. In a word, the political programme and economic policy framework was remarkably comparable to those applied in the US and Britain.[6]

Interestingly the leading liberal economists mostly come from a new generation of academics. They are working in business schools such as the Ecole Supérieure des Sciences Economiques et Commerciales (ESSEC) in Paris (Florin Aftalion) and Université de Paris-Dauphine (Pascal Salin, Christian Stoffaes), whereas Jean-Jacques Rosa and Jean-Claude Casanova are professors at the Institut d'Etudes Politiques. New universities such as the Université de Paris-Dauphine, which has one of the main business schools in France, now challenge the domination of the *grandes écoles*. Changes in the conception of the state, and changes in the nature of university research also helped to encourage new research centres which participate more fully than in the past in public and corporate debates. It is not only liberal economics that benefit from new spaces for research, for example, the Observatoire Français de la Conjoncture Economique (OFCE), attached to the National Foundation for Political Science, has become a neo-Keynesian research centre of international repute under the leadership of Jean-Paul Fitoussi and Pierre-Alain Muet, conducting many econometric studies published in its journal *Observations et Diagnostiques Economiques* (Fitoussi and Sigogne, 1994). Another independent research centre, the Centre d'Etudes Prospectives d'Economie Mathematique Appliquée (CEPREMAP), has been instrumental in the development of the Regulation School. Thus the monopoly of the public sector on successful economists, via the 'engineers', is now broken. Similarly, it is now accepted that most important corporations and financial institutions in the private sector employ economists. This started to be the case after the Big Bang of 1986 through which the financial system (banking, insurance and the stock exchange) was largely deregulated and lost its corporatist and closed structure. Some of these corporate economists now have a high profile, especially the chief economists of the main banks such as BNP, Suez or Paribas, who regularly appear in TV news bulletins in the same way as their British or North American colleagues.

As we have seen, the success of this current of thought was that significant elements were translated into the field of economic policy in such a homogeneous way that all governments since 1983 have carried out relatively similar policies, the so-called *pensée unique*. But this was not to go unchallenged for long and the recognition of the depth of social divisions in the mid-1990s gave new publicity to the opponents of such *pensée unique*. Indeed, there is an intense public debate in France on possible alternative sets of policies, fed by research from economists of opposing views.[7]

Indeed, the variety of economic currents in France was illustrated by the rainbow-like composition of the Conseil d'Analyse Economique created by the newly formed Socialist government of Lionel Jospin in July 1997. This 39–strong body provides advice to the government by preparing reports on topical socio-economic issues and its role therefore is quite different from the US Council of Economic Advisers or John Major's Wise Men who dealt with advising the UK government on financial and monetary matters. The Council reports have covered topics as varied as the reduction of working time, the role of public services in the economy, the links between growth and unemployment, and the European coordination of economic policy (Conseil d'Analyse Economique, 1998). There could not be more varied people in the membership of this council, grouping many of the main names in the profession from free-market liberals (Jean-Jacques Rosa, Gérard Maarek) to neo-Keynesians (Jean-Paul Fitoussi, Pierre-Alain Muet, Olivier Blanchard or Jean Pisani-Ferry), Regulationists (Alain Lipietz, Robert Boyer) and neo-Marxists (Philippe Herzog). There are also specialists in various fields such as monetary economics (Christian de Boissieu), industrial policy (Elie Cohen), labour economics (Edmond Malinvaud) and so on.

In other words, the Council is a microcosm in which most of the French schools of thought are represented. This variety has been made possible by the resurgence of neo-Keynesianism as a reaction to the social consequences of existing economic policies. In the mid-1990s a growing number of economists, mostly neo-Keynesians or those close to the Regulation School signed a petition requesting a reversal of many principles of economic policy which had been applied in France more or less continuously since 1983 (Appel..., 1996). Two of the main points of contention concern first the economics of the labour market, and second the monetary and budgetary policies forced onto France in order to conform to the discipline imposed by the Single European Currency project.

The issues of labour costs, labour flexibility, unemployment and cost competitiveness are among the main points of divergence between liberals and neo-Keynesians. Liberals, using the experience of the USA and the arsenal of neoclassical analysis applied to the labour markets, seek to show that the only way to reduce unemployment is to reduce labour costs. This should be achieved by eliminating wage 'rigidities' (for instance the existence of a minimum wage), by reducing social insurance premiums paid by employers, which are high in France, and deregulating the labour market in order to increase the flexibility of labour (Maarek, 1994). The response of neo-Keynesians is to show that there is no direct correlation between labour costs and employment. Other ways of reducing labour market rigidities can be found, for instance by creating jobs in high productivity areas (as the main cost indicator is labour productivity) and organizing the sharing of work by reducing working time (Hoang-Ngoc Liêm, 1996). This position has often been reinforced by tools derived from 'endogenous growth' theories, especially the work of Barro (1990) and Romer (1990).

The other major debate concerns the monetary and financial strategies followed since the mid-1980s. The 'competitive disinflation' strategy aims at reducing inflationary trends in order to increase the competitiveness of the French economy and France therefore would be able in the long term to have low interest rates; in other words, there would be a virtuous circle. Opponents of this strategy sought to demonstrate that, far from being a virtuous circle, the strategy was a never-ending race forcing France to have higher interest rates than Germany and to maintain an artificially high value of the franc; the result was increased long-term unemployment (Fitoussi, 1997). In other words, the painful means became the end. At best, the strategy could work, but after such a long lead time that the social cost would be enormous and it would be better to seek alternative policies (Fitoussi et al., 1993). For long, it looked as if the validity of this analysis had been proven by the events. As emphasized above, unemployment has soared uninterruptedly since 1982, only falling briefly in the late 1980s and then in 1998, and the number of people below the poverty line is probably over 10 million in the late 1990s, with inequalities reaching levels not known since the 1960s. The victims of this social crisis hold the *pensée unique* and the EU liberal economic strategies fully responsible for this sorry state of affairs. There were mass social movements at the end of 1995 and, more crucially, the long-term unemployed organized mass demonstrations and occupations of unemployment offices all over France at the end of 1997 and in 1998. However, the position of the liberal analysts is that the bitter medicine has not yet been applied with sufficient rigour and there are still too many constraints in France; the labour market is still to too rigid, social costs of employment and taxes still too high (Salin, 1986).

Other signs exist that many French people resent the economic medicine that has been implemented since the mid-1980s. In 1996 the writer Viviane Forrester, previously better known for her novels and cultural essays, published a book entitled *L'Horreur économique* to considerable – and unexpected – popular success (Forrester, 1996). True to its title, this book denounces the ever-increasing importance of anonymous, rigorous economic efficiency criteria for decision-making in French society, and the lack of control over unfettered market forces in the *libéralisme sauvage* that has been dominating France since the early 1980s. The attack stung mainstream economists, and a flood of articles were published defending the honour of economists and attempting to explain that Forrester had deeply misunderstood the basics of the profession and of the discipline... which was not the point of the book.

However, the Jospin government in 1998 chose a cautious middle way, maintaining a rigorous financial orthodoxy in budgetary and monetary matters, especially for the sake of the Euro project, but at the same time adopting a radically innovative strategy in relation to unemployment (Taddei and Cette, 1997). The Aubry Act, bearing the name of Martine Aubry, Minister for Employment and Social Affairs, established working time at 35 hours per week, with strict limits to overtime and partial wage compensation. Public subsidies are offered to companies in order to offset supplementary costs to the firm as long as they take on new employees, and calculations show that these subsidies are lower than the cost to the state of unemployment benefits. This policy is vigorously opposed by liberal economists and by most employers. It is supported not only by neo-Keynesians, but also by heterodox currents of economic thought.

Contemporary developments in heterodoxy: the Regulation School

The Regulation School is probably the best known innovative approach to economics to emerge from France in recent decades. It has opened a number of promising lines of research, using a relatively coherent theoretical and methodological framework. Some of the economists belonging to this school are now quite well known and are among the few contemporary French economists who are quoted internationally. Names such as Aglietta, Lipietz or Boyer, which have already appeared in this chapter, are probably the most important of them, but this school of thought has now diversified in many areas of concern and in many countries (Boyer and Saillard, 1995). The School should not be reduced to macro-economics or to political economy. Aglietta, for instance, is now better known as a specialist in international monetary economics and Boyer has researched applications of game theory. Lipietz is also known for his thinking on the economics of development (Lipietz, 1986) and the environment (for a number of years he has been the leading economics expert of the French Green Party, Les Verts). The Regulation School also often seeks support in econometric and quantitative methods, and cannot be attacked for being thin on empirical research as were previous alternative schools, such as most neo-Marxist and structuralist ones.

The singularity of the approach of the Regulation School is that it analyses markets and economic agents (such as the state and financial bodies) as complex institutions linked with others through complex and changing social relations (such as the wage relation and the monetary system), within a process of accumulation of capital going through several phases. Capitalism is analysed as a system in constant redevelopment, through conflicts, imbalances and crisis within structures. Regulation is not a set of rules, or law-like regulations, applied to a set of markets in order to regulate it. As Boyer says, it is 'the conjunction of mechanisms which combine for general reproduction, within given economic structures and existing social forms' (Boyer, 1987: 30). Regulation refers therefore to the mechanisms and processes within a specific economic structure and society which ensure the 'regularity' of its continuous functioning, or reproduction.

The main type of economic phenomenon studied by the Regulation School is the capitalist mode of production in advanced industrialized economies. These economies, explain the Regulationists, after a long period of 'extensive accumulation' (during which capitalism developed mostly through the penetration of new markets, hence the development of colonial empires), went into a period of 'intensive capital accumulation' which means a high intensity of capital used in Taylorist production management systems as well as accumulation of financial capital, which developed between the two World Wars in the USA. This Fordist regime was established on a wage relation and on a social norm of mass consumption which normally guarantee the necessary markets for mass-produced goods. It also involves a significant role for the state. However, there are differences between various types of Fordist economies. The French model in the 1950s and 1960s, for instance, gives to the state a central role in the organization of the process of accumulation in guaranteeing the social distribution of the product as well as the regularity of the labour supply through the welfare state, hence the expression 'state Fordism'.

The issue of over-accumulation of capital, which occurred from around 1967 onwards and manifested itself in the growing international monetary crisis from 1970, is seen by many Regulationists as the origin of the further general crises of advanced Fordist economies around 1974, 1979 and 1992. These crises also affected the wage relationship and the role of the state in most economies, destroying much of the fragile social compromise between social classes and bringing new forms of wage relationship and organization of production (for instance the Toyotist organization of production, or flexible labour). However, a given economy, placed in a particular point in history and in a specific country, is never the expression of a pure mode of accumulation and regulation. Many debates on Fordism and post-Fordism fail to understand that, in a country such France, varied modes of regulation and processes of accumulation operate alongside each other, depending on the sector of activity (Boyer and Durand, 1993), and their interaction is often a contributory element to dysfunction and crisis in the economy.

It is not surprising that the Regulation School appeared around the time of the mid-1970s events that signalled a crisis of the relatively successful mode of production in a country such as France. Although the starting point of the School is often identified as Michel Aglietta's seminal book on the development and crisis in the regimes of capital accumulation in the United States (Aglietta, 1976), much of the research had been done on the French economy. He was not alone in France in using the concept of regulation at the time and it was discussed in many social sciences from the 1960s onwards, notably by Canguilhem in his epistemological article for the *Encyclopedia Universalis* (Canguilhem, 1980). The concept of regulation especially appealed to a number of neo-Marxist social scientists, who saw in it a possible way out of the impasse of the Althusserian concept of 'overdetermination'. Indeed, the Marxist influence on the Regulation School has been very strong, although it has disappeared among the main protagonists, especially Aglietta and Boyer. Other noticeable influences are those of François Perroux who had a seminar on regulation at the Collège de France in the mid-1970s (Lichnerowicz, Perroux and Gadoffre, 1977), and also historians of the long term, especially Braudel (Braudel, 1979; Braudel and Labrousse, 1982) and the Annales School.

There are in fact three main currents in the Regulation School. The main one, some of whose principal ideas have been briefly summarized above, developed from work by Aglietta and by members of the CEPRE-MAP such as Boyer, Mistral and Orléan. Mainly based in Paris, it is sometimes dubbed the 'intensive accumulation' current. Two others are perhaps less well known. The so-called 'systemic school' mostly includes leading members of the old *Economie et société* journal, such as Boccara and Herzog, who developed the state monopoly capitalism theory in the early 1970s. Another one is the Marxist Regulation School that developed around the work of the Groupe de Recherche sur la Régulation de l'Economie Capitaliste (GRECC) Institute at Grenoble University. Born at about the same time as the Paris current, or even before, these two groups criticize it on various grounds. In particular, they attack it for giving too much weight to institutional arrangements (suspecting some influence from American institutionalists) and often falling into functionalist analytical traps. In their analysis, the so-called *rapport salarial* is replaced by class exploitation. However, Aglietta among others clearly makes a point of differentiating the Regulation School from Marxism; in twentieth-century Fordist capitalism, labour is integrated (and not excluded as an external class) in the core of the reproduction process (Aglietta and Brender, 1984).

Around the figures of Destanne de Bernis (better known previously for his concept of 'industrialising industries' applied to the Algerian development model in the late 1960s) and Claude Barrère, the Grenoble current keeps essential elements of Marxist economic theory, especially such concepts as the propensity of the rate of profit to fall and the trend towards equalization of profit between sectors (Destanne de Bernis, 1985). It insists on class relations and the exploitation of labour as core components of the mode of regulation (Barrère, 1985). On the side of 'systemic regulation', Boccara, who twenty years earlier had been a leading force behind the theory of state monopoly capitalism, declared that he and the other official French Communist Party economists invented the concept of regulation (Boccara, 1993) through their study of long-term cycles and over-accumulation followed by 'devalorization' of capital. He claims that they were proved right from the start by pointing out that the beginning of the crisis of Fordist capitalism should be dated 1967, rather than 1970 or 1973–4, and that the best neo-Keynesian econometric analysis performed by the Observatoire Français de la Conjoncture Economique came to the same conclusions (Jeanneney, 1989).

Other Marxist economists have been deeply critical of all the Regulation School currents. For instance de Brunhoff, a specialist in financial and monetary economics (de Brunhoff, 1976) declared that regulation is only 'an avatar of the concept of equilibrium. This concept is only relevant if society is analysed as non-contradictory in its constitution. Regulation of a society of class struggle is meaningless' (de Brunhoff and Cartelier, 1974). At the same time, it has to be recognized that the theory of regulation, in various guises, has given a new lease of life to the analysis of capitalist economies surviving and thriving through crisis, within or from outside a Marxist perspective.

Clearly, the Regulation School is very far from both neoclassical economics and modern liberalism, as its approach to market and exchange could not be more different. But it is also very different from neo-Keynesianism, as the latter is not particularly concerned with structural social processes and long-term trends. A typical difference concerns the understanding of the most recent economic recession in 1992–3. For instance, Boyer writes that 'the current recession is without precedent. Indeed, it is the expression of an unachieved as well as imperfect regulation... 1992–93 is not "a business cycle as usual"! It is rather a turning point between a decrepit Fordist regulation and still uncertain new principles' (Boyer, 1993). To this, Muet, a Keynesian from OFCE, answers in the same journal that 1992–3 is

a world recession that can be compared to the ones that followed the two oil crisis in terms of depth and geographical extent. However, the current situation differs greatly from the stagflation shocks of 1974 and 1979, and it has some common characteristics, relatively speaking, with the periodic crises in industrial economies before the Second World War.

(Muet, 1993)

In other words, according to Muet, the structure stays broadly the same, only the cycles and the policies change. However, as noted earlier, Regulationists and neo-Keynesians very often work together on questions of economic policy and short-term analysis, using each others' research, and have criticized the *pensée unique* in very similar terms.

In the above examination of heterodox currents presenting alternative analysis to the mainstream schools of economic thought, I have focused exclusively on the Regulation School in three of its main forms, but there are many other heterodox perspectives. For instance, there is the economy of conventions and the original approach of André Gorz (1988), or the Mouvement Anti-utilitariste dans les Sciences Sociales (MAUSS) group (Caillé, 1994). However, a discussion of the main currents in modern France has helped to show how economics as a social science feeds from the society in which it develops, and relates to the other great debates and issues that exist in such a society.

Indeed, although French authorities and economic leaders have broadly followed in the footsteps of the North American evolution of the discipline (especially in relation to the great split between neo-Keynesians and neoclassicists, with all its ideological overtones), the main debates and intellectual developments relate to issues specifically relating to the evolution of the French economy. In the last quarter of the century, the most important research themes, and indeed the most important developments arising from this research, concern the dramatic issues confronted by French society as a whole. Why did the relatively successful French model of development enter a long period of crisis in the early 1970s? Why and how did the brunt of the crisis fall on employment? How is the role of the state in the economy changing, especially in the context of European integration? The various currents of economic analysis provide contradictory and incomplete answers, but there are a number of enriching dialogues, especially between the Regulation and the neo-Keynesian perpectives, which bring some hope that economic research will help in developing new strategies to take the economy out of crisis.

Notes

1   This history is still relevant today and indeed one of the major contemporary think-tanks in the field of political economy was called the *Fondation Saint-Simon*. Saint-Simon, a theoretician and entrepreneur during the Second Empire, is one of the inspirers of a type of socially-aware entrepreneurial liberalism, not afraid of associating itself with the state when it sees fit.
2   Hence the creation of a mutual system of National Insurance, rather than a welfare state as in the UK. Both the unions and the employers' organizations, distrustful of institutions and of each other, wanted a stake in the management of social insurance using mechanisms that had been developed prior to the Second World War.
3   Even now, when the Plan is no longer a significant policy-making tool, the studies emanating from or commissioned by the *Commissariat* are still considered to be important. For instance, the study *France 2000*, which has a strong liberal slant, quite different from the traditional 'flexible planning' approach, had a considerable impact when it was published in 1994 (Minc, 1994).
4   The so-called *Circuit* School, represented by people such as Albertini, is also representative of this tradition. Its analysis of the economy was pedagogically useful, but it had little more to offer since it tautologically described the economy as a self-contained set of forces counterbalancing each other (Paquot and Piriou, 1989).
5   Other Marxist thinkers were influential in the field of economics, of course, even when they were not primarily working on economic issues. For example, Louis Althusser's re-reading of Marx had a strong influence on many debates in the 1960s and early 1970s (Althusser, 1964).
6   Sometimes their understanding of the libertarian free-market philosophy was quite hazy. For instance, Lepage lumped Rawls and Hayek together, although Hayek in fact bitterly opposed John Rawls' theories (Lepage, 1980). This is typical of the lack of knowledge by many French intellectuals of developments in social sciences abroad. Another illustration of this is the fact that Polyani's main book, *The Great Transformation*, was only translated and published in France in 1983, nearly forty years after its first publication in 1944.
7   These economists are indeed listened to in the political elite. Governments of the last three decades have had many economists in them, or at least top civil servants trained at the Ecole Nationale d'Administration or the Ecole Polytechnique. Of the last ten prime ministers, three were economists (Barre, Rocard and Jospin) and six were ENA graduates (Chirac, Balladur, Juppé, Fabius, Rocard, Jospin) with a strong grounding in economics.

References

Aglietta, Michel (1976) *Régulation et crises du capitalisme. L'expérience des Etats-Unis.* Paris: Calmann-Levy; translated as *A Theory of Capitalist Regulation: The US Experience.* London: New Left Books, 1979.
Aglietta, Michel (1986) *La Fin des devises clés.* Paris: La Découverte.
Aglietta, Michel and Brender, Anton (1984) *Les Métamorphoses de la société salariale.* Paris: Calmann-Levy.

Aglietta, Michel and Orléan, André (1984) *La Violence de la monnaie*. Paris: Presses Universitaires de France.

Allais, Maurice (1945) *Economie pure et rendement social*. Paris: Sirey.

—— (1984) *The Foundations of the Theory of Utility and Risk*. Dordrecht: D. Reidel.

Althusser, Louis (1965) *Pour Marx*. Paris: Maspero; translated as *For Marx*. London: Verso, 1990.

Amin, Samir (1970) *L'Accumulation à l'échelle mondiale – critique de la théorie du sous-développement*. Paris: Anthropos.

—— (1973) *Le Développement inégal – essai sur les formes sociales du capitalisme périphérique*. Paris: Editions de Minuit.

Appel des économistes pour sortir de la pensée unique (1997) *La Monnaie unique en débat*. Paris: Syros.

Barre, Raymond (1966) *Economie Politique*, 2 vols. Paris: Presses Universitaires de France.

Barrère, Claude (1984) 'L'Objet d'une théorie de la régulation', *Economies et Sociétés*. Cahiers de l'ISMEA, Serie R, no.1: L'Approche en termes de régulation 9–28. Grenoble: Presses Universitaires de Grenoble.

Barro, Robert J. (1990) 'Government spending in a simple model of endogenous growth', *Journal of Political Economy*, 98 (5): 103–25.

Baslé, Maurice et al. (1988) *Histoire des pensées économiques. Les contemporains*. Paris: Sirey.

Benassy, Jean-Pascal (1984) *Macroéconomie et théorie du déséquilibre*. Paris: Dunod.

Boccara, Paul (1976) *Traité d'économie politique: le capitalisme monopolistique d'état*. Paris: Editions Sociales.

—— (1993) 'Une Approche néomarxiste de la crise', *Alternatives Economiques*, Hors-série 16: 12.

Boudon, René (1979) *La Logique du social*. Paris: Hachette.

Boyer, Robert (1987) *La Théorie de la régulation. Une analyse critique*. Paris: La Découverte.

—— (1993) 'La Crise – sans précédent', *Le Monde des Débats*, 12: 1–2.

Boyer, Robert and Durand, Jean-Pierre (1993) *L'Après-fordisme*. Paris: Syros.

Boyer, Robert and Saillard, Yves (eds) (1995) *Théorie de la régulation, l'état des savoirs*. Paris: La Découverte.

Braudel, Fernand (1979) *Civilisation matérielle, économie et capitalisme*, 3 vols. Paris: Armand Colin.

Braudel, Fernand and Labrousse, Ernest (1982) *Histoire économique et sociale de la France, 1950–1980*, vol. IV. Paris: Presses Universitaires de France.

de Brunhoff, Suzanne (1976) *Etat et capital*. Paris: François Maspero/Presses Universitaires de Grenoble.

de Brunhoff, Suzanne and Cartelier, Jean (1974) *Financement et politique bourgeoise*. Paris: Presses Universitaires de France.

Caillé, Alain (1994) *Don, intérêt et désintéressement: Boursieu, Mauss, Platon et quelques autres*. Paris: La Découverte.

Canguilhem, Georges (1980) 'Régulation', in *Encyclopedia Universalis*, vol. 14. Paris.

Carré, Jean-Jacques, Dubois, Paul and Malinvaud, Edmond (1972) *La Croissance française*. Paris: Editions du Seuil.

Conseil d'analyse économique (1998) *Coordination européenne des politiques économiques*. Paris: La Documentation Française.

Crozier, Michel (1963) *Le phénomène bureaucratique*. Paris: Le Seuil; translated as *The Bureaucratic Phenomenon*. London: Tavistock, 1964.
—— (1970) *La société bloquée*. Paris: Le Seuil.
—— (1987) *Etat modeste, Etat moderne*. Paris: Fayard.
Destanne de Bernis, Gérard (1984) 'Sur quelques concepts nécessaires à la théorie de la régulation', *Economies et Sociétés*. Cahiers de l'ISMEA, Serie R, no.1: L'Approche en termes de régulation, 103–30. Grenoble: Presses Universitaires de Grenoble.
Dufour, Jean-Claude et al. (1970) *Economie politique du capitalisme monopolistique d'état*. Paris: Editions Sociales.
Dumont, Louis (1977) *Homo Aequalis*. Paris: Gallimard.
Fitoussi, Jean-Paul (1995) *Le Débat interdit*. Paris: Arlea.
Fitoussi, Jean-Paul and Sigogne, Philippe (1994) *Les Cycles économiques*, 2 vols, Paris: Presses de la Fondation Nationale des Sciences Politiques.
Fitoussi, Jean-Paul et al. (1993) *Competitive Disinflation: The Mark and Budgetary Politics in Europe*. Oxford: Oxford University Press.
Fonteneau, Alain and Muet, Pierre-André (1985) *La Gauche face à la crise*. Paris: Fondation Nationale des Sciences Politiques.
Forrester, Viviane (1996) *L'Horreur économique*. Paris: Fayard.
Fourastié, Jean (1979) *Les Trente glorieuses*. Paris: Fayard.
Gorz, André (1988) *Métamorphoses du travail – Quête du sens*. Paris: Galilée.
Gruson, Claude (1968) *Origines et espoirs de la planification française*. Paris: Dunod.
Hoang-Nngoc Lièm (1996) *Salaires et emploi – une critique de la pensée unique*. Paris: Syros.
Jeanneney, Jean-Marcel (ed) (1989) *L'économie française depuis 1967: la traversée des turbulences mondiales*. Paris: Editions du Seuil.
Lepage, Henri (1978) *Demain le capitalisme*. Paris: Le Livre de Poche.
—— (1980) *Demain le libéralisme*. Paris: Le Livre de Poche.
Lévy-Leboyer, Maurice and Casanova, Jean-Claude (eds) (1991) *Entre l'Etat et le marché – L'économie française des années 1880 à nos jours*. Paris: Gallimard.
Lichnerowitz, Alain, Perroux, François and Gadoffre, Gérard (1977) *L'Idée de régulation dans les sciences*. Paris: Maloine-Doin.
Lipietz, Alain (1985) *Mirages et miracles*. Paris: La Découverte; translated as *Mirages and Miracles*. London: Verso, 1988.
Maarek, Gérard (1994) *Rapport du groupe 'Perspectives Economiques'*. Paris: Commissariat Général du Plan.
Malinvaud, Edmond (1980) *Réexamen de la théorie du chômage*. Paris: Calmann-Levy.
—— (1983) *Essais sur la théorie du chômage*. Paris: Calman-Levy.
—— (1984) *Mass Unemployment*. London: Basil Blackwell.
—— (1991) *Voies de la recherche macroéconomique*. Paris: Odile Jacob.
Massé, Pierre (1959) *Le Choix des investissements*. Paris: Dunod.
—— (1965) *Le Plan ou l'anti-hasard*. Paris: Gallimard.
Minc, Alain (1994) *La France de l'an 2000*, Rapport au Premier Ministre, Commissariat Général du Plan. Paris: Odile Jacob/La Documentation française.
Muet, Pierre-Alain (1993) 'La Crise – Une récession après d'autres', *Le Monde des Débats*, 12: 3–4.
Paquot, Thierry and Piriou, Jean-Paul (eds) (1989) *La Science économique en France*. Paris: La Découverte.

Perroux, François (1948) *Le Capitalisme*. Paris: Presses Universitaires de France.

—— (1960) *Economie et société: contraintes, échange, don*. Paris: Presses Universitaires de France.

—— (1961) *L'Economie du XXème siècle*. Paris: Presses Universitaires de France.

—— (1969) *Indépendance de l'économie nationale et interdépendance des nations*. Paris: Union Générale d'Editions.

Poulantzas, Nicos (1974) *Les Classes sociales dans le capitalisme aujourd'hui*. Paris: Seuil.

Romer, Paul (1990) 'Endogenous technical change', *Journal of Political Economy*, 98 (5): 1002–37.

Rosa, Jean-Jacques and Aftalion, Florin (eds) (1977) *L'Economique retrouvée*. Paris: Economica.

Rosanvallon, Pierre (1990) *L'Etat en France de 1789 à nos jours*. Paris: Seuil.

Rueff, Jacques (1961) *Le Lancinant problème de la balance des paiements*. Paris: Payot.

Salin, Pascal (1986) *L'Arbitraire fiscal*. Paris: Robert Laffont.

Servan-Schreiber, Jean-Jacques (1967) *Le Défi américain*. Paris: Denoël.

Taddei, Dominique and Cette, Colette (1997) *Réduire le temps de travail*. Paris: Hachette, Le Livre de Poche.

9
Political Science and the Empirical Tradition

Nick Hewlett

A look at the way in which politics is studied in France suggests the following paradox: in a country whose recent intellectual history in the humanities, arts and much of the social sciences has been so famously one of elaborate theory and of abstraction, by stark contrast 'political science'[1] has been dominated by an approach which gives pride of place to facts.[2] The study of politics has been predominantly empirical and has been remarkably impervious to the huge intellectual production that has come to be known in Britain and the USA as 'continental philosophy'. For several decades after the Second World War, Marxist, neo-Marxist, structuralist or poststructuralist theory had a profound impact on the social sciences; the methodologically more liberal and more positivistic approach common in Britain and America in the postwar period was marginal in most spheres. This was not the pattern in political science, where by contrast research within a sophisticated theoretical framework was relatively rare. Explaining this paradox is a major goal of this chapter.

France has of course been home to some of the world's best-known political philosophers, including Rousseau, Montesquieu, Voltaire and Tocqueville, who have had a strong international and domestic influence and are still widely taught and written about in French universities. They are important figures in the history of political thought, and alongside more recent counterparts such as Alain and Raymond Aron – and nowadays others such as Luc Ferry and Alain Renaut – they continue to excite the interest of contemporary political philosophers. But the widespread and often rigorous study of political thought has not meant that students of politics (examining political parties, governments, public opinion, public policy and so on) have brought a strong and overarching theoretical framework to bear on their analyses. In fact the study of political thought occupies a semi-autonomous place in the politics discipline and any parallel in mainstream political science with the revolution inspired by Lévi-Strauss in anthropology, Touraine and Bourdieu in sociology or Lacan in psychoanalysis, for example, has simply not taken place.

This is not to deny the importance of much of the work on politics and government that has been carried out in universities and research centres in France since the Second World War. Writers and researchers have produced many books, articles and theses on subjects such as elections, constitutional law, political parties and public policy, and this has resulted in a wealth of information which is most useful. The writers Maurice Duverger, Jean Charlot, Olivier Duhamel, Collette Ysmal and many others have contributed greatly to our knowledge of modern politics and have presented invaluable information. But writers often remain frustratingly and uncritically close to the sources of their information and have made relatively few attempts to throw further light on their findings by setting them in a theoretical perspective. Another goal of this chapter is to point out that there have, however, been exceptions to the more descriptive, empirical rule and to highlight the attempts by non-mainstream theorists in France who also have a contribution to make to the study of concrete politics: these include Louis Althusser, Nicos Poulantzas, Michel Foucault and Pierre Bourdieu. I focus in particular on the work of Bourdieu who offers a radical, if incomplete, critique of conventional political science as well as of liberal democratic politics.

Natural science and social science

Any discussion of political science in France must take account of international factors as well as more country-specific considerations, for much of the accepted wisdom underpinning French political science is found elsewhere as well. Many mainstream political scientists in Western Europe and the USA work on the assumption that to be faithful to their discipline they must conduct it as if it were akin to a natural science. For many, political science is governed by rules which enable the accumulation of facts which, once gathered, are examined and classified. Then conclusions can be drawn and sometimes general laws induced from the data. Such claims to (natural) scientific method in political science are commonplace both in France and elsewhere and Philippe Braud sums up clearly the conception many political scientists have of their discipline in the introduction to his book *La Science politique* (now in its sixth edition) in the Que sais-je? series:

The approach of the political scientist is shaped by three main principles:

1. A separation which is as rigorous as possible between clinical examination on the one hand and a moral or partisan value judgement on the other.
2. The use of methods and techniques of investigation which are common to all social sciences. It is these which allow decisive breakthroughs as far as the establishment of facts is concerned and putting these facts in a proper context.
3. An attempt to be systematic, that is the putting forward of general analytical frameworks, and construction of models facilitating the discovery of 'laws'.

(Braud, 1995: 3)

Political science thus sets out to be scientific (in a positivistic sense) in its methods of investigation, with an emphasis on the gathering of data, and value-free and impartial in its conclusions. The generalizations and where possible general laws induced from observed facts are thus intended to be objective because empirically based; conclusions are suggested by the observation of facts rather than by reference to general theories.

This begs the (vast) question of course as to whether the objects which political scientists choose to study – but also those of sociologists, social anthropologists and economists – can be approached in the same way at the level of general method as the objects of study of physics, astronomy or biology. Many political scientists believe that if the raw facts of political life, and in particular all that is concerned with conventionally defined government, are gathered, examined, ordered and compared, then more and more will be discovered about the true nature of political life. Other, more theoretical approaches which address more overarching questions, moving further from the immediate facts of political life and dealing with broader questions of power, are dismissed as 'unscientific' and more akin to methods used in the arts and humanities (therefore inevitably less rigorous and less worthy). In the name of scientific accuracy, most political scientists have thus steered clear of general theory, as Madeleine Grawitz and Jean Leca comment in the Introduction to the vast overview of the discipline, *Traité de science politique*: 'Political science is practised in such a way that there are bits and pieces of explanation which may resemble laws – the chapters which follow contain some examples – but no "fundamental law(s)" whatsoever' (Grawitz and Leca, 1985: xi).

It is a premise of this chapter that an impartial, value-free social science is impossible, although there is not the space to discuss this in full. If one compares even briefly what is possible in political science with what is possible in biology, the differences are immediately clear. In biology experiments can be carried out where the conditions can for all intents and purposes be reproduced indefinitely. In the social sciences, by contrast, experimentation cannot be carried out in the same way; the conditions of a referendum, an election or a process of policy formation, for example, simply cannot be replicated with all the contingent socio-economic, socio-psychological and political circumstances, for the objects of study in the social sciences are necessarily historically specific. Just as importantly, the object of study in the social sciences is affected in a more direct way by the observer, who is inevitably and obviously implicated in the results of the study, and all the more so because the methodology is so weakly established in the first place. Finally, and perhaps most importantly, the social sciences inevitably involve value judgements because they take a position on issues which are in themselves matters of human choice; we are studying our own existences and inventing them at the same time, a process which makes value-free conclusions impossible (see Giddens, 1979: 244–5).

Certainly, conclusions are drawn as a result of observation of political facts, but the relatively few facts we select to support our conclusions or theories are chosen from a huge number of potential facts; this process of selection, and selection of areas of study for that matter, is already influenced by value judgements, and the same is true of the interpretations which we place on the facts. This is a premise with which many political philosophers of liberal persuasion might agree, including Alain and Raymond Aron in France; it is not the exclusive preserve of analysts influenced by Marx.

Political science claims to be value-free because it is, by contrast with other social sciences (except mainstream economics), steeped in the values of liberalism and liberal democracy; it has adopted as a constant point of reference the ideology of the time and therefore can pass as neutral. Liberal government was perhaps at its most convincing in the postwar period in many countries in the West, because this was the time when it seemed as if equality before the law, universal suffrage, open government and civil rights were able to guarantee a high standard of living, housing for all and relative absence of industrial conflict (although France was, arguably, anomalous in this respect – see Hewlett, 1998: 36–59). It seemed as if defence of the individual was the ultimate goal of just government. It seemed in other words that liberal democratic government was able to offer a better quality of life and that ultimately the job of political scientists was to reinforce this capacity. It reinforced rather than critiqued the overall system, it examined what was rather than what could be, instead of seeing liberal democracy as linked with a stage in socio-economic development that is historically specific. Political science had a profound antipathy towards historical materialism, because historical materialism denied the possibility of impartiality in looking at the nature of politics and stressed the dynamic, changing nature of politics (not to mention the limits of liberal democracy). The Cold War climate of the 1950s of course confirmed this approach. This is not social science as an objective or value-free line of enquiry, then, but an acceptance of things as they are; to be content with gathering and describing is also ultimately to condone the present order of things. This is reflected in Robert Dahl's comment in 1958 that 'in Anglo-Saxon countries, where so many interesting political problems have been solved (at least superficially) political theory is dead' (quoted in Leca, 1985: 88).

The paradox of the positivistic, empirical nature of political science in a country where theory was so important for so long is already less strange; it is explained partly by the context of the liberal democratic tradition and the relationship between the study of politics on the one hand and the practice of party and governmental politics on the other, where academic exploration and actual practice were more intimately connected than in the other social sciences.

The emergence and development of political science in France

Political science and the social sciences in general are a relatively recent phenomenon, and all emerged at roughly the same time in industrialized countries with the development of what may be described as 'modern society' and 'modern government', starting for the most part in the last third of the nineteenth century. The study of politics and society within the university is in fact an integral part of the coming of modernity and emphasizing this helps with an understanding of contemporary political science. The establishment of the social sciences came with the industrial revolution and the development of the modern university (Favre, 1985: 6–7), but the conditions of emergence of political science also include the rise of individualism, which goes hand in hand with urbanization, and what Habermas has described as the autonomization of public space as distinct from the private sphere (Habermas, 1978). The professionalization of politics is also part of this and, as indicated in the discussion above, liberalism and liberal democracy go with the establishment of political science as we know it.

In France the birth of modern political science came relatively late, at the end of the Second World War, constituting what Marcel Prélot has described as 'the end of an extraordinary deficiency' (Prélot, 1957). In a country which had produced many internationally known political philosophers, where the revolutionary ideals of 1789 had inspired governments and political movements worldwide, and where the *art* of politics had been explored for centuries, the process of modernization of the study of politics was delayed. Part of the reason for this is France's famous tendency to be conflictual and unstable and this contributed to governments' unwillingness to promote the widespread discussion of political principles in educational establishments; in an already deeply divided nation, with constant threats from abroad as well as within France, the last thing governments sought to promote was a systematic examination of political life.

The establishment of political science after the Second World War was closely related to the training of an elite which was to rebuild France from an economic, social and political point of view. The most obvious example of this was the creation of the Ecole Nationale d'Administration (ENA) in 1946, designed to train the brightest young students to serve in the state's *grands corps*. Part also of the increasing size and influence of the bureaucratic elite in the immediate postwar period was the establishment of the Paris Institut d'Etudes Politiques, another *grande école*, and a relaunch in a much more ambitious form of the Ecole Libre des Sciences Politiques which had been set up in 1871. Both had intimate links with government and leaders of large public and private sector companies, consolidating ties between the most prestigious areas of the study of political science on the one hand and the ruling elite on the other, and much teaching was performed by practitioners of various kinds rather than academics. Politics was (and is) studied and taught in universities as well, but this is almost exclusively within law faculties, where political scientists proper are in a minority (Favre, 1996: 216). The Institut d'Etudes Politiques in Paris tended (and still tends) to set the tone for the rest of the country in terms of the types of research and teaching which are carried out and which types can legitimately be called political science (there are now nine IEPs in total). This situation is hardly likely to encourage radicalism, or an approach which systematically challenges the political status quo or even the discipline's established practices;

those who do challenge are often viewed as mavericks who do not belong in political science at all.

For many years constitutional law has been an important area of study, although it is often considered to be outside the ambit of political science proper. In fact, so dominant has this area been that for many years political scientists felt they were the poor relations in *facultés de droit*. Prélot (1957: 2) comments that 'in law departments the word "politics" is said quickly and quietly, as it is not deemed to be "scientific" or "objective"' and public law is still perceived as overshadowing and dominating the study of politics more generally. Historically, this is partly because in a country which took long to establish stable government and state control, a close study of the state and constitutional arrangements (rather than raising wider issues regarding public opinion) was both practical and apparently neutral enough not to excite condemnation or accusations of political interference in a delicate political climate (Hayward, 1994: 284).

In the postwar period the ostensibly neutral area of electoral studies grew fast, building on the pioneering work by André Siegfried in electoral geography between the wars; such studies multiplied partly because the resources were there to fund them, coming from newspapers, radio and later television, whereas more theoretical research and generally research with less obvious and immediate practical application attracted little funding from outside the university system. (Meanwhile many larger businesses began to use similar techniques in order to find out more about markets, the public profile of particular firms, product image and so on.) This psephological tradition is still very strong and France remains one of the most prolific countries in the world as far as both the study of elections and public opinion is concerned (Brulé, 1988). Academics, journalists and the consumers of the studies they produce have an apparently insatiable appetite for opinion polls before elections and analyses of results after elections have taken place, and with an almost constant flow of European, presidential, legislative, regional and municipal elections, there is plenty of material to work with.

Political science today is still shaped by these influences. The tenor is set by the Instituts d'Etudes Politiques, particularly the Paris IEP, which is closely connected with the Fondation Nationale des Sciences Politiques (FNSP) and its journal the *Revue française de science politique*. These are very much the establishment institutions of political science in France, which have more resources and prestige than universities and a great deal of influence on the discipline, although the teaching of political science in some form or other is far more widespread (for details see Favre, 1996). The preoccupations of political science in order of prevalence in higher education were described in 1982 as follows: 1. institutional studies; 2. electoral behaviour (geographical and sociological); 3. political forces in history; 4. history of ideas; 5. political sociology (Dreyfus, 1982: 437). The results of a survey published in 1996 produced the following, again in order of prevalence: 1. political sociology (especially electoral behaviour, public opinion, party membership); 2. history of politics; 3. history of ideas; 4. public policy (often linked with the study of French administration); 5. area studies (such as African studies or the study of the Arab world) (Favre, 1996: 238). Even from these brief lists certain patterns are clear: the studies tend to be empirical, as discussed above, and with little reference to overarching theory. Such theory as is used is often (mainly US or British) micro-theory, such as rational choice or game theory, rather than theory which seeks to explain the fundamental power structures which political life reflects. As Pierre Favre wrote in 1981, a remark which is still relevant today, 'contrary to what one might expect, this abundance of work on French institutions is not accompanied by reflection on the theory of democracy' (Favre, 1981: 110). Favre highlights the 'local' nature of political science, the unwillingness to look at the whole, and the dearth of indigenous French political theory is illustrated by the fact that in Jean Leca's lengthy and thorough overview of contemporary political theory, very few of the bibliographical references are originally published in French (Leca, 1985).

The place of theory in political science is uneasy, partly because the discipline grew so much after the Second World War when one of the chief concerns of mainstream intellectuals was to defend liberal democracy against criticisms from others influenced by communism. With the PCF receiving nearly 30 per cent of all votes cast after the war and enjoying a huge membership, non-Communist intellectuals in France were acutely aware of Communist influence where much actual politics *was* Marxist-inspired. This expansion of political science during the Cold War has meant that any theory which deviates from defence of – or at least implicit approval of – the status quo tends to be marginalized; the *grandes écoles* and *grands corps* system and its centrality in the world of political science in France certainly reinforces this. Indeed the practical orientation of political studies in France has meant that dissenting political writing appears so much more of an immediate and obvious challenge to the status quo than in sociology, history or psychology, for example. This explains in part the profound divide between theoretical and more empirical work, reflected by Bertrand de Jouvenel when he commented in the early 1960s that:

> in political science there is a divorce between theory and concrete research which is unknown in other disciplines... The divorce between concrete research and political theory contrasts with an organic relationship in the other sciences: awareness of theory guides practical research, whose results in turn bring changes to the theory. This is not the case in political science, where theory is in any case different from elsewhere.
>
> (de Jouvenel, 1961: 364)

Jean Baudouin has also pointed out that the almost overwhelming strength of French political philosophy in the past has left today's political scientists eager to distance themselves and their 'clinical examination of facts' from political philosophy; the former is speculative and prescriptive, the latter experimental and interpretative (Baudouin, 1996: 6). Moreover, in France in the twentieth century theory has tended to be the theory of grand narratives, of salvation and emancipation, either of the extreme right, of Marxism or Republicanism. There is little established tradition of liberal political philosophy upon which to base a more theorized view of liberal political life, and the alternatives appear too great a threat to the status quo.

More recently, even from within the discipline, there have been attempts to break out of the more conventional mould described above, with publications taking a more social anthropological or feminist approach, for example (e.g. Mossuz-Lavau, 1994). The journal *Politix*, launched by young political scientists, also seeks to challenge some of the accepted wisdom of the discipline, arguing that there is a need for an 'artisanal and open' examination of politics (*Politix*, Winter 1988: 3), although more recent issues of this journal have become more conventional, if no more enamoured with the empirical.

Certainly, there are mainstream analysts of political life in France who go well beyond the simple gathering and describing of facts of political life. Maurice Duverger, for example, broke ground in 1951 with the publication of a work on political parties which emphasized the importance of organization (as opposed to programme or members' social class) when categorizing them (Duverger, 1951). Most famously, perhaps, Duverger argued that a fundamental division between modern political parties was between cadre parties and mass parties (*partis de cadres* and *partis de masses*). Broadly speaking, the former corresponded to West

European liberal and conservative parties and the latter to West European socialist parties. Jean Charlot then went on to argue that the Gaullist party was neither of these types of party, but a 'voter party', with much in common with a (conservative) 'catch-all' party found in other Western industrialized democracies where 'a minimum of shared values is enough and this enables [the party] to appeal to a very wide clientele' (Charlot, 1971: 64). The merit of such studies is that they order and classify certain aspects of political phenomena, but they do not contribute to an overall theory of power, or democracy, or conflict, for example, which could in turn be applied to more concrete objects of study.

To sum up, political science in France is particularly marked by the fact that it operates from a position of proximity to the liberal democratic state which means that it tends to be uncritical of the established order of things. This is also due to the more general conditions of its development. But political science is also very much an international phenomenon where the influence of the United States has been powerful, and it is no exaggeration to say that the Cold War was decisive in shaping political science throughout the western world; in the USA in particular it was seen as the defence of liberal democracy against Soviet communism, a way of attempting to perfect a system which had already 'got it right'. (This is a view which has, if anything, been reinforced by the breakup of the Soviet Union and the Eastern Bloc.) American-style political science, critiqued so forcefully by Bernard Crick in the late 1950s (Crick, 1959), is indeed strong and this has meant that in many countries political science has tended to be descriptive rather than underpinned theoretically, less innovative and less open than the other social sciences to influences from elsewhere, and there is a profound divide between those who are part of the mainstream and those who deviate from it. Both France's political life and much of France's intellectual life used to be radical and committed, but political science grew up in the American mould, influenced by more international, liberal intellectual traditions than those found in other disciplines in French universities and beyond. Arguably, with the decline of radicalism in French politics, famously exaggerated by François Furet, Jacques Julliard and Pierre Rosanvallon (1988; and see Hewlett, 1998), political science and the object of its interests are now far more in harmony than they were in the postwar period.

Beyond the mainstream

Significantly, given what I say above, departures from the mainstream liberal and empirical paradigm have tended not to come from within political science but from other disciplines and systems of thought. This has unfortunately meant that overarching Marxist, structuralist or post-structuralist theories touching on aspects of the conventional interests of political science have often been dismissed as being too distant from the interests of political science, 'unscientific', agitational, or several of these. They have not been integrated into the study of the more conventional concerns of political science and developed within it; they are thought of as odd strangers who have brought alien views to bear on subjects they are not qualified to understand.

Perhaps the radical theorists who have nevertheless had the most impact on political science in France, as well as beyond, are Louis Althusser and Nicos Poulantzas (who was Greek but adopted France as his country of work). In the areas of state theory and social classes in particular, their ideas became well-known (e.g. Althusser, 1971; Poulantzas, 1974, 1978) and both emphasized two points in particular in relation to the capitalist state. First, the state has 'relative autonomy' from the bourgeoisie and does not always act in the immediate interests of capital; they thus distance themselves from what they regard as the economic reductionism of traditional Marxism. Second, they argue that the state has a coercive role, in particular in the form of the police and army, but also an important ideological role through what Althusser famously described as 'ideological state apparatuses', meaning schools, the church and the media, in particular (Althusser, 1971). Some French studies of more concrete concerns have been influenced by these writers (e.g. Buci-Glucksmann, 1983), but both Althusser and Poulantzas have evoked interest above all in the realm of political philosophy, and they are now unfashionable and often dismissed in the general reaction against Marxist theory. Cornelius Castoriadis and Claude Lefort, former Marxists once associated with the journal *Socialisme ou barbarie*, have also had a certain influence on the study of democracy, for example (Lefort, 1990, 1992), but they are again outsiders and their work has not found its way into the overall approach which political scientists take towards the study of the conventional objects of interest.

Foucault, meanwhile, is also profoundly 'political', but is often regarded as being too concerned with power in general (rather than specifically state power), and too politically committed to be useful in the analysis of concrete politics. It might be argued that the French Regulation School and Alain Lipietz in particular have attempted to introduce an overall approach to the political which takes into account the general evolution of the capitalist economy and society since the early 1970s, comparing with the post-war period; there is plenty of analysis of observable phenomena here as well as theory. However, although this approach *relies* heavily on the political, as opposed to the purely economic, in particular labour relations but also government, unfortunately there has been little work on the specifically political – as opposed to political economy – by Lipietz or his colleagues in France; the political has tended to become agitational rather than analytical (Lipietz, 1994). There is, however, plenty of potential and Bob Jessop et al. (1988) have adopted and developed this framework with some success in their work on Thatcherism (for an overview of Regulation Theory, see Amin, 1994).

Finally, a slightly longer look at the contribution of Pierre Bourdieu, below, suggests both how a radical view of politics could help construct a very different way of approaching political science, and how his conception of political science itself is an integral part of his understanding of contemporary politics.

Bourdieu and political science

Some explanation is necessary as to why I have chosen to consider Bourdieu's analysis of politics and political science rather than other writers' work, not least because Bourdieu is a sociologist and not a political scientist (for a discussion of Bourdieu's contribution to sociology, see Chapter 7 of this volume). First, a considerable advantage of Bourdieu's approach to politics is precisely that he looks from outside the established world of political science and can therefore afford, professionally, to be critical of it. Second, he takes an overall view of the subject, writing in broad terms about the objects of interest of political science as well as about political science itself; he looks beyond the empirical detail which so often preoccupies political scientists and which narrows the conceptual horizons of the discipline. This is all the more the case given that he does not place the state centre-stage in his explanatory framework and locates important centres of power elsewhere. Finally, he integrates an examination of political science itself with an examination of social and political structures, an approach which, although only partially developed, is perhaps Bourdieu's most original contribution.

Bourdieu begins with the general premise that contemporary societies are structured according to the overarching division of individuals and groups into those who dominate (*les dominants*) and those who are dominated (*les dominés*), into overall power relations in other words with a clear distinction between the rulers and the ruled. Although

Bourdieu refines this considerably in some of his writing in order to introduce more subtle distinctions (e.g. Bourdieu, 1976), all social relations and social structures are best understood, ultimately, by reference to this fundamental balance of forces. However, instead of a traditional Marxist framework, Bourdieu constructs a set of organizing principles and concepts which draw on Marx but which are by no means orthodox. In particular, he uses the concept of capital in order to explain why some individuals and social groups have more power than others, but the types of capital Bourdieu is particularly interested in are 'cultural', 'social' and 'symbolic', rather than material capital, and especially capital gained through a particular form and level of education. Domination does not need to take place in a direct and obvious way in advanced capitalist societies if it can take place more subtly: 'symbolic violence is the milder and covert form which violence takes when overt violence is impossible' (1976: 131). Another important concept for Bourdieu is the 'field' (*champ*), which is used to describe many different centres of power struggle, but is ultimately a local expression of the *dominants–dominés* conflict around which society as a whole is organized. So examples in modern societies might be the fields of education, the church, the media, business or politics (including the study of politics).

Bourdieu regards a large part of the population of an advanced capitalist country as being 'dispossessed' (*dépossédée*) because it lacks the various forms of capital necessary to the exercise of power within various fields relevant to different groups and individuals. The dispossessed internalize the preconditions of (and therefore they collaborate in) their own domination, which usually makes overt repression on the part of the *dominants* unnecessary. To put it in more Bourdieusian language, a group of *dépossédés* is deprived of certain types of capital required to achieve positions of influence in particular fields and this is what guarantees the perpetuation of established power relations. For example, priests dispossess lay people of any legitimate religious competence and thus prevent them from having any real influence over the nature of religious life and discourse; in each field the *dominants* determine the types, norms, definitions and conduct which become regarded more generally as legitimate. This also applies to the division between professional politicians and most voters, a point which is explored more fully below. Institutions which are generally viewed as holding the monopoly of coercion in advanced capitalist societies (most obviously the police and the army, but more generally the state) are not directly involved in the *reproduction* of domination. This schema is influenced by Antonio Gramsci's notion of bourgeois hegemony, where the ruling class rules not only by coercion but also by shaping the ideology of the time, thus achieving the consent of the mass of the people in their exploitation with less overt violence than might otherwise be necessary (Gramsci, 1971: 245; see also the remarks above regarding Poulantzas and Althusser and their theories of the state).

Bourdieu is also keen to explain the apparently low level of interest which many citizens have in the political organization of their country. This, which is a form of dispossession, is also explained partly by the 'concentration of political means of production [or capital] in the hands of professionals' (1981: 5), which indeed is both a precondition and the result of apathy in the mass of potential voters (1981: 8), and he comments that 'indifference is only a manifestation of impotence' (1984: 406). Moreover, abstention is not so much a malfunctioning as a condition of liberal democracy (1984: 398), because liberal democracy is a political arrangement which depends for its existence on limited involvement in politics by the vast majority of the population. Indeed a great merit of Bourdieu's analysis of contemporary politics is his preoccupation with the phenomenon of political 'apathy', whether it is expressed in the form of abstention at elections or in other ways. This is something which political scientists have not integrated into a grander scheme of things.

By contrast with much of the received wisdom in political science circles, Bourdieu implies strongly that the more established an apparently consensual liberal democratic system becomes, the more elitist, closed and therefore undemocratic it becomes, partly because the division of political labour becomes more extreme. So, for example, in a highly institutionalized system, professional politicians are increasingly preoccupied with winning posts rather than winning minds (1981: 20). This layer of professional politicians, which is a very closed community in both professional and personal respects, effectively censors political discourse by imposing a restricted definition of what is considered to be the realm of the political (1981: 4). Part of this process is the transformation of politics in advanced capitalist societies into a form of spectacle, with television debates between two politicians being one of the most extreme versions of this. But the game- or theatre-like nature of politics is also expressed in both the form and content of parliamentary debates, for example. Political parties, meanwhile, are forms of extreme concentration of political capital which reinforce the dispossessed character of the mass of the electorate. But far from defending the character and behaviour of left parties, as one might perhaps expect, Bourdieu reserves his most critical comments for the (pre-1989) French and other West

European communist parties, which he implies are demagogic, elitist, mystifying and alienating for most people (1981: 5).

Turning now more obviously to the sphere of political science, it should perhaps first be said that an important part of Bourdieu's view of politics is precisely that it is not simply made up of the conventional objects of politics (parties, elections, candidates, voting systems, policy formation and so on) and that it is far more than concerns immediately related to government. In fact, in a sense everything should be seen as politics or at least everything that is subject to deliberation, choice and struggle, and not just the conventional objects of political science and professional politics which are just the visible tip of the iceberg chosen for scrutiny by those whose interests are served by this particular choice. Indeed the study of the political must, Bourdieu argues, place centre stage 'the economic and social determinants of the political division of labour' and must seek to explain a crucial feature of the political field, namely the 'monopoly of professionals' (Bourdieu, 1981: 3). For example, individuals need both free time and cultural capital (most importantly education) in order to be successful in politics, and being a man is also an important and unfair advantage.

Mainstream political science has a far from noble role to play in this scheme of things. The historic role of modern political science, he argues, is to legitimize the political status quo rather than question it or to suggest that there are other possible ways of arranging formal decision-making in modern societies. In particular, political scientists both suggest that the current arrangements are the only legitimate and viable ones and also, 'by bestowing the appearance of science on their inquiry and its analysis, they reinforce the sense of unworthiness in the "incompetent" ' (1984: 410). More generally:

> The 'political science' which is taught in specially designated institutions [the Instituts d'Etudes Politiques] is the *rationalisation* of the competence which the world of professional politics requires and which professional politicians have in a practical way: it aims to increase the effectiveness of this practical expertise by offering it rational techniques like opinion polling, public relations or political marketing. At the same time political science tends to legitimise practical politics by giving it the appearance of being scientifically based and by presenting political matters as being the preserve of specialists, who make decisions in the name of "knowledge" and not in the interests of a particular social class
>
> (1981: 6)

The Instituts d'Etudes Politiques and the Ecole Nationale d'Administration come in for particular criticism with their highly conventional approach to politics, their elitist intake and their pivotal role in forming a political, administrative, educational and journalistic elite, which means among other things further perpetuation of these approaches to politics.

Bourdieu's insights into the role and the organization of politics in advanced capitalist societies are thought-provoking and his views are more easily expressed because he is working outside the political science establishment, views which are taboo to many working within the discipline itself. Put generally, he addresses – without saying so explicitly – the question of democracy in advanced capitalist societies and in particular the question of whether liberal democracy constitutes real democracy. However, I believe several points need to be made by way of criticism. First, in his eagerness to reveal some of the profound drawbacks of contemporary politics, he understandably criticizes liberal democratic modes of organization. But there is little or nothing in Bourdieu's analysis of the political which suggests a realistic alternative, a way of reorganizing society or politics in such a way that there would be a wider, more informed participation in decision-making. There is no hint of any practical alternative, except perhaps in the more recent writings, and even there Bourdieu speaks in very general (and unexplored) terms of a 'reasoned Utopia' (1998). Second, many of Bourdieu's remarks seem to suggest that the political *dominants* are *consciously* excluding the *dominés* from positions of and a share in power in an almost conspiratorial way. This is surely not the case in most instances, although as he might point out, political scientists and others who work within a similar framework probably contribute to people's 'illusions' in liberal democracy. Third, Bourdieu's writing is itself often inaccessible, and needs several readings before the meaning becomes clearer. Certainly, social reality is itself complex and concepts used to describe it are bound also to be complex. But Bourdieu is practising some of what he criticizes, by shrouding social and political analysis in mystique by using obscure language and by creating exclusivity in the practice of social analysis. This is perhaps connected, finally, with his rather dubious claim of disciplinary autonomy for sociology, whereas the logic of much of what he says more generally is to suggest a far less bounded set of social sciences than is presently the case.

Bourdieu has been considered and rejected by some mainstream political scientists (e.g. Bon and Schemeil, 1980) although others have shown an interest in the manner in which he looks at political science as a discipline (Leca, 1982, 1991). Certainly, the degree of hostility expressed towards the discipline can do nothing to endear him to most political scientists, but an enduring merit of Bourdieu is to insist on the necessity of examining relations of power in society as a whole and to relate these to the examination of what are conventionally considered to be legitimate objects of scrutiny, that is government, parties, public opinion, public policy and so on. He insists, in other words, on looking at the bigger picture in order to understand the details. Many political scientists unfortunately shun this sort of approach.

Conclusion

Returning to the paradox indicated at the beginning of this paper, the reasons are now clearer for the under-theorized and often descriptive nature of political science in a country where theory has in general been so important. Political science on an international level suffers from its close proximity to the delicate but often unaddressed question of whether liberal democracy as practised in the West is beyond reproach. In other words its intellectual rigour suffers from having a special relationship with liberalism and liberal democracy, and any fundamental examining of the political status quo throws up questions regarding not only the legitimacy of modern government, but also about some basic characteristics of political science itself. Most political scientists have chosen not to address these broader questions, even implicitly. Because of the particular political and academic conditions surrounding the emergence and development of the discipline in France, these more general tendencies were compounded and reinforced the gulf between mainstream political scientists and others who discussed wider theories of power. Today, with the reaction against 'total' theories (which postmodern jargon dubs 'metanarratives') and the resurgence of liberalism in French political thought (Lilla, 1994), there is a danger that the study of politics and government (political science proper, as it were) will become even narrower in its preoccupations.

The study of politics badly needs to be renewed and is after all an area of crucial interest and importance not only for academics, students and other intellectuals but also for the public at large. First, there is a profound need for political scientists to take more notice of other disciplines, including sociology, anthropology, philosophy, psychology and history, without abandoning political science's current interest in economics and industrial relations. A more *interdisciplinary* approach is crucial if the discipline is to evolve in a fruitful direction, and as Colin

Leys points out, politics is not a distinct field of activity but 'an aspect of all social relations' (Leys, 1979: 11). Second, there is a need for the integration of general theories of power into more specific studies of the traditional objects of interest, working beyond the current divorce between political theory on the one hand and more concrete political analysis on the other. As David Held has said in a comment about British political science in particular, but which is equally applicable to the discipline in France and other countries, 'we seem to know more about the parts and less about the whole.... the complex character of the whole problem has remained unresolved' (Held, 1989: 248). Third, there is a need to emphasize that politics is intimately connected to all sorts of loci of power within society which usually escape the attention of political studies, including schools, families, businesses and universities. The question of social class has been virtually ignored and until recently so have the questions of gender and ethnicity (for a parallel debate regarding the international relations field, see Halliday, 1994).

Too often, political analysis closes debate instead of opening it. It is necessary to critique political science and engage in debate about it precisely because the study of politics is too important to leave largely untouched by some of the great theoretical questions, to allow it in other words to remain only semi-intellectualized. One approach to achieving movement in this respect is a thorough-going debate on the nature of democracy, which would investigate all aspects of both the concept and its practice, an area which virtually all political scientists agree is important, but which often remains unaddressed. There is some evidence that this is beginning to take place in France (e.g. Leleux, 1997; Manin, 1997) and is arguably already underway, albeit tentatively, in Britain (e.g. Held, 1993, 1996) and the USA (e.g. Elster, 1998).

Notes

1   By 'political science' I mean the teaching of and research into politics as practised in universities and other institutions (including Instituts d'Etudes Politiques) encompassing the study of the conventional concerns of political scientists, including in particular government, public policy, parties, elections and in general the activities of professional politicians. Of course, the study of politics in a broader sense also takes place in other disciplines, especially sociology, economics, history and anthropology. My reservations with regard to the term 'political science' become clear in due course, although it is used throughout the chapter for the sake of clarity.

2   I would like to thank Gregory Elliott for some valuable comments on an earlier draft of this chapter.

References

Althusser, Louis (1971) 'Ideology and ideological state apparatuses. (Notes towards an investigation.)', in *Lenin and Philosophy and Other Essays*. London: New Left Books, pp. 121–76.

Amin, Ash (1994) 'Post-Fordism: models, fantasies and phantoms of transition', in Ash Amin (ed.), *Post-Fordism*. Oxford: Basil Blackwell, pp. 1–40.

Baudouin, Jean (1996) *Introduction à la science politique*, 4th edn. Paris: Dalloz.

Bon, Frédéric and Yves Schemeil (1980) 'La Rationalisation de l'inconduite: comprendre le statut du politique chez Pierre Bourdieu', *Revue française de science politique*, 30: 1198–228.

Bourdieu, Pierre (1976) 'Les Modes de domination', *Actes de la recherche en sciences sociales*, 8–9: 122–32.

—— (1977) 'Questions de politique', *Actes de la recherche en sciences sociales*, 16: 55–89.

—— (1981) 'La Représentation politique. Eléments pour une théorie du champ politique', *Actes de la recherche en sciences sociales*, 38: 3–24.

—— (1984) *Distinction*. London: Routledge.

—— (1988) *Homo Academicus*. Cambridge: Polity.

—— (1994) 'Dialogue sur l'espace public', in *Politix. Travaux de science politique*, 26: 5–22.

—— (1998) 'A reasoned utopia and economic fatalism', *New Left Review*, 227: 125–30.

Braud, Philippe (1995) *La Science politique*. Paris: Presses Universitaires de France (Que sais-je?).

Brulé, Michel (1988) *L'Empire des sondages*. Paris: Robert Laffont.

Buci-Glucksmann, Christine (ed.) (1983) *La Gauche, le pouvoir, le socialisme. Hommage à Nicos Poulantzas*. Paris: Presses Universitaires de France.

Charlot, Jean (1971) *The Gaullist Phenomenon. The Gaullist Movement in the Fifth Republic*. London: Allen & Unwin.

Crick, Bernard (1959) *The American Science of Politics*. London: Routledge & Kegan Paul.

De Jouvenel, Bertrand (1961) 'Théorie politique pure', *Revue française de science politique*, 11 (2): 364–79.

Dreyfus, François G. (1982) 'Political Science in France', *Government and Opposition*, 17 (4): 429–43.

Duhamel, Olivier (1991) *Le Pouvoir politique en France*. Paris: Seuil.

Duverger, Maurice (1951) *Les Partis politiques*. Paris: Seuil.

Elster, Jon (ed.) (1998) *Deliberative Democracy*. Cambridge: Cambridge University Press.

Favre, Pierre (1985) 'Histoire de la science politique', in Madeleine Grawitz and Jean Leca (eds), 1985, pp. 3–46.

—— with Nadine Dada (1996) 'La Science politique en France', in Commission européenne, *La Science politique en Europe: formation, coopération, perspectives. Rapport final*. Paris: Fondation Nationale des Sciences Politiques/European Commission, pp. 214–49.

Furet, François, Jacques Julliard and Pierre Rosanvallon (1988) *La République du centre. La fin de l'exception française*. Paris: Calmann-Lévy.

Giddens, Anthony (1979) *Central Problems in Social Theory. Action, Structure and Contradiction in Social Analysis*. London: Macmillan.

Gramsci, Antonio (1971) *Selections from Prison Notebooks*. London: Lawrence & Wishart.

Grawitz, Madeleine and Leca, Jean (eds) (1985) *Traité de science politique. I. La science politique, science sociale. L'ordre politique*. Paris: Presses Universitaires de France.

Habermas, Jürgen (1978) *L'Espace public. Archéologie de la publicité comme dimension constitutive de la société bourgeoise*. Paris: Payot.

Halliday, Fred (1994) *Rethinking International Relations*. London: Macmillan.

Held, David (1989) 'A discipline of politics?', in *Political Theory and the Modern State*. Cambridge: Polity, pp. 243–59.

—— (ed.) (1993) *Prospects for Democracy, North, South, East, West*. Cambridge: Polity.

—— (1996) *Models of Democracy*, 2nd edn. Cambridge: Polity.

Hewlett, Nick (1998) *Modern French Politics. Analysing Conflict and Consensus since 1945*. Cambridge: Polity.

Jessop, Bob, Kevin Bonnett, Simon Bromley and Tom Ling (1988) *Thatcherism*. Cambridge: Polity.

Leca, Jean (1985) 'La Théorie politique', in Grawitz and Leca (eds) (1985), pp. 47–174.

Lefort, Claude (1990) *Democracy and Political Theory*. Cambridge: Polity.

—— (1992) *The Political Forms of Modern Society*. Cambridge: Polity.

Leleux, Claudine (1997) *La Démocratie moderne*. Paris: Cerf.

Lilla, Mark (ed.) (1994) *New French Thought: Political Philosophy*. Princeton, NJ: Princeton University Press

—— (1994) 'The legitimacy of the liberal age', in Lilla (ed.) (1994), pp. 3–34.

Lipietz, Alain (1994) 'Post-Fordism and democracy', in Amin (ed.) (1994), pp. 338–57.

Manin, Bernard (1997) *The Principles of Representative Government*. Cambridge: Cambridge University Press.

Mossuz-Lavau, Janine (1994) *Les Français et la politique. Enquête sur une crise*. Paris: Odile Jacob.

Prélot, Marcel (1957) 'La Fin d'une extraordinaire carence', *Revue internationale d'histoire politique et constitutionnelle*, 7: 1–16 (special issue entitled 'L'Entrée de la science politique dans l'université française').

Stedman Jones, Gareth (1972) 'History: the poverty of empiricism', in Robin Blackburn (ed.), *Ideology in Social Science. Readings in Critical Social Theory*. London: Fontana, pp. 96–115.

Ysmal, Collette (1989) *Les Partis politiques sous la Ve République*. Paris: Montchrestien.

10
An Anti-American in Paris: Lacan and French Freudianism

Grahame Lock

In 1925 Freud published his *Autobiographical Study*, a survey of the development up to that moment of the psychoanalytic movement (Freud, 1959). There he remarks that 'I now watch from a distance the symptomatic reactions that are accompanying the introduction of psychoanalysis into the France which was for so long refractory.' What might explain this refractory reaction? Accounts of 'incredible simplicity' have been proposed, he notes, 'such as that French sensitiveness is offended by the pedantry and crudity of psychoanalytic terminology', or that 'the whole mode of thought of psychoanalysis is inconsistent with the *génie latin*'.

Yet in a note to her French translation of Freud's text, Marie Bonaparte remarks that 'the French possess in their national character certain traits which make it more difficult to understand [the psychoanalytic message]: and first of all their love of logical clarity, the heritage of the classical ideal of our seventeenth century...' (Mordier, 1981: 23). She adds, it is true, that this classical ideal was itself the product of a great 'act of repression', with its own negative consequences. Thus she seems to take an ambivalent standpoint, even an embarrassed one, toward what some have regarded as the Cartesian core of the intellectual tradition in France. In reality, of course, there is no single such tradition, no 'core' of French thought, but rather a complex and contradictory history of the interplay and conflict between various so-called native or imported currents and ideas. This applies to French Freudianism too.

Shortly after the publication of Freud's study, in 1926, the first French psychoanalytic society, the *Société psychanalytique de Paris* (SPP), was set up. Among its original members were Marie Bonaparte, wife of Prince George of Greece and patient as well as friend of Sigmund Freud; Rudolph Loewenstein, a Russian Jew from Berlin, later to emigrate to the United States; Raymond de Saussure (son of the linguist, Ferdinand) and Charles Odier, both Swiss; Eugénie Sokolnicka, a Polish Jewess and analyst of two French founding members, René Laforgue and Edouard Pichon.[1] The society was well-named: more Parisian, indeed, from a certain point of view, than French.[2]

Did there really exist a French resistance to Freudianism, as Freud himself suggests and Marie Bonaparte seems anxious to confirm? Whatever the truth of the claim, Freud goes on to make the significant remark that 'in France the interest in psychoanalysis began among the men of letters'. Most spectacularly, the surrealist movement, inspired by André Breton (a psychiatrist by training), made extensive use of Freudian notions. This indicates, perhaps, that any resistance should be characterized not so much as 'French', but rather as deriving, at least in large part, though in different ways, from another source, namely from both conservative and radical currents in professional psychiatric circles. What is true is that France took longer than other countries to absorb the Freudian message.

Among the young trainee analysts who became candidate members of the SPP in the pre-Second World War period was Jacques Lacan, who chose Loewenstein as his training analyst. Lacan was a psychiatrist, but with many outside interests. He had, for instance, been struck by an article by Salvador Dali on what the latter called paranoia-criticism. (Dali was insisting at this time, for example in his *La Conquête de l'irrationel* of 1935, on the 'productive' and revolutionary effects of the 'paranoiac-critical' approach.) Lacan had already met Breton, and got to know other members of alternative Parisian literary circles, like Raymond Queneau and Georges Bataille. He was to become – and in superb fashion – the most famous or infamous representative of the French psychoanalytic profession. Even now, at the end of the 1990s, his name remains the principal reference in discussions of Freudian ideas in France.[3]

His fame began to spread only after the Second War. At the 1949 Congress of the International Psychoanalytic Association he presented a paper on 'The mirror stage as formative of the function of the "I"' (Lacan, 1966a), a new version of the paper which he had tried to read at the 1936 Marienbad congress, when he been cut short after a few minutes by the chairman, Ernest Jones. In his brief contribution, Lacan already identifies the ego (in French, the *moi*) as constituted by an 'illusion' of autonomy, by a misrecognition process – a position which implicitly established his hostility to Anna Freud and the ego

psychologists.[4] Already, then, his aversion to what he was later to identify as 'American' psychoanalysis, together with its Anna Freudian
friends, was taking shape. This aversion was later to take on ideologically
significant shape and dimensions.

In the same period, the period of the high Cold War, in which the
French Communist Party and its allies were denouncing American
attempts to establish a world politico-economic hegemony, Jacques
Lacan delivered a lecture at the Neuropsychiatric Clinic in Vienna on
what he called 'The Freudian thing' (Lacan, 1966b). Lacan declared the
need to listen once again to the Freudian message, a message which had
been forgotten in America where it was a victim of the 'cultural ahistoricism peculiar to the United States of America'.

In this lecture Lacan cites 'Freud's words to Jung'. Lacan claimed to
have them from Jung's own mouth. On an invitation to Clark University,
Jung and Freud 'arrived together in New York harbour and caught their
first glimpse of the famous statue'. At that moment, Freud is said to have
remarked: 'They don't realize we're bringing them the plague.' There is
no evidence, other than Lacan's claim, that Freud ever said such a thing
(Roudinesco, 1986: 191). But no matter, or rather, all the better: for the
report throws light on the urgency of Lacan's need for an 'anti-American'
quote from Freud to legitimate his own position. Lacan was clearly
intent on attributing to Freud an aversion to the American way of
psychoanalysis, an aversion which by this time informed his own work.

Lacan had been obliged in 1953 to resign from the established *Société
psychanalytique de Paris*, which itself was affiliated to the International
Psychoanalytic, Association (IPA). The IPA was dominated, by the simple
reason of numbers as well as in the ideological sense, by the American
analytic community – including its many originally European immig-
rant members, whom Lacan accused of having succumbed to the temp-
tation of the abandonment of principle. Thus Lacan understood his
exclusion from the Parisian Society as an event in a deep-lying, inter-
continental conflict of ideas, theories and practices.

A number of dissidents, Lacan among them, set up a new analytic
organization, the *Société Française de Psychanalyse* (SFP). But this too fell
apart a few years later, in 1963, and on the same issue: affiliation to the
IPA. For the latter demanded, as the price for the admissibility of the new
Society, the exclusion of Lacan from the body of training analysts
(Miller, 1977; Roudinesco, 1986: 581ff.).

Just after the 1953 split, the SFP held its first convention in Rome. In
that city – though at a separate conference of Romance-language
psychoanalysts – Lacan presented a long paper on 'Function and field

of speech and language in psychoanalysis'. In this and other papers of the same period he took a distance both from the American psychoanalytic tradition and from the previously dominant tendencies in the history of French analysis.

What did Lacan have against the Americans? On the one hand, of course, their interpretation of Freud, in terms of ego-psychology and adaptationist goals. We should also mention his opposition to their behaviourism, 'which has', he says, 'now completely obscured the inspiration of Freud in psychoanalysis itself.' In any case, he concludes, 'it appears incontestable that the conception of psychoanalysis in the United States has inclined towards the adaptation of the individual to the social environment, towards the quest for behaviour patterns, and towards all the objectification implied in the notion of "human relations"' (Lacan, 1966c; Lacan, 1977a: 37–8).

Let us take these remarks of 1953 seriously, in spite of their brevity. In what context is Lacan's critique of the Americans' way with Freud set?

First the theoretical context. In his paper of 1955 on 'The Freudian thing' he raises the complaint against the Americans' 'ahistoricism' to which we have already referred, a tendency, he says, 'at the antipodes of psychoanalytic experience'. For the psychoanalysts' profession in fact presupposes history 'in its very principle, their discipline being that which . . . re-established the bridge linking modern man to the ancient myths'. But the American 'horizon is too limited', and too oriented to comfort, *in casu* to intellectual comfort, the 'most corrupting of comforts'. American psychoanalysis is a 'deviation', Lacan claims. Its practice has been 'so summarily reduced to a means of obtaining "success" and to a mode of demanding "happiness"' that it actually 'constitutes a repudiation of psychoanalysis'. Many of its adherents in fact 'never wished to know anything about the Freudian discovery' – and never will understand it (Lacan, 1977b: 127–8).

Lacan had already attacked the ego-psychological current in his above-mentioned 1949 paper on 'The mirror stage', but there singling out as his target the London-based Anna Freud (who during the 1940s had been pitted against Melanie Klein in the controversial discussions inside the British Society). By 1955 his anger was extended in explicit fashion to the Americans, personified in his optic by Ernst Kris (Lacan, 1966d: 393, where Lacan quotes Kris' article 'Ego psychology and interpretation in psychoanalysis") and Heinz Hartmann (Lacan, 1977b: 132).

It is not clear that Lacan is fair in identifying 'the Americans' as his target – there is, for example, reason to doubt whether there existed or exists something that might be called the American school of psychoanalysis. But however that may be, his remarks suggest that in this period his critique of American thought is, in its political respect, based on a fairly conventional humanist ethics. In the same paper he adds, for instance, a remark on the American attachment to 'human engineering', which, he comments, 'strongly implies a privileged position of exclusion in relation to the human object' – a humanist attitude on Lacan's part that parallels a widespread 'European' feeling of the time to be found in the standpoints of very divergent political movements in France, from the Communist left to the Catholic right, and presumably rooted in part in a fear – however interpreted – of the American lead in mass-production technology, a dehumanizing trend.

A word should be said, second, about the political context in France at this time. The early 1950s were, as in some other west European lands, a period of considerable political tension. The French Communist Party had been expelled from the French, government in 1947, and was engaged in a bitter struggle against both the French government and the Americans (who were lending massive financial and political support to the anti-Communist crusade in France including material support for the anti-Communist trade union movement). Pétainists were regaining key political posts at the cost of ex-members of the Resistance. Lacan had been friendly with many left intellectuals before the war, even though he had taken no part in the Resistance movement. But it was not only the Communists and their friends who took a strongly anti-American stance in this period. R. W. Johnson notes that 'American politicians and generals ... behaved with a degree of swaggering presumption which helped push even moderate voices – most notably [the newspaper] *Le Monde* – towards a neutralist position' (Johnson, 1981: 47). De Gaulle represented a different and important current of scepticism towards America, even if anti-Communism was propelling large sections of the French population into the Americans' arms. So Lacan's anti-Americanism fitted the political mood.

For the moment, however, and indeed for some time, Lacan's readers paid little attention to his own contribution to French anti-Americanism, being more interested in his recent theoretical innovations, like the introduction of the conceptual triad of the symbolic, imaginary and real, to which we have already referred (see note 4).

But why, it might be asked, in a study of the role played by psychoanalysis in contemporary French intellectual life, put the emphasis on Lacan? Why so much honour paid to a man now regarded by many as a shaman or charlatan,[5] and by many others as in any case the representative of an age gone by, the age of structuralism? (Laplanche, 1992; Descombes, 1979). It might be held that, after all, a certain concern for Freudian ideas entered French thought, and flourished there, via quite other thinkers. Thus, for instance, both Gaston Bachelard and Jean-Paul Sartre demonstrated an interest in psychoanalysis, the former in (among other places) his essay *La Psychanalyse du feu* of 1938, the latter in *L'Être et le néant* of 1943, where he enters a plea for 'existential psychoanalysis'. But Bachelard's use of psychoanalytic ideas is a very personal one and is not an attempt to spread Freud's ideas in France, while Sartre's interpretation of Freud is eccentric by orthodox standards – and was never intended to be anything else. At a later period, to take another example, Paul Ricoeur published in 1965 a full-length study of Freudian ideas entitled *De l'Interprétation*, but this had limited impact, being a phenomenological work and therefore, so to speak, already outdated on Parisian criteria by the time it appeared. Many other examples of various kinds – of philosophers and literary figures influenced by Freudian thought, or of French analysts venturing into the general field of ideas (see especially Bouveresse, 1995) – could of course be adduced, but none is more than an exception to the general rule: that it is the name of Lacan which, for good or ill, has dominated psychoanalytical thinking in France for the last decades and will surely continue to do so for some time.

In 1966, in a letter to his analyst, René Diatkine, Louis Althusser wrote that 'at least in France, *outside of Lacan, there is at present no-one*' (Althusser, 1996: 49). And this, in a sense, remains true, for aside from Lacan – who died in 1981, but whose various works, especially the seminars, are still in course of publication – there is not yet 'anyone else', that is to say, no one who proposes an alternative theoretical strategy, with the breadth, depth, originality and appeal – but also the richness of ambiguity and even incoherence and, if you like, the intimidatory effect – of Lacan's approach. For the latter was not so much an Emperor without clothes as the contrary: a man of many and rich, sumptuous and extravagant raiments, often oddly combined, but dazzling and inspiring to many, though anathema to others, including in the first instance the greater part of the French psychoanalytic establishment.

But there are other reasons for centring a study of Freudianism in France on Jacques Lacan.

First, Lacan, in distinction from most other leading French analysts, chose partners of dialogue outside the community of medical psychiatrists or even that of his fellow practitioners of psychoanalysis. Some time in the early 1950s, says Catherine Clément, he 'abandoned the field of psychiatry for that of *Belles-Lettres*, for that of the great mediaeval tradition of Rhetoric' – that is to say, for the field in which France had originally shown, if Freud is right, its first serious interest in Freudian theory (Clément, 1981: 137).

Second, Lacan played with great tactical skill and finesse on the available 'ideological' instruments in succeeding political conjunctures. His anti-Americanism, though in his case explicitly directed against the dominant American currents in analytic theory and practice, provoked a kind of automatic, perhaps largely unreflective assent among those who, for reasons quite different from Lacan's own, opposed American 'cultural' domination in France. It has been remarked in this connection that Lacan, 'conscious of the state of expansion of Freudian ideas [in the 1950s], . . . turned his gaze in the direction of two institutions which seem to him to be important for the future: the Catholic Church and the Communist Party' (Roudinesco, 1986: 273). Both, he seems to have hoped, might – however much he was in disagreement with their ideological positions (and Lacan had abandoned Catholicism, while he never became a Communist)[6] – help him in his struggle against the Americans.

Lacan's opposition to 'American psychoanalysis' in the 1950s seems indeed to lie as much in an aversion to all things American as in a critical judgement on analytical ways there. We already suggested that it would be wrong to suppose that there was such a thing as a single American school of psychoanalysis. Many currents were in contention there, three of the principal tendencies being the culturalist stream associated with the names of Karen Horney and indirectly with Erich Fromm; the Chicago School, established by Franz Alexander; and the above-mentioned ego-psychology, a movement led by Heinz Hartmann, Ernst Kris and Lacan's ex-and indeed only analyst Rudolph Loewenstein, who had left France in 1942 for a career in the United States.

Lacan's scorn was directed especially to this third current. We might speculate about the reasons for this. It is unlikely that the presence of his own former analyst among the leading figures of ego-psychology – though the two men were not on the best of terms – can explain his attitude. More likely, it seems to me, is that Lacan's antipathy to the 'American way to happiness' led him to target as 'typically American' that current in psychoanalytic doctrine which could most persuasively be presented as an expression of this American way, of the American inclination, as he saw it, to prize and promote above all things the adaptation of the individual to his social environment. It is not, however, that Lacan ever spells out a theory or even a plausible account of America, of American culture or of the American way of life. Rather, he seems to be swimming in an anti-American current widespread, as we saw, in the France of these years.

Even so, a puzzle remains. Many of the leading figures in the SPP were just as attached to a more or less dogmatic adaptationism as were the Americans. The attribution, within a structure of mental agencies or instances, of a central role to the ego was not, after all, a new idea. Henri Ellenberger notes that

> to define the ego as the coordinating organization of the mental processes in a person was reminiscent of [Pierre] Janet's function of synthesis, and ego strength was not very different from Janet's psychological tension. The ego was an old philosophical concept in new psychological dress. [Sacha] Nacht's definition of the ego as 'the entity through which the individual becomes conscious of his own existence and of the existence of the external world' is almost identical with that which Fichte had given in philosophical terms.
>
> (Ellenberger, 1970: 516–17)

In other words, the 'typically American' emphasis on the ego has its roots in venerable ideas of the European tradition.

The names of Janet and Nacht are, by the way, also relevant to our story. Janet is often quoted as a personified example of the French resistance to Freudian psychoanalysis. Roudinesco remarks that 'Janet's psychology, like Bergson's philosophy, represents an essentially "French" moment of the new scientific spirit in the domain of the understanding of psychic phenomena' (Roudinesco, 1982: 239). Janet, she notes, 'had chosen atheism against religion, a liberal spirit against chauvinism, but...had developed in his childhood a kind of phobia against the German language which made it impossible for him to read Freud's works in the original.'[7] Thus he thought of the Freudian (as opposed to the Gallic) psychoanalyst as a kind of 'detective terrorizing his victims and tracking down their infantile traumas'. He represents a sort of 'French-style scientific anti-Freudianism'. And yet he defended Freud in 1914, insisting – against the latter's principled enemies – on the scientific value of Freudian psychoanalysis.

Between Janet and Nacht – the latter, of Jewish-Romanian origin, was to become during the German occupation a member of the French Resistance[8] – stands a third figure of importance, the paediatrician, psychoanalyst and grammarian of the French language Edouard Pichon. Born in 1890, he was in 1926 to be a co-founder of the *Société psychanalytique de Paris*. Pichon became Janet's son-in-law. A Catholic by family background and political conviction, he opposed the Jewish and Protestant 'spirits' and joined Action Française, Maurras' extreme right-wing, anti-semitic political movement. Pichon's aim was to construct a 'French' version of psychoanalysis, one compatible with the 'Latin genius'. His interest in the unconscious, as Roudinesco points out, derived in large part from his passion for the French language and its many usages and dialects. He was particularly attached to his father-in-law and to the latter's work. Together the two men borrowed the juridical notion of foreclusion, using it to denote a special grammatical operation of negation or exclusion (of the foreclosing of facts). Lacan was later to borrow the term, in order to make his own translation of the Freudian concept of *Verwerfung*, thus producing what was to become a central concept in his scheme.

In 1938, following on his election as a full member of the SPP, Lacan had published an encyclopaedia article on 'The family' (Lacan, 1984). This piece was immediately reviewed and severely criticized by Pichon. The relevance of the article and of Pichon's critique to our topic is that both publications take up, in different and often opposed ways, the themes of 'French civilization' and 'French psychoanalysis'.

Here is how Roudinesco sums up Lacan's article in the relevant respect:

> Lacan went back, through Maurras, to an attitude inherited from the positivism of Comte, according to which society is made up of families rather than of individuals. It was also through Maurras that Lacan rediscovered Aristotle as a theorist of the social identity of the individual.

Lacan's style, she adds, 'was as purely French as the style of Maurras, Lacan's model, yet at the same time as iconoclastic and cosmopolitan as the Enlightenment idea that was another constant source of inspiration to him' (Roudinesco, 1997: 143–4; cf. Ogilvie, 1987).

I leave aside here all aspects of the article on the family except those which bear on the question of Lacan's 'Frenchness'. One thing to be said in this connection is that the 'detours' in his piece are often by way of French thinkers: of Maurras, as we saw; of the psychiatrist Gaëtan Gatian de Clérambault; of the psychologist Henri Wallon; of (the originally Russian) Alexandre Kojève; of the philosopher Henri Bergson and his contrast between the moralities of obligation and of aspiration, translated by Lacan into a polarity of maternal or closed morality on the one hand and open or paternal authority on the other. But Pichon, in his review of and assault on Lacan, attacks him just for his lack of loyalty to the traditions of French thought.

Lacan, he claims, substitutes German 'culture' for French 'civilization'; makes use of a German conception of dialectic; ignores the French psychoanalytic tradition, which by contrast links psychoanalytic insights to questions of morality, insisting for instance – it is Pichon's own doctrine – on the 'immoral origins of the neuroses'. Pichon claims that 'the French psychoanalysts have, each in his own way, demonstrated that, in essence, they belong to the most humanist of all civilizations, French civilization. For French civilization, so lively and so vigorous, conserves its precious character of humanism in spite of, first, the Reformation, then the bloody masquerade of 1789–99 and the democracy that sprang from the Fourth of September movement' (Pichon, 1980). Lacan, in his attachment to Hegel – and, Pichon suggests, to Marx – had become a 'German'. Which is to say: Pichon's view was that Lacan was *not French enough*.

Note that in this quarrel America was not an issue. But when, much later, after the Second World War, Lacan started to articulate an anti-American position, *he* became identified – though in a sense different from Pichon's – with a specifically French approach to psychoanalytic thought, and even came to be regarded as the theorist of the 'French exception': France 'as odd man out', as a special case.[9] On this view, France's special status (Roudinesco argues), 'derived in the first place [*pace* Pichon!] from the revolution of 1789'. To that birth of political modernity might be added the genesis of modern French literature in the persons of Baudelaire, Rimbaud and Lautréamont (Roudinesco, 1997: 263–4). Lacan was familiar with these traditions.

Pichon had defined France as the land of humanism. But Lacan's 1950s Frenchness – which was in reality a residue of a French Husserlianism, of a French Hegelianism (as we saw, Lacan was acquainted with Alexandre Kojève, who had famously lectured on Hegel in the Paris of the 1930s), of a French Heideggerianism (though of a very different kind from that of Sartre)[10] and later of a French structuralism – produced a very different kind of 'typically French' system: an *anti*-humanism. Roudinesco, again, notes that Lacan became indeed not just a structuralist, but a radical one: an opponent of merely moderate structuralism, which continued to pander to the ideal of the 'human' sciences (Roudinesco, 1997: 326). He might indeed be called a permanent radical, always ready to take just one step more than his fellows.

Louis Althusser, reading Lacan in the early 1960s, was impressed by his 'implacable war against humanism, scientism and personalism' and against American psychoanalysis: he thus expressed himself in a lecture of 1963 (quoted in Roudinesco, 1997: 303–4).[11] In 1964 Althusser published in the Communist journal *La Nouvelle Critique* an article on 'Freud and Lacan' (Althusser, 1971a). This piece is both a defence of Freud against the hostility or indifference to psychoanalytic theory and practice characteristic of official French Communist Party doctrine, and an apology of Lacan's own 'return to Freud'. Althusser had been reading Lacan with his students at the Ecole Normale Supérieure of the rue d'Ulm; the 1963 lecture referred to above was prepared in this context. In 1964 he took a public position: 'We must', Althusser now wrote, 'return to Freud', that is to say, combat 'the relapse into childhood in which all or a part of contemporary psychoanalysis, particularly in America, savours the advantages of surrender.'

Althusser's name for this relapse into childhood is *psychologism*. He knows of course that this psychologism is not an exclusively American phenomenon. But it seems, in its psychoanalytic variant, to be typically American, in any case when it is reduced – as American analysis is said to tend to reduce it – to 'a technique of "emotional" or "affective" readaptation, or to a reeducation of the "relational function", neither of which have anything to do with its real object – but which unfortunately respond to a major demand.' Through this bias, he adds, 'psychoanalysis has become an article of mass consumption' (Althusser, 1971a: 187).

What does America here represent? For Althusser, it usually meant, of course, advanced capitalism, in its imperialist variant. Is there then a specifically imperialist form of the corruption of psychoanalytic theory and practice? And was it the special position of France in the international political and economic order, or perhaps rather its revolutionary tradition, which somehow helped the French Freudians, at least in certain cases – at least when the (by this time substantial numbers of) Lacanians are entered into the account – to avoid suffering the same fate? Or, to put it another way: had Lacan's early cosmopolitanism, his interest in German theory, needed to transform itself into an anti- Americanism, itself something like a counterfeit of the French suspicion of the United States, common in the 1950s (as we noted) to the Communist and the Gaullist movements? Is Lacan's position in respect of Freudian theory an example of the French exception, or on the contrary a reflection of a true internationalism, just for that reason directed against the fake internationalism of the International Psychoanalytic Association? These questions are of course themselves too crude to admit of an interesting or unambiguous answer, yet they point in a relevant direction.

Althusser's account defines the object of psychoanalysis as 'the unconscious', understood as an effect of the 'humanization' of the baby of the species homo sapiens; that is to say, of the transformation of that animal baby into a masculine or feminine subject (a theme to which Althusser returns, in a different context, in his essay of 1970 on 'Ideology and ideological state apparatuses' – Althusser, 1971b: 121–73).[12] Lacan had produced, he says, a new – though properly Freudian – theorization of this object on the basis of the insights of Saussurian linguistics. The Oedipal drama is thus interpreted as a forced initiation, beyond the stage or mode of imaginary identification, into a law of Order, that is to say, into a law of the Symbolic, one 'formally identical with the order of language'.

Althusser, though giving Lacan the credit for his 'discovery' of the new theory adequate to the Freudian object called the unconscious, had in fact by 1964 produced his own concise version of Freudian theory, a variation on Lacan. What interested Althusser was the possibility of a materialist reading – in his own sense – of Freud. The 'culturalism' of which he accused himself in a letter of 1969 to the English translator of his text was in fact no mere oversight, but an (admittedly not very successful) attempt to grasp the mechanisms – understood in a materialist sense, for instance, in something like the sense of 'institutions' – which allow the above-mentioned process of 'humanization' to operate. And this without falling into psychology, as had, much earlier, the Communist thinker Georges Politzer in his critique of Freud (Politzer, 1969).

Dominique Lecourt has drawn attention to an important, perhaps crucial point in this connection: that in his essay (1964) Althusser seems to have 'surrendered to the effect of intimidation from which Lacan's work draws a good part of its force – an intimidation which derives, in the last resort, from the manner in which Lacan constructed a real philosophy of psychoanalysis, in the most traditional sense of the word "philosophy" ' (Lecourt, 1982). This is a conclusion which Althusser himself drew, at least in part, in a later paper entitled 'Dr Freud's discovery'. Some time ago I wrote that 'in "Freud and Lacan", Althusser offers an enthusiastic and largely uncritical defense of Lacan's thought. But in his "Dr Freud's Discovery" (in Althusser, 1996), he paints a different, almost aggressive picture.' Lacan, he says,

> tried to do what Freud had not been able to do; *he tried to produce a scientific theory of the unconscious* . . . But instead of a scientific theory of the unconscious he presented to an astonished world *a philosophy of*

psychoanalysis..., a fantastic philosophy of psychoanalysis which fascinated intellectuals...He fooled everyone, and very likely, in spite of his extreme artfulness, he even fooled himself.

What is the line of Althusser's critique? Lacan, he complains, produced a whole theory 'distinguishing between the real, the symbolic and the imaginary' – a gigantic theoretical construction, which is ceaselessly proliferating – and for a good reason, namely, because it could only pursue an object outside its reach, since this object did not exist.' But it is true (I added) 'that Lacan is not *just* a philosopher...His work is an enormously complex – Althusser says "baroque" – mixture of elements, empirical and metaphysical, of historico-scientific and philosophical references' (Lock, 1996: 85–6).

Although his paper contains manifest weaknesses (Althusser, 1996: 79–80), it also contains a number of 'emancipatory' formulations, in the sense of formulations which help counter the above-mentioned intimidatory effect. Thus Althusser refers to Lacan's seminar on Poe's *The Purloined Letter*, in which Lacan makes his claim that 'a letter always arrives at its destination' – that is, the unconscious message is somehow always successfully transmitted and received. It is, Althusser comments,

> a line excessively encumbered with meanings and echoes of a philo-
> sophy of the signifier, the letter, the unconscious as signifier. To that
> declaration, which is supported by a whole philosophy not of the
> addressee but of destiny or fate, and thus of the most classic finality, I
> will simply oppose the materialist thesis: *it happens that a letter does not
> arrive at its destination.*
>
> (Althusser, 1996: 91–2)

But this seminar on *The Purloined Letter*, which opens Lacan's *Ecrits*, was just the text which had also led to a contradictory debate between Lacan and Jacques Derrida. In 1975 Derrida published his essay on 'Le facteur de la vérité' (Derrida, 1980). There he 'deconstructs' Lacan's account of Poe's story. The details of this operation do not concern us here. What matters is Derrida's approach. The latter was to note, later, that just in this period (and Lacan's choice of the seminar on *The Purloined Letter* to open the *Ecrits*, published in 1966, was one index of the sense of the operation),[13] Lacan was effecting a remixing of his writings 'which made the most powerful and most powerfully spectacu-lar use of all the *motifs* that in my view were just asking to be deconstructed, were already being deconstructed' – including the motif of the *parole pleine* (cf. Derrida, 1996: 72).

Derrida comments that Lacan seems to be trying to use a literary text in order to establish a truth external to the text in question. For Lacan's reading of Poe is in fact directed against Marie Bonaparte, who had produced a much earlier psychoanalytic interpretation of the same story. But Lacan is not just in accidental disagreement with the princess. Bonaparte was after all the member of the *Société psychanalytique de Paris* whose 'treachery' – her abandonment of Lacan for his rival, Sacha Nacht, in the 1953 controversy – was responsible for Lacan's 'excommunication'. Like the minister in Poe's story, she had 'stolen' a letter, Lacan's letter of recommendation, his letter of credit. Thus, Lacan identifies with Poe's hero, Dupin, whose task is to 'put the world to rights'. The external truth which Lacan wants to impose is that 'a letter always arrives at its destination' (cf. Milner, 1985; Major, 1987). Lacan recounts his version of the events involving Nacht and Marie Bonaparte in a letter to Rudolph Loewenstein of 14 July 1953 (Miller, 1976). René Major, referring to the same letter, comments that Nacht is for Lacan 'an unprincipled man', like the minister in Poe's story – Dupin's 'double' because (at least metaphorically, so it is argued, and perhaps in 'reality', as Jean-Claude Milner holds) his brother. Nacht, Lacan's brother analyst, was confirmed in power, against Lacan, by a third party, a woman, Marie Bonaparte. She, according to Lacan, had betrayed him (Lacan talks about 'the most patent and harrowing treason'), playing a double game, signing a secret pact with Nacht, for which she was later rewarded.

The relation to the 'double', to the *semblable*, is on Lacan's own account an imaginary relation; in the analytic situation 'an imaginary transference on to our person of one of the more or less archaic *imagos,* . . . which, by an act of identification, has given its form to this or that agency of the personality'. But in such a case 'the slightest pretext is enough to arouse the aggressive intention, which reactualizes the *imago* . . . ' (Lacan, 1977c: 14). Lacan's aggression seems, however, to be directed, at least in the published texts, not so much against Nacht (who, he tells Loewenstein, even if he is unscrupulous, at least deserves credit for never deviating from or abandoning his goal) as against Marie Bonaparte. She it is who is mocked in an offhand and cryptic manner in the seminar on *The Purloined Letter*; it is she who is identified as the 'cook' from the kitchen, in the sense of the gossip, who concerns herself only with unimportant matters – and who thus, presumably, misses the crucial point (Lacan, 1966e: 36).

Althusser, in his first letter to Lacan, tells him: 'You are not alone.' In other words, we are comrades-in-arms, brothers – perhaps even *semblables*... (Althusser, 1996: 148, 151). For while I, Althusser, was making a return to Marx (to his rejection of the *homo economicus*) you, Lacan, were making a return to Freud (to his rejection of the *homo psychologicus*). Lacan answers: I find my questions in your work. And so the correspondence continues, Althusser playing, as it has been said, the role of the 'father-of-the-father', Lacan more reticent, absorbed in his own concerns (Roudinesco, 1997: 301; Ogilvie, 1993: 36–9).

Let us recall that the conclusion that Althusser for his part draws in respect of the seminar on *The Purloined Letter* is that the 'truth' which Lacan wants to establish is in reality a philosophical thesis *of teleological tendency*. Yet in his autobiographical essay *L'Avenir dure longtemps* Althusser modifies his assessment of the disagreement with Lacan: for Lacan, confronted with Althusser's reversal of his own thesis, had replied that Althusser was not a practitioner. 'I understood', Althusser comments, 'that he was right'! In the transference relation linking analyst and patient, there is no void – whatever unconscious message is sent out there really does always arrive. Althusser does not say whether he thinks that this interpretation of Lacan's claim removes any teleological features which it might have been thought to possess. But, Althusser adds, 'I was right too: for Lacan was speaking from the point of view of analytic practice, while I was speaking from the point of view of the practice of philosophy.'

The intimidation effect had, it seems, now reimposed itself on Althusser. Indeed, he adds that Lacan's reaction only reinforced his respect for the latter's perspicacity – and this 'in spite of the equivocal character of some of his usages' – especially of the concepts of *parole vide* and *parole pleine* found in 'Function and field...', the Rome Lecture of 1953. But the question is whether these phrases are indeed accidental excrescences on an otherwise materialist theory. Lecourt for one thinks not.

Lacan's great strategic innovation, Lecourt argues, was not to have returned to a set of authentic Freudian meanings, but to have produced a unification of those concepts which seemed to him necessary in order to grasp the unconscious via a single theoretical reference. Freud, in contrast, had borrowed from many sciences (moving back and forwards between dynamics, biology, political economy, 'energeticism', psychology, psychiatry and so on). Lacan's innovation lay in restricting his borrowings, as far as the scientific domain is concerned, to a single theoretical zone, namely structural linguistics, with some support from a structuralist ethnology, the whole system turning around a notion of *desire* – and this, we might add, in a Kojèvian sense: 'Man's desire finds its sense in the desire of the other, not so much because the other holds the key to the object desired, as because the first object of desire is to be recognized by the other' (Lacan, 1966c: 268). Thus, in *parole vide* or empty speech the subject 'can never become one with the assumption of his desire'. How to transform *parole vide* into *parole pleine?* The key to the problem lies to hand. What, after all, is – on Lacan's view – the problematic *of parole vide and parole pleine* but a problematic of the 'true subject'? And the true subject is 'the subject of the unconscious' (Lacan, 1966f). For, as he puts it, 'what the subject who is speaking says, however empty his words may at first be, takes on its effect from his thus approaching the word in which he may fully convert the truth which his symptoms express'. Psychoanalysis as the way, the path to a truth transcending the conscious experience of the subject.

Roudinesco comments speculatively on the fact that 'Lacan and Althusser shared a religious background that probably had something to do with their shared religious conception of the decentred subject and of structure as *absent causality.*' Was it not necessary, she asks, 'if one wanted to save one's soul, to tear oneself away from oneself and merge into a history stripped of all historicity, or into the *one* in the signifying chain?' (Roudinesco, 1997: 301). A religious background can indeed explain many things. But is it not equally likely – and Roudinesco provides the information to support such an idea – that Lacan's varied and indeed eclectic philosophical borrowings have a more indirect relation to religion? This would be true, for instance, of his idea of (unconscious) desire, whose signifier (he calls it object *a*) is the representative of the 'object of lack' (*manque*). This and some other Lacanian notions, it is true, are difficult to decipher. Roudinesco indeed insists, in another context, on Lacan's 'capacity for the production of ambiguity'. But they certainly have a spiritualist ring to them. In some respects they derive from Kojève, who speaks in his commentary on Hegel's *Phenomenology of Spirit* of desire as 'the revelation of a void' (Roudinesco, 1997: 103); but in other regards they seem to be inspired by Bergson, as we have already seen. And Bergson is indeed one of the great spiritualists, a member of that 'archetypically French' tradition of a philosophy of consciousness and authenticity.

In Lacan, the subject progresses from lack to desire, and 'in moving from desire to demand alienates itself in language', as it had earlier alienated itself in imaginary representation, that is, in the image of the ego-object (Lemaire, 1977: 129, 161). So there seems to be a double alienation. The former alienation is, says Lacan, the 'doing of the subject', which is paradoxically to say that it is the expression of the fact that 'no subject can be its own cause (for it is not God, nor could even God be like that)' (Lacan, 1966g: 840). That is why there is an alienation at all, a separation, a 'splitting of the subject'. What psychoanalytic practice offers then is a prospect of 'reintegration and harmony, . . . even reconciliation' (Lacan, 1966h: 514, 523).

Where, however, in the face of these difficulties, Freud compromises, Lacan seeks a solution in philosophical eclecticism. That is to say: on the one hand he insists on the radical difference between his own treatment of 'the subject' (of its splitting, of its alienating identifications and so on) and the psychological approach; on the other hand he makes use where he can, in order to solve specific 'theoretical problems', of whatever philosophical tools come to hand. Thus spiritualist instruments are put to work too, and especially notions of authenticity and the like, now linked not to consciousness as in the original spiritualist tradition,[14] but to the unconscious. There is an unconscious subject, or rather, since the unconscious is defined as the 'discourse of the other' (after the mid-1950s, of the 'Other'), there is a 'true subject', which is, as we saw, the subject of the unconscious, condemned to speak the 'language of its symptoms' – until, as we also saw, it succeeds in 'fully converting the truth' of those symptoms. In 'Variantes de la cure-type' (Variations on the standard treatment), an article written for the *Encyclopédie médico-chirurgicale*, though rejected by the encyclopaedia's editors, Lacan returns to the attack on American psychoanalysis which has adulterated Freud. At the same time he insists on the need for the analyst to open himself to the 'authentic speech' of the other (Lacan, 1966i: 352).

Now this *authenticity* is reminiscent of the Heideggerian notion, as Anthony Wilden remarks. But Wilden also correctly points up, in this context, a general difficulty in reading Lacan: 'Many problems of interpreting Lacan', he notes, 'are difficult to resolve because he does not approach the developments of his own theory in an unequivocal fashion. I cannot recall many published passages in which he says, for instance, that at such and such a time he thought one thing whereas now he thinks another. His views are always presented *en bloc* as if they had never evolved, with the result that one tends to assume that any formula or aphorism which is repeated always means more or less the same thing, whereas closer examination shows that this can not be so.' However that may be, in the 1950s Lacan still has an ' "existential" concern . . . for the fate of the individual in the neo-Freudian theories of social adaptation', as reflected in 'his apparently approving references to

[Maurice] Leenhardt's Westernized "man in his authenticity"' (Wilden, 1968: 181–2). Later, without ever taking an explicit distance from his earlier formulations, Lacan launched a new attack on the 'Cartesian subject', in the context of the production of a concept of the 'subject of the unconscious' – though one that hardly turned out to fit well with Freud's system. Roudinesco calls this later development a logicistic rewriting of structuralism, 'an astonishing patchwork of Frege and Gödel, mixed together in a sort of metaphorical bucket' (Roudinesco, 1986: 412–13). The subject, which is divided, foreclosed, 'ex-centric', is said just for that reason to be a new subject of science, that is to say, of a 'science of the incomplete', of a science of the impossibility of a complete formalization of its object (Lacan, 1966j: 5–28; Lock, 1987). 'The subject on which we operate in psychoanalysis', Lacan commented during the seminar series of 1965–6, 'can only be the subject of science, even if this looks like a paradox...' But this science is not a 'science of man' because the 'man' of science does not exist... Indeed, the term 'human sciences' designates, he thinks, something like a (temporarily successful) attempt by psychology to secure its survival by offering its services to technocracy: engaging 'even, as a sensational article by [Georges] Canguilhem concludes, in a Swiftian tone of humour, in a toboggan slide from the Panthéon to the police station' (Lacan, 1966j: 10–11).

By the 1960s, then, Lacan had radicalized his conception of the subject, without having explicitly renounced his earlier views. But whereas the earlier Lacan insisted on a distinction between the subject (of the unconscious) and an 'alienated', misrecognized ego – a Hegelian-Kojèvian account seasoned with a 'Heideggerian' or quasi-spiritualist, more or less explicitly open dependence on a problematic of inauthenticity and authenticity – the later Lacan prefers to talk about 'a topology intended to account for the constitution of the subject', 'the topology proper to our experience as analysts', the 'topology of the subject', which he represents as a 'Möbius surface' or 'Möbius strip' (Lacan, 1979: 90, 403). It may indeed be said that Lacan moves, in his account of subject and ego, from saying to showing.

Leaving aside the question of Lacan's odd exploitation of topological figures, which became one of his obsessions in the last years of his life (Roudinesco calls it his trip to 'planet Borromeo' on account of the role played in the obsession by the 'Borromean knot'), it becomes clear that by this time Lacan's eclecticism had led him to embrace a theoretical formalism and a practice which 'reduced psychoanalysis to zero'. (Roudinesco, 1997: 385ff. uses this phrase in connection especially with the short, finally as good as non-existent psychoanalytic session practised by Lacan.) But this return to zero seems to be explicable, at least in part, by an impasse in which Lacan found himself, that of the impossibility of a durable combination of what Lecourt calls a 'materialism of the signifier and a spiritualism of authenticity'. Lecourt adds:

> It is doubtless because Althusser, in consequence of his own, still substantialist conception of materialism, only noticed and grasped the former [element], that he could have fallen into the blind alley which finally led to his article ['On Freud and Lacan'] of 1964. And it is probably because they discovered the second that the pleiad of disappointed ex-militants of the movement of May 1968 were able to discover in Lacanianism a refuge for their disillusions, thus restoring vigour, in a hardly recognizable form, to a national philosophical tradition which seemed to have been dead and buried for at least ten years.
>
> (Lecourt, 1982: 119–20)

Lacan's relation to his philosophical sources was of a kind I called eclectic, a term recalling, I think, at least for the French, the famed eclecticism of Victor Cousin, his 'fusion of all that is best in philosophy', based on the idea that every system contains some truth. It was Cousin who inspired the renewal of interest in the work of Maine de Biran, the founding father of spiritualism.

There is a moment, duly transcribed in the published version of Lacan's 1964 seminar, which seems to sum up his manner of theoretical operation as well as the problems associated with such an eclectic use of sources in the field of rapidly moving intellectual fashion. Lacan, in one of the sessions of the seminar, expounds a generally Kojèvian- Hegelian account of 'lack' (see above) and alienation. It is in Hegel, he again claims, that he was able to discover a 'legitimate justification' for his terminology (the so-called 'alienating *vel*'), used to denote a process of 'the production of the primary alienation, that by which man enters into the way of slavery. *Your freedom or your life!* If he chooses freedom, he loses both immediately – if he chooses life, he has life deprived of freedom.' And so on. In the brief period following Lacan's exposition devoted to 'Questions and answers', Jacques-Alain Miller (who was to become his son-in-law, institutional heir and editor of the published seminar) asks somewhat impudently:

> 'Do you not wish to show, all the same [that is, whatever you actually said], that the alienation of a subject who has received the definition

of being born in, constituted by, and ordered in a field that is exterior to him, is to be distinguished radically from the alienation of a con-sciousness-of-self? In short, are we to understand – Lacan *against* Hegel?'

Miller – the pupil at this time of Althusser – is reminding Lacan that time has moved on, that the reference to Hegel is the wrong one; the whole argument has indeed been couched in the wrong terms. But there is no need to panic: the argument can be turned around: why not simply redub it *anti*-Hegelian: 'Lacan *against* Hegel'. Lacan, without hesitation, takes the hint. 'What you have just said is very good,' he responds.

> It's exactly the opposite of what [André] Green just said to me – he came up to me, shook my paw, at least morally, and said, 'The death of structuralism, you are the son of Hegel.' I don't agree. I think that in saying Lacan *against* Hegel, you [Miller] are much closer to the truth, though of course it is not at all a philosophical debate.

At which point Green is recorded as contenting himself with the remark: 'The sons kill the father' (Lacan, 1979: 215).

Nearly thirty years later, in an interview, André Green comments that the kind of alienation which interested Lacan was the alienation of his followers in his own person. For he was a man who would do anything in order to be idolized, in the manner of a sect leader. Lacan was above the law which he himself laid down. The short session – terminated by Lacan at any moment, sometimes before the patient had a chance to say more than a few words[15] – set up a sado-masochistic relation as a model. Elisabeth Roudinesco comments: '[His theory] denounced the omnipo-tence of the ego..., though he himself asserted the supremacy of his own.' It is often said that a clear line has to be drawn between Lacan the man on the one hand – a 'worthless' character – and Lacan the 'marvel-lous' practician on the other. Green, however, disagrees: they were, he insists, the same man (Green, 1993: 20).

The intellectual landscape in France, in the period of Lacan's most intensive activity – roughly the period of his seminars, but especially the 1960s – was, it seems, one in which Lacan was sometimes able to 'get away' with anything: what the French call the 'n'importe quoi'. Many of the members of his audience had in any case little idea of the line or sense of his argument, whatever it may have been, nor were they in any position to take a critical attitude to his exposition.[16]

Stuart Schneiderman comments that Lacan was 'hysterical' and 'histrionic' and saw analysis as akin to theatre. But the theory, he claims, 'was the base on which the practice was built' (Schneiderman, 1983: 35, 37). Yet the theory, if rich, was often incoherent. Lacan borrowed from anyone who was willing to lend him – at no charge, of course – an idea. Nearly anything could be pressed into service. We saw that Roudinesco credits him with a gift for ambiguity. In this respect the collections of his spoken word have some similarity with sacred texts, at one and the same time mandatory in their force and yet open to the most varied interpretations. I say 'word', for in many cases the effect of what he said was a function not so much of argument as of a happy (or unhappy) *trouvaille*: 'Lacan's spoken word had always imitated the language of the unconscious, but from 1975 on...he almost drowned his own teaching in puns, allographs, portmanteau words, and neologisms that were often reminiscent of the basic signifiers in his life and teaching' (Roudinesco, 1997: 374). As in the case of aphoristic writers, it is the reader who does much of the work, projecting – in a manner which Ludwig Feuerbach might have considered with profit – his own results onto the author.

And yet – Lacan, who had no academic training in the field, was regarded by many as something like a philosopher, even as a great one. One might imagine that this could only have been the case in a country like France, where philosophy has an existence outside of the academic institution, where most 'educated' people have taken at least a basic course in philosophy at secondary school, and where philosophical essays are sold in relatively large numbers to a fairly general public – that is to say, in a country with a tradition of cultivated amateurism. But 'in the English-speaking countries [too], as in most of northern Europe, Lacan's work was regarded as belonging to the history of French philosophy and never as a clinical doctrine' (Roudinesco, 1997: 375).

As far as its influence in France is concerned, Lacan's work hardly touched the field of the *beaux-arts* and *belles-lettres*. This state of affairs might perhaps have been expected, given that Lacan himself, though he had many friends in literary and artistic circles, seems to have been primarily interested in what Derrida called an external use of literature and art as sources of illustrative examples or even proofs of his psychoanalytic theses. But there are two main domains in which his activity did have a very considerable influence.

The first of these domains is that of philosophy in the broad sense, but including academic philosophy, in France and elsewhere. An important reference in this connection is the generation of *normaliens*, students of the Ecole Normale Supérieure in Paris, some of whom, under the influence of their teacher Althusser, had begun as we saw in the early 1960s to make a study of Lacan's work. This group, which set up the journal *Cahiers pour l'Analyse*, produced – or recruited from outside of its original ranks – many of the most brilliant young thinkers of the postwar period. Thus, among the first editors of the *Cahiers pour l'Analyse* were Jacques-Alain Miller (see above), Jean-Claude Milner, later to become a theorist of linguistics (see, for example, Milner, 1983) and François Regnault. The last was to publish works on literature and theatre as well as a set of 'Lacanian theses' on Thomas Aquinas (Regnault, 1985). Michel Tort, also by origin an Althusserian, pursued a Freudian career. A rather different example is provided by Michel Plon. Trained outside of Paris in psychology, Plon published in 1976 an outstanding, acerbic study, inspired by Althusser and Lacan, of the theory, ideology and politics of game theory (Plon, 1976). Standing in a quite different relation to Lacan is another ex-student of the Ecole Normale, Alain Badiou. The author of a number of impressively brilliant and erudite works on philosophy, politics, mathematics and poetry (for instance Badiou 1982, 1988, 1989), he early became a Maoist and inspired the activities of a group of intellectual militants. Three of the members of this group produced an attack (Boons et al., 1975) on psychoanalytic theory and, more particularly, on the Lacanian 'metaphysics of language' (as well as on Deleuze).[17] But Badiou's own position on Lacan was more subtle and polyvalent. In his *Manifeste pour la philosophie* he tries to establish the nature of Lacan's contribution to philosophy – or anti-philosophy – and to situate the latter's work in the politico-theoretical 'conjuncture' of the years 1965–80. We should also mention the name of Pierre Legendre, who, after an ecclesiastical training, became both an analyst and a recognized academic expert on administrative law and medieval legal theory. Legendre published in 1974, in Lacan's series *Le Champ freudien*, a curious but magnificent Freudian study of legal and political institutions (Legendre, 1974) which he has followed up with a series of *Leçons* (among which Legendre, 1983, 1988, 1992).

Many other examples could be given of thinkers indebted to or heavily influenced by Lacan. But one of the characteristics of these thinkers – all of them younger, some much younger, than Lacan – is that their more or less independent development of Lacanian themes has been such as to produce results that have generally been much better regarded by the academic establishment than is the work of Lacan himself. And there is a reason for this: simply, that their work tends to take a distance from the imposture considered by many to be an essential aspect of Lacan's style and perhaps of the content of his work.

The second field influenced by Lacan is that of psychoanalytic practice itself. There are now some five thousand practising analysts in France – the highest in the world in proportion to the population – of which less than a thousand are members of the two societies affiliated to the IPA (the SPP and the Association Psychanalytique de France that succeeded the SFP). The others are mostly more or less Lacanian, members of one of the more than a dozen schools and groups which sprang up after the dissolution in 1980 of Lacan's Ecole freudienne de Paris.[18]

By the 1990s a substantial normalization of French psychoanalytic practice had taken place, even if not in the manner once intended by the IPA. The 'Lacanians', of varied plumage, are apparently – at least as far as the new generation is concerned – no longer so interested in spectacular theoretical or philosophical discoveries. They are less well-educated, in the general sense, than earlier generations, and less concerned with matters not directly relevant to psychoanalytic practice. They tend to have a background in psychology rather than in medicine and psychiatry on the one hand or academic philosophy on the other. France, Roudinesco has recently commented, 'does not have to face the virulent wave of anti-Freudianism that exists in the United States. Neither Freud nor psychoanalysis itself is under attack. But the schools of psychoanalysis are severely criticized' (Roudinesco, 1998). The response of the psychoanalytic profession, whether 'orthodox' or 'Lacanian', has been to withdraw into the world of clinical practice. This tendency, indeed, reflects the attitude of the patients, who are now much more likely than in the past to treat psychoanalysis as just one potential medicine among others, more or less effective than others on offer, to be judged in comparison with its competitors on the basis of short-term therapeutic success (Roudinesco, 1997: 428ff.).

Lacan's theory, for many of these practicians, including the Lacanians, has thus been reduced to a textbook doctrine – which is probably no more nor less useful or dangerous than similar textbook summaries of Freud's own doctrine. A few ideas now orient the young Lacanian analyst's practice: that the unconscious is 'structured like a language' (which justifies the method of the 'talking cure'); that the child creates a sense of identity – an ego – in the mirror stage; that this ego is an imaginary construction (*pace* the ego-psychologists, who still play the role of theoretical bugbears); that as against this imaginary ego, a subject of the symbolic order, of language, of the unconscious, of science, can be posited; that the laws of the unconscious can be formalized (in the matheme)[19] and taught – for example at the university – in this formalized version; and so on. Indeed, the doctrine is so taught. Since 1968 there has existed a Lacanian department of psychoanalysis at the University of Paris-VIII (Vincennes). It was founded by Serge Leclaire, but taken over and brought under control by the 'legitimists' under the leadership of Jacques-Alain Miller (Roudinesco, 1986: 557ff.). There are even psychoanalytic textbooks for schoolchildren, which, as a French publisher recently announced, are intended to introduce pupils to 'Freud, Lacan, Jung and Melanie Klein' (Monde des Livres, 1987).

The normalization of French psychoanalysis has been paralleled by a normalization of French social, ideological and political life. The Cold War has come to an end in Europe. The French Communist Party has been reduced to a fraction of its previous size, and its influence diminished even further. The Catholic Church for its part had already in the 1960s, with the Second Vatican Council, effected a modernization of some of those elements of its doctrine and liturgy which offended the contemporary liberal conscience; now it is under severe pressure to take further steps along the same road. And French civil society is in a rapid process of Americanization, especially among the younger generations.

In this situation, a continuation of something like Lacan's 'intellectual adventure' would make little sense. For the success of this adventure was parasitic on the febrile atmosphere of a country divided for most of the century, yet at the same time enlivened, by bitter but productive ideological conflicts. Nearly all of these currents are to be found reflected and transformed in Lacan's developing thought – he was a friend of and borrowed from Marxists, Hegelians, surrealists, Maurrassians, Catholics, psychiatrists, poets, philosophers, mathematicians and others.

But there is a category which does not figure on this list. In spite of his political caution, Lacan never had much time for liberalism.[20] And in an epoch of an apparently triumphant neo-liberal ideology, this fact must have consequences for the fate of his intellectual heritage. Moreover, it may be roughly true, as Régis Debray argues, that 'an Americanized intelligentsia in a Europeanized France puts the emphasis on smiles, good teeth, nice hair and the adolescent stupidity known as petulance' (Jenkins and Kemp-Welch, 1997: 14, quoting Debray, 1981). Lacan lacked some (though not all) of these qualities, and is in any case now dead, with only a kind of intellectual administrator as heir and successor.

The adventure, it might be concluded, is over. Or, from another point of view, it might be said that an end has come to a 'very Parisian phenomenon, a fashion, a folly, a snobbish mode'. I quote these words from Catherine Clément, a Lacanian journalist, who only adds that there is an explanation of this collective passion, which 'avoided all criticism, even the most serious, from outside', this explanation being called *love* – a love projected onto Lacan, the beacon and guide believed to show the way, in Clément's own nebulous formulation, to 'a different kind of thinking...' (Clément, 1981: 27).

In a fine turn of phrase, it has been said that Lacan 'sought to inject death, subversion, and total disorder into the Freudian body as he found it. He then shoved the dead body of psychoanalysis into a vat of vinegar to ferment in a sea of excrement' – his gift to the next century (Dominguez, 1998). It is always difficult to know what the dead might think of a critic's appreciation of their 'lifetime achievement', as the much-detested Americans call it. But I imagine that Lacan would have thought that these words, if they do not quite hit the right note, were at least in an appropriate key. They provide, it might be said, a symbolic framework within which a kind of mourning can take place for a 'French psychoanalysis' which once was but will be, in that guise of passion, adventure and delirium, no more.

Notes

1 Making up the original group of ten were Angelo Hesnard, René Allendy and Georges Parcheminey.

2 For most of the historical information contained in the chapter, I am – as are all commentators on the history of psychoanalysis in France – indebted to the work of Elisabeth Roudinesco. On important matters I indicate the precise source in Roudinesco's writings.

3 Marion Michel Oliner, whose intention is to relate 'the fate of Freud's heritage in France', notes that 'many Americans have the mistaken impression that Jacques Lacan represents the views of most Freud psychoanalysts. He does not, but... [his] presence has been pervasive, even to those who rejected him from the start.' This impact, she adds, 'was both political and theoretical' (Oliner, 1988: xiii, 5). Oliner distinguishes between the 'orthodox' and the 'Lacanian' analysts. She devotes two chapters of her book to Lacan, more space than to any other French analyst. But she does discuss at greater or lesser length the work of, among others, Michel Fain, Janine Chasseguet-Smirgel, André Green, Béla Grunberger, Michel de M'Uzan, Marthe Robert and Didier Anzieu. Oliner's point of view is that there is a typically 'French approach' to psychoanalysis, distinguished from the American by the former's more speculative and intuitive traits. 'The French are more daring'; 'by comparison Americans are modest and most methodical'. Oliner notes that the 'unique character of French psychoanalysis is related to the nation's cultural milieu: its erudition, its reverence for tradition, and its intellectuals' capacity for incisive logic and passion for independence', but she does not systematically discuss the lines of influence (Oliner, 1988: 3, 305–6). Rather, she summarizes various strands of

argument in psychoanalytic theory (for example on narcissism, perversion and reality) to be found in the French authors. In the present short study there is no room for a discussion of the work of such authors, however welcome that might be.

4   According to the theory of the mirror stage, the young child (between 6 months and 18 months old) learns to 'identify' with the 'other' represented by its own mirror image. Lacan here borrows from and transforms an idea of Henri Wallon (from the latter's notion of the role of the 'mirror stage' or 'mirror ordeal' in the unification of the ego) and from a conception of Alexandre Kojève. Kojève had already, on the basis of his reading of Hegel's *Philosophy of Spirit*, developed a notion of ego as will, therefore source of error, distinguished from an 'I', site of thought and desire (Roudinesco, 1997: 105). On Lacan's subsequent account, the field of (necessary) misrecognition in which the ego is produced is called the *imaginary*. This field is contrasted not only with the *symbolic* order, relayed by the Name-of-the-Father, but also with the *real*, which is said to be the 'impossible', that is to say, whatever is left over when a symbolic order has finished cutting up the world, or whatever such an order 'fails to get hold of'. Anika Lemaire comments that 'the normal man will be characterized by an economy balanced around these three poles [Real, Imaginary and Symbolic], the neurotic by a disturbance of internal metabolism between them, and the psychotic by a radical and original alteration in the use of the linguistic sign . . . The neurotic has effected the transition to the symbolic order, whereas the psychotic . . . never effected it completely' (Lemaire, 1997: 227; cf. Lock and Roudinesco, 1983–4).

5   See, for example, Raymond Tallis (Tallis, 1997: 20):

> Lacan . . . is one of the fattest spiders at the heart of the web of muddled not-quite-thinkable thoughts and evidence-free assertions of limitless scope, which practitioners of theorrhoea have woven into their version of the humanities . . . His lunatic legacy . . . lives on . . . in departments of literature whose inmates are even now trying to, or pretending to, make sense of his utterly unfounded, gnomic teachings and inflicting them on baffled students.

Cf. Sokal and Bricmont (1997).

6   The French Communist Party was hostile to Freudian theory and practice, which it considered a 'bourgeois' phenomenon. In 1949, a group of Communists engaged in the psychiatric and cognate professions published in the journal *La Nouvelle Critique* – under pressure – a text entitled 'Autocritique: La Psychanalyse, idéologie réactionnaire'. Among the signatories was the psychoanalyst Serge Lebovici, one of the leading figures in the SPP and an opponent of Lacan. Lebovici was later to become the first French President of the IPA.

7   So some part at least of the 'French resistance to psychoanalysis' might be accounted for not just in personal but in political terms: the Franco-Prussian war of 1871 and the annexation of Alsace and Lorraine had stirred anti-Germanic feelings in many French spirits.

8   Which was not Lacan's case. Roudinesco quotes Georges Bernier (Lacan's first analysand) to the effect that Lacan 'felt that he had a superior mind and

belonged to the intellectual elite. So he saw to it that the events that history forced him to confront should have no effect on his way of life' (Roudinesco, 1997: 155).

9 Catherine Clément (Clément, 1971: 42) writes: 'I recognize myself as French in Lacan. Not, indeed, for "national" reasons, but for reasons of culture... No more Jerusalem, no more Moses; but the Jansenist cross, Port-Royal... Lacan succeeded in establishing, in his person, the first plausible image of French psychoanalysis.' It thus sounds as if, for Clément, this image is at least in part Catholic.

10 Roudinesco writes (Roudinesco, 1997: 61):

> From 1932 on [Lacan] could look to a new philosophical heritage... Pointing to the extreme poverty of French philosophy as it was then, plunged deep in Bergsonian spiritualism, academic neo-Kantianism, or a Cartesianism diverted from its original inspiration, the materialist avant-garde liked to contrast this deplorable state of affairs with the splendour of German thought. They saw this as both Hegelian and Marxist but also enriched by the gospel of certain great contemporaries: Husserl, of course, but also Nietzsche and Heidegger, who had just (in 1926) published his famous *Sein und Zeit*... Lacan, having been thus dubbed a materialist, accepted the mirror held up to him by the avant-garde... [He] converted to a different Husserl and a Hegelian-Marxist materialism. But it would take him four years to come to grips, though the teaching of Kojève and Koyré, with Hegel's *Phenomenology of Mind* and Heidegger's philosophy.'

Yet matters, as we shall see, were even more complicated.

11 But it should not be forgotten that Lacan (unlike Althusser) made profitable sorties to speak at American universities, for example at Yale and at the Massachusetts Institute of Technology in 1975. At Yale he characterized himself as a 'psychotic' in respect of his 'attempt at rigour'.

12 Cf. Lock (1996: 78): '[Althusser's] theory of the constitution of the subject is not a "sociological" theory because it is hardly a "social" theory at all. It is fairly clearly modeled... on Lacan's account of the "mirror stage" in the constitution of the human individual...'

13 See Roudinesco (1997: 326):

> In the biographical note, 'Concerning my Antecedents' [appended to the *Ecrits*] Lacan [interpreted] the history of his earlier texts in the light of his present doctrine... A book, he was saying in substance, should be read in terms of its later evolution... That being so, the best introduction to a reading of the *Ecrits* was not so much the 'Seminar on "The Purloined Letter"' as its two appendices (the 'Presentation' and the 'Parenthesis'), which led on to a text called 'Science and Truth'... In this text Lacan had carried out what I have called a *logical revision* of his structural theory of the subject and the signifier...

14 The spiritualists tended generally to argue that psychology is unable to provide a complete or an adequate account of intellectual phenomena; that the

spirit is somehow superior to the faculties of the body or to the material sphere; that it is necessary (as Félix Ravaisson claimed) to develop a spiritualist realism, capable of taking account of the ego's role as a power endowed with liberty, able to assert its authenticity by an act of will, and so on.

15 Stuart Schneiderman makes a valiant attempt to provide a 'theoretical' justification for the short session (in Schneiderman, 1983: 136, 138):

> [A] brief look at the principle of free association will help to clarify what Lacan was doing with the short sessions. Most analysts have felt that the process of free association takes place *within* the analytic session... What Lacan added was a free association that took place *between* sessions... People in analysis often yield up a mass of verbiage whose purpose is to confuse the issue and to cloud over the question. Lacan must have felt that talking too much often was used as a resistance... Through the experience of short sessions the analysand [the patient] learns first to get right to the point and second to say as much as possible quickly.

16 What the Austrian ex-student Frieda Meisner-Blau (Meissner-Blau, 1993) has to say about her first visit to the seminar, in 1968, is germane. 'I had the feeling', she recalls, 'of entering a temple, so thick and tense was the atmosphere... Silence reigned, a solemn silence, a silence of expectation. I stood open-mouthed: I could understand each word, taken separately, but I couldn't make the slightest sense of the least phrase!' And this reaction is, it seems, not untypical.

17 Boon et al. are very hostile to Lacan, claiming for example that his 'ethics of truth' is a lie and a fake. Gilles Deleuze had, with Félix Guattari, published in 1972 a work entitled *L'Anti-Oedipe*, in which the authors radicalize the theory of the Oedipal drama and of the symbolic order, turning it against Lacan, to advocate a new practice of 'schizo-analysis'.

18 These are divided between the 'legitimist' *Ecole de la Cause freudienne*, led by Jacques-Alain Miller, and many 'dissident' groups, some with hundreds of members, others with only a handful.

19 See Lettres de l'Ecole (1977).

20 It is true that Lacan once, in 1968, provocatively told the students of Vincennes that 'I'm only a liberal, like everyone else', but glossing liberalism as an 'anti-progressive' position (Roudinesco, 1997: 342). Compare Georges Bernier's story, dating from 1944: Bernier, who 'had become a fervent advocate of parliamentary democracy, ... asked Lacan and his entourage if they ever voted. The result was general stupefaction, roars of laughter, and a chorus of noes...' (Roudinesco, 1997: 170).

References

Althusser, Louis (1971a) 'Freud and Lacan', in *Lenin and Philosophy and Other Essays*. London: New Left Books.

Althusser, Louis (1971b) 'Ideology and ideological state apparatuses: notes towards an investigation', in *Lenin and Philosophy and Other Essays*. London: New Left Books.

·Althusser, Louis (1996) *Writings on Psychoanalysis: Freud and Lacan*. New York: Columbia University Press.

Badiou, Alain (1982) *Théorie du sujet*. Paris: Editions du Seuil.

Badiou, Alain (1988) *L'Être et l'événement*. Paris: Editions du Seuil.

Badiou, Alain (1989) *Manifeste pour la philosophie*. Paris: Editions du Seuil.

Boons, M. C., B. Sichère and F. Manesse (1975) *Marxisme-léninisme et psychanalyse*. Paris: Maspero.

Bouveresse, Jacques (1995) *Wittgenstein Reads Freud: the Myth of the Unconscious*. Princeton: Princeton University Press.

Braunschweig, D. and M. Fain (1971) *Eros et Antéros*. Paris: Payot.

Clément, Catherine (1981) *Vies et légendes de Jacques Lacan*. Paris: Grasset.

Debray, Régis (1981) *Teachers, Writers, Celebrities: The Intellectuals of Modern France*. London: Verso.

Derrida, Jacques (1980) *La Carte postale*. Paris: Aubier-Flammarion. (Original publication in *Poétique*, 1975, no. 21.)

Derrida, Jacques (1996) *Résistances de la psychanalyse*. Paris: Galilée.

Descombes, Vincent (1979) *Le Même et l'autre: Quarante-cinq ans de philosophie française*. Paris: Editions de Minuit.

Dominguez, Ricardo (1998) 'Jacques Lacan, by Elisabeth Roudinesco'. www-text at http://www. thing.net/mag/ttreview/octrev 97.01.html

Ellenberger, Henri (1970) *The Discovery of the Unconscious*. New York: Basic Books.

Freud, Sigmund (1959) 'An autobiographical study', in James Strachey (ed.), *The Standard Edition of the Complete Psychological Works of Sigmund Freud*. London: Hogarth Press, pp. 7–74 (first published in 1925 as *Selbstdarstellung*).

Green, André (1993) 'Le Père omnipotent: un entretien avec André Green', *Le Magazine Littéraire*, no. 315.

Jenkins, Jeremy and Anthony Kemp-Welch (1997) *Intellectuals in Politics*. London: Routledge.

Johnson, R. W. (1981) *The Long March of the French Left*. London: Macmillan.

Lacan, Jacques (1966a) 'Le Stade du miroir comme formateur de la fonction du Je telle qu'elle nous est révélée dans l'expérience psychanalytique', in Jacques Lacan, *Ecrits*. Paris: Editions du Seuil.

Lacan, Jacques (1966b) 'La Chose freudienne ou Sens du retour à Freud en psychanalyse', in Jacques Lacan, *Ecrits*. Paris: Editions du Seuil.

Lacan, Jacques (1966c) 'Fonction et champ de la parole et du langage en psychanalyse', in Jacques Lacan, *Ecrits*. Paris: Editions du Seuil.

Lacan, Jacques (1966d) 'Réponse au commentaire de Jean Hyppolite', in Jacques Lacan, *Ecrits*. Paris: Editions du Seuil.

Lacan, Jacques (1966e) 'Le Séminaire sur "La Lettre volée"', in Jacques Lacan, *Ecrits*. Paris: Editions du Seuil.

Lacan, Jacques (1966f) 'Introduction au commentaire de Jean Hyppolite sur la "Verneinung" de Freud', in Jacques Lacan, *Ecrits*. Paris: Editions du Seuil.

Lacan, Jacques (1966g) 'Position de l'inconscient', in Jacques Lacan, *Ecrits*. Paris: Editions du Seuil.

Lacan, Jacques (1966h) 'L'Instance de la lettre dans l'inconscient', in Jacques Lacan, *Ecrits*. Paris: Editions du Seuil.

Lacan, Jacques (1966i) 'Variantes de la cure-type', in Jacques Lacan, *Ecrits*. Paris: Editions du Seuil.

Lacan, Jacques (1966j) 'La Science et la vérité', *Les Cahiers pour l'Analyse*. Paris: Editions du Seuil, 1966, no. 1–2.

Lacan, Jacques (1977a) 'Function and field of speech and language in psychoanalysis', in *Ecrits* (English edition). London: Tavistock Publications.

Lacan, Jacques (1977b) 'The Freudian thing, or the meaning of the return to Freud in psychoanalysis', in *Ecrits* (English edition). London: Tavistock Publications.

Lacan, Jacques (1977c) 'Aggressivity in psychoanalysis', in *Ecrits* (English edition). London: Tavistock Publications.

Lacan, Jacques (1979) *The Four Fundamental Concepts of Psycho-analysis*. Harmondsworth: Penguin Books.

Lacan, Jacques (1984) *Les Complexes familiaux dans la formation de l'individu*. Paris: Navarin. (Originally published in 1938 under the title 'La Famille'.)

Laplanche, Jean (1992) 'Le Structuralisme devant la psychanalyse', in *La Révolution copernicienne inachevée*. Paris: Aubier.

Lecourt, Dominique (1982) 'Lacan', in *La Philosophie sans feinte*. Paris: Albin Michel.

Legendre, Pierre (1974) *L'Amour du censeur*. Paris: Editions du Seuil.

Legendre, Pierre (1983) *L'Empire de la vérité*. Paris: Editions du Seuil.

Legendre, Pierre (1988) *Le Désir politique de Dieu*. Paris: Editions du Seuil.

Legendre, Pierre (1992) *Les Enfants du texte*. Paris: Editions du Seuil.

Lemaire, Anika (1977) *Jacques Lacan*. London: Routledge & Kegan Paul.

Lettres de l'Ecole (1977) *Lettres de l'Ecole. Bulletin Intérieur de l'Ecole freudienne de Paris*: 'Les mathèmes de la psychanalyse'.

Lock, Grahame (1987) 'Analytic philosophy, psychoanalytic theory and formalism', *Revue de Synthèse*, no. 2, April–June.

Lock, Grahame (1996) 'Subject, interpellation, and ideology', in Antonio Callari and David F. Ruccio (eds), *Postmodern Materialism and the Future of Marxist Theory*. Hanover, NH and London: Wesleyan University Press.

Lock, Grahame and Elisabeth Roudinesco (1983–4) 'Jacques Lacan en het eind van de "Ecole freudienne"', *De Gids*, Amsterdam, 528–35.

Major, René (1987) 'La Parabole de la lettre volée', *Etudes freudiennes*, no. 30.

Meissner-Blau, Frieda (1993) 'Instantané du séminaire', *Le Magazine Littéraire*, no. 315.

Miller, Jacques-Alain (ed.) (1976) *La Scission de 1953: La Communauté psychanalytique en France I* (supplément au numéro 8 d'*Ornicar?*). Paris: Champ freudien.

Miller, Jacques-Alain (ed.) (1977) *L'Excommunication: la Communauté psychanalytique en France II* (supplément au numéro 7 d'*Ornicar?*). Paris: Champ freudien.

Milner, Jean-Claude (1983) *Les Noms indistincts*. Paris: Editions du Seuil.

Milner, Jean-Claude (1985) 'Retour à la lettre volée', in *Detections fictives*. Paris: Editions du Seuil.

Monde des Livres (1997) *Le Monde des Livres*, 7 November 1997, p. viii.

Mordier, Jean-Pierre (1981) *Les Débuts de la psychanalyse*. Paris: Maspero. Citing Marie Bonaparte's note to Sigmund Freud, *Ma vie et la psychanalyse*.

Ogilvie, Betrand (1987) *Lacan, le sujet*. Paris: Presses Universitaires de France.

Ogilvie, Bertrand (1993) 'Lacan, Althusser: figures croisées', *Le Magazine Littéraire*, no. 315.

Oliner, Marion Michel (1988) *Cultivating Freud's Garden in France*. Northvale, NJ: Jason Aronson.

Pichon, Edouard (1980) 'La Famille devant M. Lacan', *Cahiers Confrontation*, Paris, no. 3.

Plon, Michel (1976) *La Théorie des jeux: une politique imaginaire.* Paris: Maspero.

Politzer, Georges (1969) *Ecrits. 2: Les Fondements de la psychologie.* Paris: Editions Sociales.

Regnault, François (1985) *Dieu est inconscient.* Paris: Navarin.

Roudinesco, Elisabeth (1982) *Histoire de la psychanalyse en France. 1, 1885–1939.* Paris: Editions Ramsay.

Roudinesco, Elisabeth (1986) *Histoire de la psychanalyse en France. 2, 1925–85.* Paris: Editions du Seuil.

Roudinesco, Elisabeth (1997) *Jacques Lacan.* Cambridge: Polity Press.

Roudinesco, Elisabeth (1998) 'Psychoanalysis at the end of the 20th century. The situation in France: clinical and institutional prospects', at http://www.ipa.org.vk/roudin.htm.

Schneiderman, Stuart (1983) *Jacques Lacan: Death of an Intellectual Hero.* Cambridge, MA: Harvard University Press.

Sokal, Alan and Jean Brinkmont (1997) *Impostures intellectuelles.* Paris: Edtions Odile Jacob.

Tallis, Raymond (1997) 'The shrink from hell', *The Times Higher Education Supplement,* 31 October 1997.

Wilden, Anthony (1968) *The Language of the Self.* Baltimore, MD and London: Johns Hopkins University Press.

11
Beyond Theory? The Empowering of Feminist Philosophy

Máire Fedelma Cross

In the history of Western thought, woman has been treated as something peculiar, unrepresentative of any essence of humanity (Battersby, 1998: 1). Not only that but women were considered incapable of serious thought. They were mere thinking muses (Allen and Young, 1989: 1). In recent developments in French thought feminist intellectuals challenge this treatment and attempt to construct a way of thinking which sees the female as the norm. They have been more successful in the former.

This chapter looks at the shaping of feminism as an intellectual field in France since 1945. It will show that for feminism, the links between theory and practice present the greatest dilemma in view of the continued inequality of gender relationships in French society and the persistence of the exclusion of women from decision-making processes. My suggestion is that this exclusion poses a particular problem of impotence for feminist philosophy which other intellectual disciplines do not encounter. Feminism is an enormous challenge to the established order and women's writing could have made considerably more impact on intellectual life in France if it were not for this inequality.

Feminism as a declared set of principles and as an organized movement has been in existence in France and elsewhere since the nineteenth century (Bard, 1995; Smith, 1996). It has been an intellectual activity ever since it left written evidence of its avowed philosophical search for the cause of this oppression or its political theory of liberation (Cross, 1997). Traditionally this intellectual activity was inspired by collective action, by women combating their oppression (Scott, 1996). Since 1945 in France there has been a conjunction of feminism and intellectual thought, beginning with Simone de Beauvoir's *Le Deuxième Sexe*, published in 1949.[1] According to Allen and Young (1989), French feminism was given a stimulus in post-war France when existential philosophy and phenomenology gave a new priority to everyday lived experience which defined relationships between men and women in phenomenological terms.

Furthermore one of the consequences of the fragmentation of intellectual currents in France after the Second World War was a new emphasis on the psyche, language, body and desire, which empowered women to contribute to intellectual discourse in a new way. Hitherto there had been no place for women nor for their specific concerns in the logic of eighteenth- and nineteenth-century thinkers. The development of Freudian psychoanalysis, existentialism, phenomenology and post-structuralism all challenged the abstract way of defining human beings and their existence and paved the way for a questioning of accepted modes of human behaviour and relationships in gender terms. However, this seemed to create a further conundrum for feminist intellectuals in France, that of identifying a female-specific intellectual identity. Feminist philosophy was concerned with constructing an identity for women as a group as if they shared a common experience which, according to some (Badinter, 1997), was the source of their cultural imprisonment in the first place. To segregate female identity was too artificial. The female experience was part of humanity. The pioneer in this intellectual effort was Simone de Beauvoir.

Questions of female identity are never posed in a theoretical vacuum. When she set out to write a systematic account of what it was to be a woman in the prime of her life, Simone de Beauvoir had already chosen her intellectual parameters. As a humanist she had found an alternative meaning of life to religion; as an existentialist she considered the individual's life to be interpretable in terms of freedom to make choices. Marxism was an attractive ideology too, with the example of the Soviet Union still appealing as a counter to western capitalism. Indeed, the ultimate solution for de Beauvoir, in as much as she considered any solution to oppression, was that the advent of state socialism would ensure the emancipation of women. She began, however, by wondering why women accept their subordinate position in society:

Why do women not challenge male sovereignty?

(1949a: 17)

> How is it that the world has always belonged to men and that things
> are only beginning to change now? Is this change for the better? Will
> it lead to men and women sharing the world on equal terms?
>
> (1949a: 22)

As an existentialist she looked for the meaning of life for women:

> What circumstances limit a woman's freedom and can she overcome
> them? These are the fundamental questions I would like to elucidate.
> That is to say that as I am interested in the question of an individual's
> potential I would define this potential in terms not of happiness but
> of freedom.
>
> (1949a: 32)

From the outset de Beauvoir was looking for a theory of oppression
and liberation which could apply to women from within her already
defined philosophical stance. By its open-ended nature feminism
empowered her philosophy: she was seeking a definition of woman, an
explanation of how relationships between the sexes had been determined and how women's lives which had altered during her lifetime as
well as over the centuries could alter in the future. She drew on historical
sources and anecdotal first-hand experience of other countries. She
claimed that women's condition was universal by citing examples of
the pattern of their lives from the contemporary scene in the USA,
USSR, Britain, Italy and examples from ancient Greece, Rome, the
Bible, medieval France, the *ancien régime*, the 1789 revolution and the
Industrial Revolution. The search for this definition led her to conclude
that one sex dominated another through social engineering. The main
focus of her analysis of oppression centred on the biological functions of
marriage and motherhood, which were commonly represented as 'natural'. She proclaimed that these were social functions according to economic needs of society and that women were socially conditioned to
fulfil their so-called natural roles. Thus women's subordination was
engineered, not static, but constantly evolving according to economic
changes in society:

> Therefore the triumph of patriarchy was neither by chance nor the
> result of a violent revolution. From the beginning of mankind, men's
> biological privilege has enabled them to assert themselves as the sole
> sovereign subjects; they have never rescinded this privilege, they
> alienated part of their existence in Nature and in Woman; but they

subsequently reconquered it; condemned to play the role of the Other, woman was also condemned to possess only a precarious power; slave or idol, it has never been she who chooses her lot in life.

(1949a: 130)

De Beauvoir's conclusion, therefore, was that women were different from men because of their social function defined by men. 'Anxious to maintain masculine prerogatives', men have created the divisions between the sexes (1949a: 114). On this view women are alienated from their true selves; they are condemned by their social conditioning to endure their natural functions of wife and mother. While she provided evidence to illustrate this alienation through social conditioning to the benefit of men, de Beauvoir's project for fulfilment was flawed. She equated biological functions with oppression because she reduced the value of motherhood to a basic existence and for this she was much criticized subsequently:

To characterise women's procreative and nurturing activity as reproduction is to deny its creativity... In our opinion this suggestion seriously undervalues the variability and the complexity of women's creative and nurturing activity as well as its possibilities for historical development.

(Jaggar and McBride, 1985: 192)

In France the debate over the social determination of motherhood was continued by Elizabeth Badinter who identified closely with de Beauvoir's argument:

Over thirty years ago a philosopher, Simone de Beauvoir, questioned maternal instinct. So too did psychologists and sociologists, mostly women. But as these women were feminists their arguments were dismissed as those of militants and not scientists. Instead of discussing their theories, many commentators made ironic remarks on their deliberate sterility or their aggressive, virile characteristics.

(1980: 27)

Badinter was arguing against biological essentialism in the same way as was de Beauvoir. She contributed further by writing a history of the manner in which the social function of motherhood was constructed in France (1980). In the subsequent development of feminism the nature of womanhood became one of the most contentious issues among feminists. For some, biological essentialism held the key to liberation as well as being the source of difference. This of course was not the first time the questioning of female functions was placed at the heart of any intellectual debate. One of the recent developments in intellectual feminism in France has been a revaluation of previous feminist campaigns. Thanks to the work of contemporary feminist historians we are discovering more and more about the feminist movement which existed before de Beauvoir (Bard, 1995; Perrot, 1984; Riot-Sarcey, 1994; Fraisse, 1989; Fauré, 1985). Many issues of equality had been debated by articulate women and men who campaigned ceaselessly for an end to political, social and economic oppression and who believed in political and economic equality for the benefit of the whole society. Traditional opinions on motherhood, women's education and civil rights were expressed by philosophers, philanthropists and public policy-makers. Indeed women's issues were rarely far from public debate during the life of the Third Republic (Smith, 1996; Accampo et al., 1995).

While she sought to analyse systematically the history of dominant thinking on women, de Beauvoir scarcely acknowledged her own contribution to a feminist tradition, movement or school of thought. Although she saw women as a historical group, when writing *Le Deuxième Sexe* she dismissed categorically any possibility for women to act collectively as agents for their own liberation. Yet, in keeping with common practice for philosophers, she sought out comparisons with eminent predecessors such as Hegel, Marx or Engels or with contemporaries such as Lévi-Strauss. She sought to act as their equal. Her lack of identification with feminist predecessors meant that there was no sense of the continuity of a growing corpus of feminist philosophy. I would suggest that this absence of dialogue between feminists ends with de Beauvoir, as the following generation of intellectual feminists used her claims as a benchmark from which to carry on the debate. She began something truly significant for feminist intellectual activity. But unlike her successors, de Beauvoir did not present the actions of earlier women writers as role models. In the eyes of many contemporary radical feminists in the 1970s and 1980s, any flaws or omissions in her arguments were redeemed to a certain extent when she engaged directly in the women's movement towards the end of her life.

Traditionally biological differences were used to justify women's inferiority or to campaign for legislation to make them better mothers, as mentioned above. De Beauvoir set the scene for a new intellectual use of difference. Henceforth it was to be used to search for the real identity of women liberated from an imposed social conditioning. It was to be used to emphasize their potential for solidarity as a class and it was used in their demand for a reconstruction of knowledge to include female specificity. This pattern of identifying sexual difference as the cause of oppression, and as the potential end of that oppression, has continued to dominate feminist thinking ever since. Luce Irigaray argues: 'Sexual difference is one of the important questions of our age, if not in fact the burning issue. According to Heidegger, each age is preoccupied with one thing, and one alone. Sexual difference is probably that issue in our own age which could be our salvation on an intellectual level' (cited in Moi, 1989: 118).

Let us return to the pioneering efforts of de Beauvoir. Having identified the cause of oppression, de Beauvoir privileged a further two key areas in her study of potential changes towards liberation: economic status and literary output. The circumstances of the author, mingled with her own conditioned values (i.e. blind spots), produce some interesting statements. The USA, she declared, was on its way to becoming a civilization without sexes as American women tried to deny their femininity. De Beauvoir also treated women writers in Britain and Italy scornfully, whereas in France, she maintained, 'we have seen that because of the extent of the sophistication of high society and its close links with intellectual life, the situation of French women is a little more favourable' (1949a: 182).

De Beauvoir claimed that French intellectual life was exceptional, and she considered that it had an empowering influence on women. Her own ease of access to intellectual activities was certainly essential for the development of intellectual feminism. However, it must be stressed that, contrary to what has been argued by outsiders – particularly by some of the subsequent generation of American feminist academics – the intellectual debate in France was never to the the exclusion of other feminist activities (Marks and Courtivron, 1980; Fraser, 1989; Moi, 1989). While breaking new ground herself by empowering philosophy with liberating potential for women, de Beauvoir was by no means the first to acknowledge that emancipation is possible through economic change. 'It is through work', she asserts, 'that woman has conquered her human dignity: but it was a particularly slow and tough struggle' (1949b: 431).

Although she recognized, as had many feminists of the nineteenth and early twentieth centuries such as Flora Tristan, Jeanne Deroin, Pauline Roland, Hubertine Auclert and Madeleine Pelletier (Gordon and Cross, 1996; Scott, 1996), that economic independence is the key to personal liberty, she sought to demonstrate through her existentialist philosophy that something more vital is necessary to be able to express one's true self. If women were to be something more than the Other, they needed to find themselves through culture. Intellectual activity offered personal fulfilment and more importantly was even the key to the emancipation of women. She pointed out (1949a: 180) that in the past, throughout the *ancien régime*, the cultural sphere had been the most accessible to women who sought to assert themselves. The realm of ideas was where they could find fulfilment as writers and as women and not just as appendages of men.

Culture was given priority by de Beauvoir for the expression of women's aspirations because it was the most open to her. Unlike many of her predecessors working to end women's oppression, de Beauvoir largely ignored the political question of the exercise of power exclusively by men in the past. Yet she was by no means apolitical. As an intellectual she was highly critical of the Establishment. Along with her fellow intellectuals she not only took positions in international debates during the Cold War, but also took part in many protest movements during the Algerian crisis, for instance (Chebel d'Appollonia, 1991). This tradition of intellectual *engagement* had been part of French specificity since the Dreyfus affair. Along with many of her fellow intellectuals, however, de Beauvoir remained aloof from party politics, particularly after the Communist Party had left government in 1949. As a feminist Simone de Beauvoir considered it impossible for women to intervene in politics, although she was aware of some improvement in women's rights. 'The French Civil Code no longer cites obedience among the duties of a wife and every female citizen has become a voter', she noted (1949b: 431). One the one hand, then, de Beauvoir the philosopher admitted that there had been limited progress towards equality of the sexes in her time; on the other, in 1949 de Beauvoir the feminist was suggesting an impasse, not a solution. Women would not be able to find fulfilment and become fully emancipated or to act either individually or as a group in politics. Socially conditioned women were condemned because they could not constitute an effective group:

> Feminism itself has never been an autonomous movement: it has been partly a tool in the hands of politicians, partly an epiphenomenon reflecting a deeper social conflict. Women have never constituted a separate social caste: and really they have never sought to play a role in history as a gender.
>
> (1949b: 439)

This left many questions raised but unanswered. The search for institutional changes as a solution to women's oppression was not an intellectual priority in itself for de Beauvoir in 1949. She was aware of previous political campaigns for greater freedom for women but chose not to emphasize that aspect of the past in *Le Deuxième Sexe*. Rather, the book was first and foremost a successful and articulate analysis of women's inferior status in society, but more importantly for her it empowered her to claim intellectual freedom and her own female identity. Defining femininity as a socio-economic and cultural phenomenon and not as a biological determinant, de Beauvoir contributed to contemporary feminist theory by challenging the whole of society as a patriarchal order from her intellectual home base of existentialism. In doing so she drew feminism into philosophy, a privileged male sphere. It must be remembered, however, that intellectualism was also, and continues to be, a privileged class sphere: she was, after all, part of the Parisian elite with a voice, having access to publishers. Her underrating of politics was part of the intellectual, bourgeois remoteness from the harsh reality of other women's daily lives. Questions of freedom and self-fulfilment had been posed in the abstract. This potent mixture of an individual philosopher's search for generic female identity using an already existing body of thought, and her new affirmation of self while recognizing that social determinism should be applied to the cause of gender oppression, was to be repeated by the next generation of feminists in other intellectual currents of structuralism, psychoanalysis and postmodernism. The same tensions remain: the contradictions between intellectual theory and political reality, difference and equality, determinism and voluntarism, belonging and exclusion from contemporary intellectual thinking.

Since its publication de Beauvoir's work has been read abroad as much as in France and has been thoroughly criticized by succeeding generations of feminists who have tried either to develop some aspects or to reject others. A genuine debate continues around the very central issues raised by de Beauvoir. She herself evolved and changed her mind about certain feminist issues and later became an important symbolic figure valued for her personal engagement in feminist causes as well as a respected intellectual who had yet to be recognized in her own right (Fullbrook and Fullbrook, 1998; Kruks, 1993; Simons, 1995). She set the trend for contemporary professional intellectual women in late twentieth-century France. Therefore her influence on feminism extends a good way beyond the tenets of *Le Deuxième Sexe*. Her enduring legacy to contemporary philosophers is her challenge to knowledge as a gender-neutral system and her central focus on categorizing gender differences.

But it is my contention that de Beauvoir also anticipated her successors by both her aversion and her attraction to politics: intellectually she justified the initial absence of any relationship with politics in 1949, and subsequently she sought to rectify this derogation of responsibility by a practical engagement in feminist struggles beyond *Le Deuxième Sexe.*

What happened to feminist theory after the publication of *Le Deuxième Sexe* was contingent upon the further development of intellectual thought and the socio-economic changes in France which had a direct effect upon women's lives. During the fifty years since the publication of *Le Deuxième Sexe* feminism in its many forms has been particularly influenced by the formal, theoretical nature of intellectual developments because women like de Beauvoir had access to these analytical tools and more generally to education. Subsequently further improvements to women's lives occurred: mass secondary and university education of women, greater employment possibilities in the tertiary sector, sexual liberation and political emancipation made it seem as if the circumstances were right for greater freedom for individuals. The flourishing of a new wave of feminist intellectualism after May 1968 occurred because of the frustrations of many that the end of gender oppression proved to be as elusive as ever. The creation of an educated female intelligentsia gave a voice to these frustrations. The intellectual crisis of Marxism and the traditional left which had long insisted on the hegemony of the class struggle over all other conflicts together with the increasing fragmentation and diversity of intellectual activity provided the opportunity.

For all the theoretical sophistication and in spite of their aloofness from politics, intellectual feminists have been inspired and boosted by grassroots movements of women campaigning in political struggles before and particularly since 1968. In spite of gaining the vote there was an absence of institutional politicization by women such as de Beauvoir in the 1950s and 1960s in almost the same way as there had been an alienation of the working class from party politics until the Front Populaire in 1936. Intellectual feminism only became recognized as a social phenomenon because of its links with the wider struggle beyond the written form. Antoinette Fouque remarks: 'There are two sexes. This is a reality which history should henceforth take as its fourth principle after liberty, equality and fraternity if it wishes to be worthy of its ideals' (1995: 53). Here feminist intellectuals experienced a new sense of belonging born out of an exclusion from male-dominated politics

(Fouque, 1995: 55). When women in left-wing movements in May 1968 discovered that the emancipatory politics proclaimed did not necessarily extend to gender equality they felt confident to create their own groups. In doing so they also subsequently found that feminist politics could be just as intransigent and prone to divisions, power struggles and hierarchy (Moi, 1989: 33–79; Gunew, 1991: 29, 39). However, for a short period there was an idea of common cause achieved in France in particular around the 1970s abortion campaign. More often, the diversity of women's social and economic positions and interests soon became apparent in the flourishing of this second wave of intellectual feminism and contributed to the wealth of ideas expressed.

At one stage during the early moments of second-wave feminism it was felt that solidarity among women could achieve results. Alongside the radical challenges to male-dominated intellectual thinking, the early 1970s saw the great moment when it was felt that a small breakthrough had been achieved in politics, when the personal became political. Male deputies in the Assemblée Nationale on the right and on the left were compelled to discuss the 'private' matters of contraception and abortion. For a moment there was a sense of optimism and freedom in the 1970s among activists and intellectuals that it was possible to achieve something. De Beauvoir equated the importance of the Abortion Act with the granting of a 40–hour or 39–hour week. She meant this symbolically. Radical feminists could see that this was only a limited reform (Moi, 1989: 47–56). Indeed they felt as alienated from politics as de Beauvoir had been in the 1940s and 1950s. They felt that involvement in politics was the ultimate connivance with phallocentric power. That was for the liberal or egalitarian feminists. Yet here is where de Beauvoir intervened and finally became involved, lending her name to the different causes in the name of her belief in universal freedom, while others turned their backs on the formal politics of the Fifth Republic. More recently the wheel has turned full circle and the new generation of professional women is knocking at the door of institutional politics, demanding and obtaining posts of responsibility in government, campaigning for parity (no longer satisfied with quotas) and an end to the *cumul des mandats* as the most immediate way of widening political access to all citizens, including women.

Many intellectuals, including Simone de Beauvoir, felt it was time to act politically to empower women rather than to cogitate as women. More importantly, whatever impact direct political action achieved, the aftermath of the events of 1968 unleashed a new feminist intellectual energy. Furious debates then took place over the traditional liberal, the dogmatic Marxist and the new radical interpretations of the causes of gender oppression. Few feminist intellectuals could identify with liberal feminists' belief in campaigning for reform to gradually ensure equal opportunity for all within the existing capitalist and increasingly globalized system of the end of the twentieth century. The liberals' general assumption is that, given equality of opportunity, women will act like men (i.e. as competently) because they are inherently equal. They emphasize sameness and therefore minimize difference. They are most often criticized by Marxists and radicals who scorn their belief in the efficacy of gradual change, just as de Beauvoir did in 1949. Traditionally Marxists have believed that only a complete overthrow of capitalism can bring emancipation and that the few improvements to women's position in French society since the Second World War have come about without a fundamental change to power structures of patriarchal capitalism which has itself evolved. Indeed increasing feminization of poverty (Fouque, 1995: 68, 95) would indicate that capitalism continues to benefit from having a female workforce which is flexible and amenable to poor working conditions. For all that, with the collapse of the hegemony of the left after May 1968, liberal feminists were often allies with their severest critics among more radical feminists who were tired of waiting for the socialist revolution as the panacea for all ills. By the 1970s de Beauvoir herself tried the idea of tackling causes of oppression in a piecemeal way and supported many groups fighting for rights or combating violence against women.

In the feminist search for the ability to find an outlet for women's true identity as Subject, in their attempt to oppose the hegemony of male cultural domination, intellectual feminists have continued the trend developed by Simone de Beauvoir and used the very tools of their masters both in their analysis of oppression and in their attempt to create a new alternative feminist intellectual expression. Feminism has therefore tried to break free of dominant ideology from the inside. Feminist intellectuals have enjoyed the fruits of structuralism and postmodernism, particularly in investigation of new self-expression through language and the subconscious.

The most experimental intellectual feminists have been inspired by the radical claim that struggle against gender oppression should take precedence over resistance to class oppression. Here the emphasis is on difference. It is impossible here to include a full analysis of the breadth of intellectual activity where feminists have challenged patriarchy: in philosophy, psychoanalysis, history, socio-linguistics and many other cultural fields, particularly literary theory. Where contemporary French feminism has tended to privilege variations of theories of difference, in every case the intention is to propose a female norm which would be culturally as strong as the established male norm. Some would claim in true post-Freudian fashion that contemporary feminists are turning their backs on de Beauvoir's (the mother's) theories of social determinism and universal notions of freedom and equality and insisting instead on celebrating biological differences as an emancipatory process (Kaufman McCall, 1987). The use of psychoanalysis has been found to be appropriate because it fits in with the politics of difference. The investigation of self-fulfilment begun by de Beauvoir continues in relation to understanding one's origins, in relation to the enabling process of new expression through the subconscious.

The post-1970s era has been a particularly rich time for the convergence of culture and psychoanalysis with philosophy. Structuralists, situationists and postmodernists delved into all types of cultural expression in the attempt to codify, decode, unravel and construct the meaning of knowledge and the relationship of power and knowledge. This is what provided the opportunity and intellectual energy to probe further into the question of relationships between gender and power:

> The new French feminisms cannot be understood diachronically as part of the history of feminism in France. The significant differences between the old and new feminisms are best perceived by situating the new feminisms synchronically in relation to the profound changes in the orientation of French intellectual life.
>
> (Marks and Courtivron, 1980: 30)

Equally feminist intellectuals have been frustrated by their continued exclusion from the Establishment or from other benefits. Their contribution to the diverse branches of French contemporary thinking is not always recognized. In this collection, for instance, there is little recognition in the other chapters of feminists' contribution to the many intellectual disciplines included. For the objectives of feminism, the further question is whether this intellectual exploration has succeeded in providing a way out of unequal relationships between men and women, which is after all its fundamental aim. For those interested in results, intellectual debate among feminists seemed to paralyse the nascent liberation movements and lead to further political impotence.[2] However, although many women insisted on giving their support to causes specifically related to women, claiming that their priorities were for action, the greatest intellectual drive which took place in France lay in the search for an explanation of gender differences. This theoretical search for the cause of oppression rather than action to achieve specific reforms shaped the feminist movement of the 1970s and 1980s. Feminist philosophy seemed to want to bridge the gaps in feminist political struggles.

However, since the late 1980s feminist intellectuals have again been questioning the distance between theory and reality. Prominent writers such as Christine Delphy, Michèle Le Doeuff, Luce Irigaray and Antoinette Fouque are inspired by the belief that a political solution of equality is necessary and that equality which recognizes difference is possible. Political parity has become a rallying cry of the 1990s. This begs the question that de Beauvoir raised about women as a class or as an identity. Feminist philosophers in France do not agree on this. Fouque and Irigaray have both attempted to engage intellectual attention towards political change. They realize that removed from the public eye feminists are powerless. Significantly perhaps, they have both sought outlets outside France. Antoinette Fouque is active in European politics as a *député*. Luce Irigaray has been militant with the Italian communist party.

While feminism since de Beauvoir has continued to energize intellectual currents in France, and while women are no longer totally invisible as subjects of study or as intellectual actors, Christine Delphy, among others, claims that little progress has been made in the question of the value of female activity (Moi, 1989: 108). She argues that by continuing to emphasize sexual difference in the allocation of new social roles for men and women and by searching for a new identity feminists are in danger of prescribing a new set of imposed codes of behaviour for women.

At the same time the fragmentation of French philosophical activity was of considerable benefit to feminists, although in every case theory has continued to remain a privilege, accessible to an elite and aloof from the experience of the majority of women suffering hardship in oppressed or underprivileged situations. Still, the pattern of feminist debate in this privileged intellectual space has continued to challenge the hegemony of the masculine subject in philosophy. In turn the space created has produced intense differences among women intellectuals and new conflicts arising from interpretations of women's ability to construct new language and signifiers. Although not as numerous as male writers, a greater number of women are pursuing the same route established by de

Beauvoir, writing to empower feminism in an intellectual sphere. Julia Kristeva, Hélène Cixous, Monique Wittig, Christine Rochefort, Benoîte Groult, Luce Irigaray and Marguerite Duras are among those women intellectuals who have published works searching for the means to express their interpretation of the female as Subject.

The consensus among observers, particularly English-speaking observers, is that the overriding image of French feminism is associated with difference (Moses, 1993; Moi, 1989), and furthermore that French feminist theorists have engaged in a complex philosophy which has little to do with practical feminism. It is my contention that this is having a stifling effect on political engagement of intellectual feminists. Due to the sophistication of French intellectual feminism, another common perception from the outside is that feminism has progressed beyond equality politics and is far ahead of feminisms in other countries (Deutscher, 1997). If women have achieved their rights in France, some might think that equality politics could be outdated anyway. Feminism itself as a concept might even be redundant in philosophy if women had achieved anything like equality. It is claimed now that a revolution occurred thirty years ago, as if there had been a sea change to set women once and for all on the road to emancipation. Antoinette Fouque responds: 'Some would have us believe that the women's movement is over, dead even, that the struggles are behind us now, whereas they are only just beginning; they take their misogynistic desires for reality' (1995: 96–7)

Whatever the success or failure of the most recent feminist intellectual wave, many of the key terms of feminism are now to be found in claims by philosophers to counter feminist arguments: difference and equality remain the key issues. Lipovetsky (1997) claims that women have reconciled their private lives with their careers, and that because they are in control of their own destiny, they are on an equal footing with men; he too insists on the permanence of sexual differences. He sees women finding their autonomy on an individual basis, although he accepts that economic exploitation is a reality. He has no time for what he terms aggressive American feminists who have declared war on men and he hopes France will be spared this indignity because of its ancient traditions of courtesy, Gallic gallantry and, of course, French femininity. Social roles have been defined historically according to sexual differences and will go on socially reproducing, according to Lipovetsky. It is not a matter of biology. Whatever his justification, he insists on gender difference, but likes to think men and women are equal in their socially determined separate roles. Echoes of Proudhon!

For Deutscher (1997) there has been a conflation of many intellectuals around feminism of difference, overshadowing those committed to feminism of equality and giving little space to this theory. Fouque and Irigaray, two theorists associated with the feminism of difference, are now concerned to link their theories to practical feminism. Knowing that the odds are against women in patriarchal society they realize that it is not enough to claim to express women's identity. Economic inequality is a harsh reality for the majority of women. Economic equality is as remote a goal as ever. With each new gain, new forms of exploitation are coming into being. If women do not act as agents of their own liberation through egalitarian campaigns, they would be denying their existential heritage as human beings with a claim to still echo beyond the gender question, beyond sex. Both Fouque and Irigaray try to combine difference and equality in their theory. They argue for a gendered equality.

In this chapter I have explained briefly how *Le Deuxième Sexe* set parameters for the next generation of feminists. I also explained that the subsequent debate on the contemporary scene has resulted in tensions between theoretical discourse on feminism and the grassroots level of feminist struggles which is in itself an essential aspect of French feminism. I have criticized the remoteness of theory and suggested that feminists are looking beyond the tools of analysis of a highly introverted contemporary intellectual scene and are engaging in other equally powerful feminist traditions involving active campaigns to find a new synthesis of intellectual empowerment.

The durability of the issues raised by de Beauvoir is attributable to their universality and the unresolved aim of intellectual feminism, which is to find real fulfilment for women as Subjects and in doing so to end all systems of oppression of one gender by another. Although there are limitations to her own arguments, they have helped to establish the very necessary development of a philosophical debate in order to test the validity of issues raised. The debate centres around two main problems: the feasibility of finding this female identity in a patriarchal system and the resolution of whether the maintenance of difference is desirable in the female search for fulfilment as Subject. It is no coincidence that of all the current developments in French intellectual activity, feminist writers have made most use of linguistic approaches, psychoanalysis and philosophy.

Intellectuals are never comfortable in the prosaic world of party-political power struggles, feminist intellectuals even less so. Radical feminism was about turning away from male-controlled society. Political institutions were part of the man's world in which many feminists felt oppressed. This was what de Beauvoir had felt when writing *Le Deuxième Sexe*. Yet the experience of collective action for women in the 1970s cast the problem of equality and difference in a new light and marked the return of the most problematic issue for contemporary intellectual feminism, the definition of female identity.

Notes

1 For an account of the circumstances of its publication, see Günther (1998).
2 See, for instance, Antoinette Fouque's differences with other feminists over the MLF patent (Fouque, 1995) or Christine Delphy's critique of Annie Leclerc's *Paroles de femme* (Moi, 1989).

References

Accampo, Elinor, Rachel Fuchs and Mary Lynn Stewart (1995) *Gender and the Politics of Social Reform in France 1870–1914*. Baltimore MD: Johns Hopkins University Press.

Allen, Jeffner and Iris Marion Young (1989) *The Thinking Muse. Feminism in Modern French Philosophy*. Bloomington: Indiana University Press.

Appignanesi, Lisa (ed.) (1989) 'Ideas from France', in *The Legacy of French Theory*. London: Free Association.

Badinter, Elizabeth (1980) *L'Amour en plus. Histoire de l'amour maternel (XVIIe–XXe siècle)*. Paris: Flammarion.

—— (1997) 'Nous ne sommes pas une espèce à protéger', *Le Nouvel Observateur*, 23–29 January: 38–40.

Bard, Christine (1995) *Les Filles de Marianne: histoire des féminismes 1914–1940*. Paris: Fayard.

Battersby, Christine (1998) *The Phenomenal Woman: Feminist Metaphysics and the Pattern of Identity*. Cambridge: Polity Press.

Beauvoir, Simone de (1949a and b) *Le Deuxième Sexe*, 2 vols. Paris: Editions Gallimard.

Bryson, Valerie (1992) *Feminist Political Theory*. London: Macmillan.

Chebel d'Appollonia, Ariane (1991) *Histoire politique des intellectuels en France, 1944–54*, vol. 2. Paris: Complexe.

Cross, Máire (1997) 'Feminism', in Christopher Flood and Laurence Bell (eds), *Political Ideologies in Contemporary France*. London: Cassell/Pinter, pp. 162–79.

Deutscher, Penelope (1997) 'French feminist philosophers on law and public policy: Michèle Le Doeuff and Luce Iragaray', *Australian Journal of Feminist Studies*, 34 (1): 24–44.

Duroux, Françoise (1997) 'La Cité et les femmes', *Australian Journal of Feminist Studies*, 34 (1): 7–23.

Fauré, Christine (1985) *La Démocratie sans les femmes*. Paris: Presses Universitaires de France.

Fouque, Antoinette (1995) *Il y a deux sexes. Essais de féminologie 1989–1995*. Paris: Gallimard.

Fraisse, Geneviève (1989) *Muse de la raison. La démocratie exclusive et la différence des sexes*. Paris: Alinéa.

Fraser, Nancy and Sandra Lee Bartky (1992) *Revaluing French Feminism: Critical Essays on Difference, Agency and Culture*. Bloomington: Indiana University Press.

Fullbrook, Edward and Kate Fullbrook (1998) *Simone de Beauvoir. A Critical Introduction*. Cambridge: Polity Press.

Gordon, Felicia and Máire Cross (1996) *Early French Feminisms. A Passion for Liberty*. Cheltenham: Edward Elgar

Gunew, Sneja (1991) *A Reader in Feminist Knowledge*. London: Routledge.

Günther, Renate (1998) 'Fifty years on: the impact of *Le Deuxième Sexe* on contemporary feminist theory', *Modern and Contemporary France*, 6 (2): 177–88.

Irigaray, Luce (1989) *Le Temps de la différence*. Paris: Livre de Poche.

—— (1990) *Je, tu, nous. Pour une culture de la différence*. Paris: Grasset.

Jaggar, Alison M. and William McBride (1985) ' "Reproduction" as male ideology', *Women's Studies International Forum*, 8 (3): 185–96

Kaufman McCall, Dorothy (1987) 'Simone de Beauvoir: questions of difference and generation', in Hélène Vivienne Wenzel (ed.), *Simone de Beauvoir: Witness to a Century*. Special issue of *Yale French Studies*, 72: 121–31.

Kruks, Sonia (1993) 'Genre et subjectivité: Simone de Beauvoir et le féminisme contemporarine'. *Nouvelles Questions féministes*, 14 (1): 3–28.

Le Bras-Chopard, Armelle et Janine Mossuz-Lavau (eds) (1997) *Les Femmes et la politique*. Paris: L'Harmattan.

Lipovetsky, Gilles (1997) *La Troisième Femme*. Paris: Gallimard.

Marks, Elaine and Isabelle de Courtivron (1980) *New French Feminisms*. Brighton: Harvester.

Moi, Toril (1989) *French Feminist Thought: A Reader*. Oxford: Blackwell.

Moses, Claire and Leslie Rabine (1993) *Feminism, Socialism, and French Romanticism*. Bloomington: Indiana University Press.

Perrot, Michelle (ed.) (1984) *Une histoire des femmes est-elle possible?* Marseille: Rivage.

Reynolds, Siân (1996) *France between the Wars. Gender and Politics*. London: Routledge.

Riot-Sarcey, Michèle (ed.) (1993) *Femmes pouvoirs*. Paris: Kimé.

—— (1994) *La Démocratie à l'épreuve des femmes*. Paris: Albin Michel.

Scott, Joan (1996) *Only Paradoxes to Offer. French Feminists and the Rights of Man*. Cambridge, MA: Harvard University Press.

Simons, Margaret A. (1995) '*The Second Sex*: from Marxism to radical feminism', in Margaret A. Simons (ed.), *Feminist Interpretations of Simone de Beauvoir*. Pennsylvania: Pennsylvania State University Press, pp. 243–62.

Smith, Paul (1996) *Feminism and the Third Republic: Women's Political and Civil Rights in France 1918–1945*. Oxford: Oxford Historical Monographs.

Wenzel, Hélène Vivienne (ed.) (1986) *Simone de Beauvoir: Witness to a Century*. Special issue of *Yale French Studies*, 72.

12
Film Theory and the New Historicism

Jill Forbes

It is in great measure the reputation of *Cahiers du cinéma* which forged the link between film theory and France. The *politique des auteurs*, as well as Marxist, Althusserian and Lacanian approaches to the cinema, were all developed by *Cahiers du cinéma* between its creation in 1951 and its relaunch in 1974. *Cahiers* was not alone in this, but its influence was incomparably wider than that of any other journal both inside France itself (Baecque, 1991) and in the English-speaking world where the broad dissemination of a version of its ideas took place (Forbes, 1987). The international significance of *Cahiers* can be seen in the journals *Movie* and *Screen* in Britain and *October* and *Camera Obscura* in the United States. An English language version of *Cahiers*, edited by Andrew Sarris, was published in the United States in 1966 and 1967, selections of articles have also been translated into English (Hillier, 1985, 1986; Browne, 1990) and in France the early volumes have been reprinted in book form.

However, in the wake of the events of May 1968 *Cahiers* came to treat cinema, essentially, as a prism through which ideology could be apprehended, studied and exposed. Thus publication of translations of Eisenstein's writings began in February 1969; in October of that year came the start of the series 'Cinéma, idéologie, critique'; in May 1971, the series 'Technique et idéologie'; by 1972 the journal's central debate concerned 'Politique et lutte idéologique de classe', and by December 1972 'Quelles sont nos tâches sur le front révolutionnaire?' Just as the years 1973–4 marked a watershed in French politics and economics, so *Cahiers du cinéma* fell victim to the post-68 cultural *tristesse* so powerfully articulated in Jean Eustache's film *La Maman et la putain* (1973) in which the protagonist remarks: 'We've had the Cultural Revolution, the Rolling Stones, May 68, the Black Panthers, the Underground, but nothing else for two or three years' (Eustache, 1986: 65) and the relaunch which transformed *Cahiers*, under the editorship of Serge Daney and Jean Narboni, from political pamphlet into glossy, upmarket, film magazine, also signalled the decline of its international theoretical influence.

From 1973 the study of film became more academic. *La Revue d'esthétique* published a special number, somewhat misleadingly entitled *Cinéma: Théorie, Lectures*, which sought to position film as an art (Noguez, 1978). This was done by relating contemporary French film theory to earlier traditions in Germany, Britain and the US, and by demonstrating a continuity between the theoretical and practical concerns of the 1970s and those of the French, German and Italian *film d'art* of the 1920s and the American Underground of the 1960s, as well as through an entire section (265–369) devoted to 'non-representational or non-narrative cinema'. The editor, Dominique Noguez, endeavoured to promote the view that the cinema is the 'seventh' art, as well as to claim that it is not only as legitimate and interesting as painting, sculpture, architecture or music, but also in some sense the *summum* of them all: 'It would now be difficult to conceive of an aesthetic which did not grant an essential, perhaps *the* essential position to what ought, perhaps, to be called the most important of the arts' (2–3). This approach met with some success. The special issue was reprinted in 1978 as a book which now included sections devoted to earlier texts on film aesthetics (Arnheim, Kracauer and Balázs), ideological criticism (Comolli and Lebel), semiological approaches (Barthes, Pasolini, Metz) and texts by avant-garde practitioners such as P. Adams Sitney, Jonas Mekas and Claudine Eizekmann. Underlying this was the post-68 belief that film practice, embodied in Godard's aim 'to make political films politically', was much more important than film analysis or film theory. Changing ways of seeing was now more important, in other words, than changing theories of film.

In a parallel move, film studies in the 1970s began a process of academic institutionalization in three different Parisian sites representing different ideological, political and, to some extent, aesthetic positions: within the history of art at the Institut d'art et d'archéologie; as ideological practice at Vincennes; and as a branch of semiotics under Christian Metz at the EHEES (Metz, 1968, 1971, 1972, 1977). There, the semiological and structuralist revolution in language and literary studies begun in the 1960s was now applied to film and, aided by the prestige of the EHEES, Metz's devoted students gradually populated the Communications department at the Université de Paris III which became an important centre for film theory of the semiological persuasion.

Noguez and others denounced the trend towards 'microscopic decoding [and] towards conducting what may soon become the most unpro-
ductive kind of film analysis. As is well known, there is a very thin line
between patient decoding and semiological mania (in the medical sense)
or analyses that are completely insane' (Noguez, 1978: 6). However, the
semiological approach to film had advantages which rendered it particularly attractive in the 1970s: it required special knowledge and the
mastery of a particular critical language which could endow film with
the respectability that would allow it to be taken seriously; it also
avoided crude politicization so that at Vincennes, for example, Michèle
Lagny, Marie-Claire Ropars and Pierre Sorlin were able to marry Marxism
and semiology in their seminar on Eisenstein's *October* (Lagny et al.,
1976). In the 1960s, therefore, the study of film in France was the
province of cinephiles, journalists, collectors, writers and occasionally
theorists; in the period 1968–74 it belonged to political militants; while
the 1970s saw the dominance of aestheticians, practitioners, structuralists and semioticians and the start of institutionalized film studies.

But 1968 sowed the seeds of a different debate. In February of that year
the government attempted to replace Henri Langlois as the Secretary of
the Cinémathèque française for political reasons ostensibly based on
dissatisfaction with Langlois's programming policies (Roud, 1983). Prominent film-makers, especially *nouvelle vague* directors like Truffaut
whose film education had been provided by Cinémathèque screenings,
rallied to support Langlois. The Langlois Affair is often viewed as an
example of Gaullist hubris and a warning sign of the cataclysm which
was to take place in May of that year when questions of the power of and
over images were starkly posed by the role of television in reporting, or
failing to report, demonstrations in the streets. Much of the discussion in
film journals like *Cahiers du cinéma* and in media journals such as *Communications* immediately after the Events, turned on the 'loss of inno-
cence', the impossibility of the neutral or objective image, the
realization that, as Barthes put it, there is no such thing as an image
without a 'rhetoric', that all images belong within an economy of persuasion and interest (Barthes, 1964).

The Affair also posed questions about the ownership of images. Langlois treated the Cinémathèque's collection as though it were his own –
as, indeed, in some sense it was, for much of what it contained had been
given to him personally. His objective was accumulation not conservation and he allegedly paid little attention to the conventions of intellectual property. His excellent relations with film-makers, who often
bequeathed copies of their films, made it possible for him to conduct

the Cinémathèque's affairs in this way. But the disadvantage was that material was not properly stored (particularly worrying in the case of nitrate film) and there was no catalogue. Indeed, Langlois claimed: 'I am the catalogue'. In retrospect, therefore, the confrontation between Langlois and the civil service seems an early indication of the way control and ownership of the audio-visual archive was moving up the public agenda. Indeed, it might be interpreted as a first step in wresting control of cinema history from amateurs, film-makers and theorists and handing it over to the state.

This bureaucratic warning sign had a parallel in film-making. Marcel Ophuls's *Le Chagrin et la pitié* (1971), attempted to 'demystify history' (Ophuls, 1971) by disrupting the unities of time and place on which documentary was conventionally based. Hitherto, it had generally been assumed that in documentary, unlike fiction, the film-maker had to 'be there', to be 'in situ' so that the camera 'recorded the reality' which was authenticated by the bodily presences of the film crew, their 'avoir-été-là' (having been there). Ophuls, however, ignored this convention by juxtaposing material from 'now' (that is the late 1960s and early 1970s) and 'then', that is from the archive. He used disparate, and sometimes contradictory, material from different archive sources (German and British as well as French) and he applied the principle of montage to the soundtrack as well as to the images. The effect was to render the 'truth' of the document both relative and contingent. Whereas in the French documentaries of the 1950s, of which Resnais's *Nuit et brouillard* (1955) would be a good example, past and present are clearly distinguished (colour/black and white, sound/ silent, still/moving photography), and we are clearly aware that this is a point of view now on an event then, because the temporality ('temps') of the narrative ('récit') is clear, and the voice-over commentary provides the emotional or dramatic synthesis guiding the spectator. In *Le Chagrin et la pitié* the film-maker remains an enquirer; he asks questions and is occasionally seen as an actor in his own film, but his discourse carries no greater weight or authority than that of the interviewees or of the soundtracks attached to the newsreel images. In basing *Le Chagrin et la pitié* on an elaborate montage of disparate material, Ophuls called in question the relationship of that material to a previous 'reality' and, in particular, questioned the value of the archive as a depository of facts while revealing its immense potential as a source of fictions.

Ophuls was far from being the first film-maker to demonstrate the creative possibilities of montage. Several of Godard's fiction films, notably *Pierrot le fou* made in 1965, have a palimpsest structure in which different 'times' are superimposed on, or juxtaposed with, one another (Forbes, 1999). However, in taking a period of history for which a deliberate effort had been made to present a single version and vision (Rousso, 1987; Lindeperg, 1997), and showing instead a multiple vision, in doing so at great length, and in succeeding in having the film broadcast on virtually all the major European TV channels except those of France, Ophuls ensured that his undertaking would be immensely influential. As Marc Ferro wrote: '*Le Chagrin et la pitié* represents a sort of October Revolution in the history of documentary film. The position it adopted created a tremendous stir and the repercussions were probably linked to its subject-matter' (Ferro, 162). In addition to promoting a revisionist history of the Occupation years, *Le Chagrin et la pitié* marked an important historiographical shift which was taken up both in writing about the documentary cinema from the late 1960s (Comolli, 1969) and in fiction films such as André Téchiné's *Souvenirs d'en France* (1975), but which is best illustrated in Louis Malle's *Lacombe Lucien* (1974), the first feature film made for a general audience to present a view of the Occupation which did not conform to the previously ubiquitous *resistancialiste* narrative (Forbes, 1992: 243–5; Rousso, 1987: 353–9). If 'historicism' is 'the name given to [the] apparent relativising of the past by getting to know the different interpretations to which it is open and deciding between them on grounds expressing our own, contemporary preoccupations' (Hamilton, 1996: 19), then by analogy with the new approaches to the English Renaissance, this shift may be described as a 'new historicism' which, as Hamilton puts it, 'recasts history as a battle over fictions, a battle of communication'.[1] The achievement of *Le Chagrin et la pitié* was to reveal the significance of the content and ownership of the resources of audio-visual archives in the pursuit of the new historicism. In this way, the theoretical investigations which began in earnest in the 1980s can be traced back to the power struggles over the ownership and interpretation of images which took place in the 1970s.

One very important reason why writers and theorists had concentrated on the detailed, linguistically and semiologically inspired analysis of film was because of the difficulties encountered in gaining access to film archives in France or even in knowing what they contained. This was made explicit in a seminal article by Pierre Sorlin and François Garçon in which they wrote:

In France film analysis is carried out on the basis of collections built up haphazardly, which have been assembled by chance and which are unlikely to be representative; the poor viewing conditions almost inevitably lead the historian to lower his sights as far as concerns analysis: the combination of these difficulties means that researchers tend to write studies of single films.

(Garçon and Sorlin, 1981: 354–5)

The authors quote the following reply from a curator whom they had asked whether a film was available: 'Dear Sir, I am not sure I wish to help you' (350, n.26) and, as we have seen, much of Sorlin's own research in the 1970s was devoted, perhaps inevitably, to the exhaustive analysis of just one film, Eisenstein's *October*.

The topic was revisited in 1985 both in a special issue of the Franco-American journal *Iris*, in which Sorlin contrasted the differing objectives of 'film theory' and 'film history' and suggested that the latter was merely a branch of history in general (Sorlin, 1985), and at a symposium (Aumont, 1989) at which Jean-Pierre Jeancolas, referring to the 'signal weakness' of film history in France, linked the lack of an academic base for film studies to an 'amateurish' approach to film. In Jeancolas's view, those whose ambition was to write about the cinema, as opposed to individual films, did so essentially on the basis of memory and subjective judgements. French film historians such as Maurice Bardèche and Robert Brasillach, Jean Mitry and Georges Sadoul, all of whom 'were working from first hand information which for the most part cannot be corroborated', deriving from the people they knew, the films they happened to have seen and their personal memories of events, had all 'established divisions, classifications and a terminology which we all rely on' (Jeancolas, 1989: 79–80). An excellent illustration of Jeancolas's thesis, though not one he uses, is the 'invention' of 'film noir' by two French critics Raymond Borde and Etienne Chaumeton who, in the preface to their *Panorama du film noir américain* of 1955, explained how their identification of a new genre arose from the unique circumstances of the late 1940s when a large number of previously-banned American films were screened in Paris. Similarly, the title of one of Jeancolas's own books *Quinze ans d'années trente* (1983) points to the author's impatience with an earlier historiographical practice whereby, for obvious ideological reasons, the French cinema of the Occupation years was separated from that of the 1930s in a way that, Jeancolas argued, could not be justified in the light of continuity of personnel and aesthetic practices.

The absence of viable catalogues and difficulties of access were increasingly things of the past by the mid-1980s with respect to film, as Jeancolas stressed, when close collaboration between seven Francophone

archives brought about dramatic changes and permitted the identification and location of much material that as recently as the 1970s had
been assumed lost. However, the television archive, which includes
newsreel material such as the *Actualités françaises* from the Vichy period,
was a different matter. Until 1974 television was controlled by a Ministry
of Information which acted as a political gatekeeper, but in addition its
archive was managed essentially for commercial (sale to foreign television companies) and in-house purposes. The increasing technological
convergence and financial imbrication of film and television during the
1970s did not lead to the creation of a national film and television
archive in France, as it did in other countries like Britain, but it did
mean that the questions of ownership and access applied to television
as much as to film.

Reflection on and creative exploitation of the possibilities of the television archive was made possible by the reform of the Office de Radio-
diffusion-Télévision Française (ORTF) undertaken by President Giscard
d'Estaing in 1974. The break up of the monolithic ORTF led to the
creation of the more independent Institut National de l'Audiovisuel
(INA) in 1975, which inherited conservation (management of the
archive) and research (production of experimental material) among its
missions (Forbes, 1984), and it encouraged various experiments in the
creative exploitation of archive holdings, to some extent inspired by *Le
Chagrin et la pitié*. Produced by Thierry Garrel and Louisette Neil the
programme series 'Hiéroglyphes' (1975), 'Rue des Archives' (1978–81)
and 'Juste une image' (1982) confirmed the potential richness of INA's
holdings and were motivated, in the words of the television archive's
curator, Francis Denel, by a conception 'that sees memory as a source of
creativity' (Forbes, 1984: 17).

In 1968 Marc Ferro had courageously appealed for historians to take
film seriously: 'It is astonishing that this particular source of information
remains unused. If historians or sociologists looked at it and exploited it
they would have to revise both their methods and their findings' (Ferro,
1968). In 1973 he attempted to explain historians' continuing neglect of
the cinema by recalling, after Foucault: 'The sources used by the established historian form a corpus which is as elaborately hierarchical as the
society for which he writes his work' (Ferro, 1993: 32). In other words, if
the historian wanted to be taken seriously and exercise the influence
which was his due – for in the same article Ferro underlines the
complicity between power and history – his materials had to mirror in
their 'nobility' the 'nobility' of his calling. But in the 1980s things began
to change and, by the 1990s, as Rémy Pithon recalls, respected film

scholars such as Lagny (1992) and Bourget (1992) published works discussing the relationship between cinema and history, while works by foreign scholars such as Allen and Gomery (1993) were translated into French.

Le Chagrin et la pitié had demonstrated the significance of audiovisual material in revising the history of the Occupation years and, in the 1980s, promoted film and television archives to a position of central importance. With the trial of Klaus Barbie, again reported on by Ophuls in the film *Hôtel Terminus* (1988), this reached the heart of the state (Rousso, 1987: 216–30). At issue was the control and exploitation of visual memory, the relationship between history and memory, between official history and personal memory, and also between competing official 'memories' (Namer, 1983: 143–63). The formation of a socialist government, after almost a quarter of a century of rule by the right, also played its part in the revisionism of the period. The Socialists came to power in 1981 committed to depoliticizing the control of images by distancing the government from television, but at the same time they signalled their determination to wrest control of memory from their opponents through Mitterrand's symbolic tribute to left-wing heroes at the Panthéon on the occasion of his inauguration (Namer, 1983: 199–204).

The concern with popular memory explored by Foucault in the 1970s (Foucault, 1974) and the quest to exploit different and less official or 'noble' archives (Le Goff and Nora, 1986) had their impact on the conduct and writing of history in which film and television played a part. But so did techniques deriving from the treatment of film sources. This can be seen in the massive volumes of Pierre Nora's *Les Lieux de mémoire*, which are composed of a montage of fragments or condensed images, albeit immensely erudite, fragments brought together in a manner which mirrors the technique made familiar from *Le Chagrin et la pitié* with no attempt at the unitary narrative which is the traditional prerogative of history and the practice of the historian. The implication is that the whole will somehow be greater than the sum of its parts and that the reader of the *Lieux*, like the viewer of Ophuls's film, will, from personal experience or the habits of reading or viewing, fill in the missing links and thus enable a continuity to emerge as it does from the discrete frames of a reel of film.

The confluence of memory and history and the application of the techniques and habits of memory to the practice of history were realized in the work and, indeed, in the person of Jean-Noël Jeanneney. In 1977, in collaboration with Monique Sauvage, he established a research seminar on television history at the Institut d'Etudes Politiques de Paris, some of whose proceedings were published under the title *Télévision nouvelle mémoire*, with a preface stating the urgent necessity to undertake the investigation of the television archive, despite the apparent technological and economic difficulties which such an enterprise posed (Jeanneney and Sauvage, 1982: 7–17). By 1987 Jeanneney had been placed in charge of preparing for the public commemoration of the Bicentenary of the French Revolution in 1989, and by 1992 he had become the prime mover in the enactment of a new statute providing for the deposit of all audio-visual material made in France together with a right of access to existing and future audio-visual archives.

Like literary studies, film studies in France have come to be interested in the 'paratext' – both upstream and downstream. The centenary of the cinema in 1995 reminded researchers that those early practitioners who were still alive were very elderly and that their recollections must be collected and recorded or lost for ever, while under the influence of reception theory as well as of Foucauldian and Barthesian structuralism, the critical history of a work, the reception of a film or films over time, has come to seem extremely significant. As Sylvie Lindeperg, following Genette, put it in her introduction to *Les Ecrans de l'ombre*:

> Thinking of the work of cinema as a palimpsest means foregrounding a procedure which consists in 'scratching' the surface of a film in order to reveal successive layers of writing which are invisible to the viewer. The first synopsis, intermediate shot lists and versions of the dialogue, and storyboards, are all pieces of evidence which, when they are closely examined and placed in order, reveal a series of shifts, reworkings, additions and cuts.
>
> (Lindeperg, 1997: 11)

But for film studies to be able to exploit all the archival and documentary sources surrounding the making of films, then it is not merely the film archive which requires an accessible and comprehensive catalogue, but also those of production companies, public bodies responsible for licensing, censorship and subsidy, agents' records, and so on (Jeancolas, 1989: 85).

In this way, from the 1980s onwards and with increasing momentum, the film archive became the focus of academic interest and debate. In France, if not elsewhere, the creation, ownership, selection and classification of archives is viewed as a political activity. As Francis Denel recalled:

archives are seen as the foundation of national unity...the creation of the archive and the creation of the nation state go hand in hand. Paper archives were created with the Revolution. The one and indivisible French Republic was based on the collective memory deposited in the Archives Nationales!

(Forbes, 1984: 17)

In this respect images are no different from paper-based documents: they may, and indeed in Foucault's formulation they must, provide the basis on which the 'popular memory' can be reactivated as an agent of militant struggle (Foucault, 1974: 7–8). Thus the attempt to move away from the Gaullist narrative and to rewrite the history of Vichy, while it did not reveal the significance of the audio-visual archive, certainly helped to ensure that the audio-visual media were fully recognized as an important historical and political source. Since what is felt to be at stake in the archive is the identity of the nation and the capacity to narrate its history, it is perhaps inevitable that its ownership and exploitation should be contested, but in the process a particularly fascinating tension is exposed. On the one hand, there is the belief, evoked almost poetically by Arlette Farge, that if the archives are made accessible the truth will emerge in all its univocal splendour: 'Pieces of the truth have remained and are now spread before the eyes: their clarity and credibility is blinding. There can be no doubt, the discovery of an archive is a kind of manna which fully merits the description of "source"' (Farge, 1989: 14–15); on the other hand, there is the knowledge that each successive generation, and within that each social class, remakes its own version of the past through its fictions.

The recognition of the importance and richness of audio-visual archives had a practical consequence in the statute enacted in June 1992 instituting the statutory deposit of all radio and television material produced in France and the right of access to the archive thus constituted. The scepticism with regard to film noted by Marc Ferro in the 1970s had thus completely dissipated by the 1990s when a large group of distinguished academics and intellectuals wrote an open letter to *Le Monde* entitled 'Mémoire interdite', complaining about delays to this project (Denel et al., 1994: 15–16). Similarly, Régis Debray described the initiative as the founding moment of a new era, of comparable significance to the statutory deposit of printed material since it transformed images into heritage objects:

... in 1537 the Edict of Montpellier made it compulsory that one copy of any printed work put on sale in the kingdom should be deposited in the Royal Library... in this way ordinary documents were transformed into archives. The electronic image is superficial, perishable and short-lived, but the law of 22 June 1992 stipulates that a copy of every image shall be placed on deposit... The heritage-effect is not a luxury but a necessity for the mind.

(Debray, 1994: 6)

Bringing the apparatus of classification and criticism to bear on material which had hitherto been considered materially, and therefore intellectually, ephemeral undoubtedly changes the status of that material. However, this process is the consequence of present economics as well as of past history. It is when the materiality of the real is in doubt, as Barthes remarked, that heritage objects are used to confirm it (Barthes, 1968). Just as the Musée des arts et traditions populaires was created in response to modernization – to retard it as well as to throw it into relief – so the 'record' of the past held, however virtually, on film and video has also become a means of holding back and compensating for an equally traumatic process of globalization.

On the one hand, the French media privatizations carried through in the 1980s with the creation of La Cinq, M6 and Canal Plus and the privatization of TF1, and the creation of media conglomerates in the 1990s via Hachette, Havas, Matra, Thomson and Alcatel, responded to the imperatives of globalization. On the other hand, the policy of film subsidy pursued by the socialist government (Austin, 1996: 142–70), the deliberate promotion of heritage productions such as Claude Berri's *Jean de Florette* (1986), the celebration of the Bicentenary of the Revolution and the *loi sur le dépôt légal* of 1992 were attempts to compensate for, or even retard, the impact of new technologies and of deterritorialization. This was outlined by Jacques Derrida, in a televised interview in 1993:

The global effect of television, of the telephone, of fax, of satellites, of the more rapid circulation of images and discourses, etc., is that the here and now becomes uncertain and that people's moorings, their rootedness, their sense of belonging are radically challenged. The impulse to turn or return inward increases in proportion to the violence of technological expropriation and displacement [délocalisation].

(Derrida, 1994: 108)

The postwar period in France has offered a succession of theories of film, as art, as language and communication, as historical document, as heritage and cultural object, all of which have had a more or less wide international resonance. The current designation of film and video as heritage objects is clearly of immense political and ideological significance and offers vast new areas of investigation. The recent publication of a seminar held at the Institut d'histoire du temps présent between 1995 and 1997 entitled *De l'histoire au cinéma* (Baecque, 1998) underlines not only that cinema has entered the mainstream of historical research but also the wealth and variety of new avenues of exploration which are or have been opened up as a consequence. But perhaps of even more interest are the possibilities offered by the new technologies that are the source of the public anxiety described by Derrida. In making its archive accessible, INA has also introduced a sophisticated system of digital retrieval and cross referencing which, over time, will enable fulfilment of the creative potential of the material which it has in store, creating, thereby, the next theoretical frontier. But these technologies will inevitably increase the real or imagined 'delocalization' which has haunted political and ideological approaches to the media in France since the 1940s. Indeed, it might be argued, as Derrida suggests, that by permitting an assault on temporal and spatial certainties, the new historicism in film and television has reawakened the anxiety about cultural expropriation and colonization which informed French discourse in the 1940s and 1950s.

Note

1   The 'new historicism' is usually associated with Stephen Greenblatt and studies of the English Renaissance. See, however, Roger Chartier, 'La vérité entre fiction et histoire', in Baecque and Delage (eds) (1998), pp. 29–44

References

Allen, Robert C. and Gomery, Douglas (1985) *Film History: Theory and Practice*. New York: Alfred Knopf; trans. Lévy, Jacques (1993) *Faire l'histoire du cinéma: les modèles américains*. Paris: Nathan.

Aumont, Jaques (1989) *L'Analyse des films*. Paris: Nathan.

Austin, Guy (1996) *Contemporary French Cinema*. Manchester: Manchester University Press.

Baecque, Antoine de and Delage, Christian (1998) *De l'histoire au cinéma*. Paris: Editions complexe.

Barthes, Roland (1964) 'Rhétorique de l'image', in *Communications*, 4: 40–51.

Barthes, Roland (1968) 'L'Effet de réel', *Communications*, 11; reprinted in Gérard Genette and Tzetvan Todorov (eds) (1982) *Littérature et réalité*. Paris: Editions du Seuil.

Bourget, Jean-Loup (1992) *L'Histoire au cinéma: Le passé retrouvé*. Paris: Gallimard.

Browne, Nick (1990) *Cahiers du cinéma. Vol. 3, 1969–72: The Politics of Representation*. London: Routledge.

Chartier, Roger (1996) 'La Vérité entre fiction et histoire', reprinted in Baecque and Delage (1998), 29–44.

Comolli, Jean-Louis (1969) 'Le détour par le direct', *Cahiers du cinéma*, 209: 48–53.

Debray, Régis (1994) 'Le seuil décisif', *Dossiers de l'audiovisuel*, 54: 6–8.

Derrida, Jacques (1994) 'Postface. Entretien avec Jacques Derrida'. In *Dossiers de l'audiovisuel*, 54, pp. 104–11.

Eustache, Jean (1986) *La Maman et la putain: scénario*. Paris: Editions Cahiers du cinéma.

Farge, Arlette (1989), *Le Goût de l'archive*. Paris: Editions du Seuil.

Ferro, Marc (1968) 'Société du XXe siècle et histoire cinématographique', *Annales ESC*, May–June: 581–5.

Ferro, Marc (1993) *Cinéma et histoire*, Paris: Gallimard.

Forbes, Jill (1984) *INA, French for Innovation*. London: British Film Institute.

Forbes, Jill (1987) 'French film culture and British cinema', in Ceri Crossley and Ian Small (eds), *Imagining France*. London: Macmillan.

Forbes, Jill (1992) *The Cinema in France: After the New Wave*. London: Macmillan.

Forbes, Jill (1999) '*Pierrot le Fou* and Post New Wave French cinema', in David Wills (ed.), *Pierrot le fou*, New York: Cambridge University Press.

Foucault, Michel (1974) 'Entretien avec Michel Foucault', in *Cahiers du cinéma*, July–August: 5–15.

Garçon, François and Sorlin, Pierre (1981) 'L'Historien et les archives filmiques', in *Revue d'histoire moderne et contemporaine*, 28: 344–57.

Hamilton, Paul (1996) *Historicism*. London: Routledge.

Hillier, Jim (1985) *Cahiers du cinéma. Vol. 1: The 1950s*. London: Routledge & Kegan Paul.

Hillier, Jim (1986) *Cahiers du cinéma. Vol. 2, 1960–68*. London: Routledge & Kegan Paul.

Jeancolas, Jean-Pierre (1983) *Quinze ans d'années trente: Le Cinéma des Français 1929–44*. Paris: Stock.

Jeancolas, Jean-Pierre (1989) 'L'Histoire du cinéma français: pour une approche immédiatement opératoire', in Jacques Aumont (ed.), *L'Histoire du cinéma: nouvelles approches*. Paris: Publications de la Sorbonne.

Jeanneney, Jean-Noël and Sauvage, Monique (1982) *Télévision: nouvelle mémoire*. Paris: Editions du Seuil/INA.

Lagny, Michèle (1992) *De l'histoire du cinéma*. Paris: Armand Colin.

Lagny, Michèle, Ropars, Marie-Claire and Sorlin, Pierre (1976) *Octobre: Film, Histoire, Politique*. Paris: Albatros.

Le Goff, Jacques and Nora, Pierre (1986) *Faire de l'histoire*, 3 vols. Paris: Gallimard.

Lindeperg, Sylvie (1997) *Les Ecrans de l'ombre*. Paris: CNRS Editions.

Metz, Christian (1968) *Essais sur la signification au cinéma*, vol 1. Paris: Klincksieck.

Metz, Christian (1971) *Langage et cinéma*. Paris: Larousse.

Metz, Christian (1972) *Essais sur la signification au cinéma*, vol. 2. Paris: Klincksieck.

Metz, Christian (1977) *Le Signifiant imaginaire*. Paris: UGE.

Namer, Gérard (1983) *La Commémoration en France 1944–82*. Paris: SPAG/Papyrus.
Noguez, Dominique (1978) *Cinéma: Théorie, Lectures*. Paris: Klincksieck.
Nora, Pierre (1984–92) *Les Lieux de mémoire*, 7 vols. Paris: Gallimard.
Pithon, Rémy (1995) 'Cinéma et histoire: bilan historique', *Cinéma: le temps de l'histoire, Vingtième siècle*, 46, April–June.
Roud, Richard (1983) *A Passion for Films: Henri Langlois and the Cinémathèque française*. London: Secker & Warburg.
Rousso, Henry (1987) *Le Syndrome de Vichy de 1944 à nos jours*. Paris: Editions du Seuil.
Sorlin, Pierre (1985) 'Promenade dans Rome', *Iris*, 2(2): 5–16.

Film references

Berri, Claude (1986) *Jean de Florette*
Eustache, Jean (1973) *La Maman et la putain*
Godard, Jean-Luc (1965) *Pierrot le fou*.
Malle, Louis (1974) *Lacombe Lucien*.
Ophuls, Marcel (1971) *Le Chagrin et la pitié*
Ophuls, Marcel (1988) *Hôtel Terminus*.
Resnais, Alain (1955) *Nuit et brouillard*.
Téchiné, André (1975) *Souvenirs d'en France*.

Index